OUR RECOVERY OF JESUS

Our RECOVERY of
JESUS

By WALTER E. BUNDY

Professor of English Bible in DePauw University

Author of THE RELIGION OF JESUS

The Bobbs-Merrill Company

Indianapolis   Publishers

FIRST EDITION

To

MAURICE E. BARRETT

γνησίῳ πατρὶ ἐν πίστει

SIR, WE WOULD SEE JESUS.

John 12, 21

CONTENTS

CHAPTER   PAGE

PREFACE   ix

INTRODUCTION—THE WILL TO RECOVER

JESUS   1

I   THE RECOVERY OF JESUS IN THE NEW

TESTAMENT   20

II   THE ROAD TO THE RECOVERY OF JESUS....   67

III THE RECOVERY OF JESUS' SOCIAL MESSAGE   139

IV   THE PERSONAL PROBLEMS OF JESUS......   198

V   VISIONS AND VOICES...................   268

VI   MORE ABOUT THE PRAYING OF JESUS......   298

BIBLIOGRAPHY   323

INDEX OF SUBJECTS   331

INDEX OF SCRIPTURE PASSAGES   345

PREFACE

THE present volume is a companion to the author's recent study, *The Religion of Jesus,* in the preface of which the substance of this volume was outlined. The earlier chapters of the present volume deal with the special problem of recovering Jesus as a human, historical and religious figure. The later chapters turn again to the religious experience of Jesus, to brief psychographic studies of his exclusively religious personality.

The conviction running through this series of studies is identical with that which appears in *The Religion of Jesus.* Here as there, the author feels that it is Jesus as he was who will mean most to us. Further, the conviction maintains itself that Christianity must be more than a Christ-cult, more than a powerful and efficient organization. A Christianity that is in any appreciable measure true to the Galilean genius that gave it birth must be a spiritual movement that claims and commands the hearts of men, that supplies men as individuals and as groups with those inner resources that are necessary for the living of human life religiously.

To Professor Clyde W. Votaw, of the University of Chicago, I am indebted for his helpful interest in the publication of these two volumes, especially for certain very valuable suggestions with regard to the present study. Again I must express my appreciation to Professor William A. Huggard, of DePauw University, for many helpful criticisms of the original manuscript.

Greencastle, Indiana   W. E. B.
Old Gold Day, 1928

OUR RECOVERY OF JESUS

OUR RECOVERY OF JESUS

INTRODUCTION

THE WILL TO RECOVER JESUS[1]

IN THE historical expressions of the Christian faith, in the essence of Christian experience, the influence of Paul and John has been far greater than that of Jesus. The simple Synoptic story has had very little influence on Christian thinking, and it has not been in the light of the religious experience of Jesus himself that Christianity has understood itself and interpreted its task. The church has followed Paul and John both in the nature and in the substance of its religious experience. Christian piety has turned to the Gospel of John and to the letters of Paul rather than to the first three Gospels for its devotional reading within the New Testament, for the Christian consciousness has always felt a closer kinship with Paul and John than with Jesus. The traditional picture of Jesus has been that of the Fourth Gospel—the Christ of faith, not the Jesus of history. Paul and John rather than Jesus have been the great authorities; they have furnished the norms and standards for the Christian life and faith. Even to-day we are more Pauline and Johannine in our religious experience than we are like Jesus.

In view of this fact, it is only natural that the church would neglect the personal religious experience of Jesus.

---

[1]A large portion of the materials in this introduction appeared in various of the Methodist *Advocates*, April 15 and 22, 1926.

The church seems to have feared a religious Jesus, for such would seem to conflict with the principal substance of its official faith. Such borders on a heresy, that dread word that strikes fear into the orthodox heart. But in its fear of heresy the church has often been dangerously near apostasy, a virtual denial and rejection of his spirit. The whole tendency of the Christian faith from the first has been to overlook, even to suppress, the religious experience of Jesus. The Christian consciousness has never been generally aware of the fact that he himself was religious, a man of deep personal piety, the most religious personality of history. He has always been the principal substance of the Christian faith, its distinctive object of worship. Christianity as *a religion about Jesus* has almost totally obscured Christian vision for *the religion of Jesus*. Even to-day in liberal circles there is very little real sensitiveness to the profound religiousness of Jesus himself. Yet it is the greatest single treasure deposited in the New Testament.

The church has always been proud of the fact that it lighted the lamps of learning. Although many institutions have broken off from the church that gave them birth, nevertheless the church has always been more successful as an educator than it has as a prophet. There is hardly a field of learning to which the church has not given, sooner or later, its hearty support and some of its most gifted minds. But the church has not welcomed too much unbiased investigation in its own peculiar field. As far as the church's scholars have gone into the historical foundations of the Christian faith, their chief task has not been to conform the church's experience to that of its acclaimed Founder. The church has neglected the study of its greatest single body of religious subject-matter.

During the first eighteen centuries of its history only the second generation of Christians, from which the first three Gospels came, showed any appreciable interest in the human historical Jesus.

Such study of the life of Jesus as has been undertaken within the church at large has been so strongly dominated by the theological, homiletical, exegetical and traditional point of view that the resultant picture has not been a reproduction of Jesus as he thought and taught, preached and prayed, but rather a picture in the colors of the Christian imagination and quite far from the Jesus of history. It has not resulted in the recovery of Jesus and his religious experience for the church itself. Faith and its necessary supports have prevailed over a desire for fact. The life of Jesus has been studied, quite unconsciously for the most part, from the point of view of confirming theological prejudice rather than from the point of view of learning to know him as he actually was, independent of all tradition, as a resource and reinforcement for religious living. Theology, homiletics and exegesis may study the life of Jesus ever so diligently, even profitably, and yet miss the clearest meaning which he has in the way of religion. The recovery of Jesus by modern research has as yet had little influence on the nature and substance of the church's experience. The life-of-Jesus research has no desire to burden the church with all its technicalities and academic paraphernalia, but it can give Jesus to the church, which is no little gift.

The neglect of the life of Jesus on the part of the church in general has been natural enough in view of its traditional points of emphasis. It has been presupposed that ministers and laymen would read the Gospels, and they have. The church has tacitly assumed that its ministry and laity know all about Jesus—all one needs do is turn to the Gospels and read—an assumption as natural as it is inadequate. Very little respectable study of the life of Jesus has been done by the church for its ministers and laymen. To strive to know Jesus as we would know any other man of history has been a rare enterprise, one seldom undertaken even in our theological seminaries. In the past all emphasis has been laid upon the theological training of the ministerial candidate. He has been led to the New Testament through the devious paths of theology and homiletics. His introduction to the life of Jesus has exhausted itself in questions of date, authorship, literary character, composition and general historical reliability of the Gospels. He has been trained to defend the Gospels rather than to discover the rich religious values deposited in them. Thorough academic courses that seek to recover the human historical Jesus and his religious experience are still at the innovation stage. Young ministers graduate from our American seminaries with little or no preparation in the spirit of the task they are undertaking.

The very nature of the minister's task in society makes him, if he is true to his task, a student of many things, but he must be a specialist in one thing—the life, religious mind and experience of Jesus. He is primarily a seeker and sharer of this experience. It has not been so many years since it was possible for men preparing for the ministry to be graduated from some of our proudest colleges and seminaries without having had even the opportunity to pursue a thorough course of study in the life of Jesus. There are great numbers of earnest men in the ministry to-day who have had exactly this experience. The ministry of the church to-day knows all too little about the life of Jesus, and the ministry is not to be blamed. The fault lies with the college and the seminary where any real training in the life of Jesus has been neglected in favor of theology and exegesis. And back of this neglect lies the lack of any vital interest on the part of the church in this chief of all subjects.

The average minister to-day has had more training in the life and work of the great interpreters of Jesus than he has had in the actual study of Jesus himself. He is more at home in the thought and teaching of the great Christian theologians, philosophers and reformers than he is in the thought and teaching of Jesus. He knows more about the Christianity of Paul, Augustine, Luther, Wesley, Fox and the rest than he does about the religion of Jesus. In fact, many ministers have gone through college and seminary without ever being told and without their seeing that Jesus had a religion and that his personal piety is the clearest single feature of the Gospel picture. The ministry to-day is full of messageless men, powerless preachers, who have never come in contact with that fire which Jesus came to cast upon the earth— his own deep experience of God and religion. In the one thing which they need most they have had least preparation. It is only later that some wake up to the fact that the New Testament and Jesus are much more than their theological training has found them to be. And this fresh experience is a veritable Damascus road when they discover within the New Testament the only thing that will give content and conviction to their message.

"And it shall be, like people, like priest." (Hos. 4,9.) It could not be otherwise. The attention of the layman has never been fastened upon the rich religious values in the life of Jesus. The average layman to-day has a better idea, a truer impression, of almost any popular hero of history than he has of Jesus. And yet there is nothing to which the layman will respond more readily than to the simple and swift presentation of the meaning of God in the human experience of Jesus. His response is readier because he feels that Jesus then comes close to him and his religious needs.

What has been said thus far has not been in a spirit of unfriendly criticism of the church in general, nor of the minister and layman in particular. It is a simple testimony out of actual experience, out of personal religious experience, out of a startling awakening ten years ago to the religious life of Jesus and to the infinite religious values deposited there.

It is now a certainty that we must come to a more intimate, a truer acquaintance with Jesus simply as a human historical figure because of the direct relation he bears to our organized religion and to our personal and practical piety. Jesus must really live for the church and the churchman, if he is to make a real contribution to the life of either.

JESUS AND CHRISTIANITY

In recent times various questions have been asked concerning the relation of the church to Jesus. Is the church the work of Jesus? Is historical Christianity with all of its outgrowths a faithful reproduction or a natural development of the religion of Jesus? How close is Christianity to the One it claims as its Founder? It is now a familiar matter among students of the history of Christianity and the life of Jesus that there is a wide gap between official and organized Christianity and Jesus himself. It is a gap that has existed from the first, a gap that came as the result of the nature of the experiences of the first Christians. For this wide departure from Jesus and his religion there are perfectly natural historical reasons. But the question confronts us: Is this gap necessary and essential to-day? Do we owe our loyalty to the forms of faith that came from Paul and John? Or do we owe our chief loyalty to Jesus and the essential substance of his experience of God? Is *a religion about Jesus,* such as Christianity has always been, to furnish the body of our faith, or are we to turn to *the religion of Jesus?* There are many earnest Christians to-day, both ministers and laymen, who feel the deep religious need of a resolute return to Jesus.

No one feels this more keenly than the serious student of the life of Jesus. On the basis of the New Testament itself the historical student is forced to distinguish between Christianity and the religion of Jesus. Christianity is not the religion of Jesus, and the religion of Jesus is not Christianity. Although they have been identified in Christian thinking for eighteen centuries, they are really two distinct religions. They differ in their objects of worship, in their centers of devotion, in their points of emphasis, in their loyalties and loves, in their goals for attainment.

The historical student has no criticism of the church to offer. He feels that this great institution has steered a marvelous course through nineteen centuries of storm. At times, harbors had to be sought that were not desirable. But to-day the historical student sees no reason why Christianity and the church should not become greater than they have ever been in the past. The historical and psychological situations of the first and subsequent centuries no longer exist. With all respect for Paul and John and the fathers of the faith that followed, there is no reason why the church should not become true to the best of its genius and go back beyond all the historical expressions of the Christian faith to the richest and most reliable of all its sources—to Jesus himself.

It would be a mistake to suppose that this whole question of the relation of the church to Jesus is just a technical and dreary academic issue. The feeling of a disparity between the Christ of faith and the Jesus of history, between Christian experience and the religious experience of Jesus, is not confined to the professional student of the New Testament and the history of Christianity. Leading men of the Orient who reject outright official and organized Christianity as the dry crust of Western civilization are quite inclined to look to Jesus as the bread of life. Matter-of-fact men of the West who remain cold toward conventional Christianity warm at once to a show of spirit that suggests Jesus. It is an issue that is rapidly invading the life of the church itself. It is the real crux of the controversy that now disturbs many communions, although it has rarely been stated in such terms. This feeling of the wide gap that exists between official and organized Christianity in its traditional theological forms and the simple yet profound religion of Jesus is not confined to the clergy. It has invaded the ranks of the laity for the simple reason that it is a question of vital concern to all personal and practical piety. Many laymen are realizing the remoteness of theology from the problem of living life religiously. The weakness and waywardness of conventional Christianity and the inadequacy of ecclesiasticism for the deep religious needs of men are clearer than ever before. Plain men feel the need of a genuine religious spirit such as the human historical Jesus exhibited.

The issue has to do with the fundamental problem of the essence of the religion that names itself after Jesus. Is it to be doctrine and dogma, creed and confession, officialism and orthodoxy? Or is the essence of a religion worthy of the name of Jesus to find its primitive fountain of faith in his own personal piety? Is it to seek its spontaneous sources of power in closeness to Jesus himself, its issue in individual character and social conduct that conform to the divine will which Jesus himself sought to learn and to perform? The whole issue involves the sources of our religious light and strength. To whom shall we go for the highest religious hope and helpfulness? To the traditional theological beliefs, or to the profound religious faith that possessed him? To a religion about Jesus, or to his own personal piety, to those intimate sources that he knew and drew upon, to the experience of God that was his? What are the marks of the Christian? Orthodoxy of opinion and unfailing fidelity to fixed forms of faith? Or is the religious experience of the follower of Jesus something warmer and more living—a personal loyalty to Jesus himself and all that he reveals and represents in the way of religion?

That there is a wide gap between organized and official Christianity and the personal piety of Jesus is clear enough in the so-called *Apostles' Creed*. It is a creed about Jesus. With the exception of the first article, it contains none of the important elements of Jesus' own personal faith. It skips from "born of the Virgin Mary" to "suffered under Pontius Pilate"; in fact, it skips the whole life of Jesus. From it we would never know that Jesus preached the Sermon on the Mount, that he taught the *Golden Rule,* that he uttered the *Lord's Prayer,* that he announced the kingdom of God, prayed for its coming, consecrated himself to it and championed it even to the cross. The one great religious foundation of his life and work, the kingdom of God, is not even mentioned in the church's official statement of its faith. And this omission is characteristic of the neglect of the religious life and experience of Jesus throughout the history of Christianity.

The *Apostles' Creed* has valid historical reasons for its existence, and there are valid religious reasons for its survival and continued repetition to-day. But it must be remembered that it is the creed of the old Catholic Church, not the creed of Jesus. It is far removed from an adequate expression of the distinctive substance of his religious experience. Although religious faith was the very essence of Jesus' personality, although he is absolutely unintelligible apart from it, nevertheless the expression, "I believe," as a formal statement, never crosses his lips. Jesus had no creed, no formal statement of his faith, no confession that he required of his disciples. The one great command of Jesus was, "Follow me." It is the only command he ever gave a disciple in the way of religious requirements. He did not require that his disciples believe certain things *about* him, but that they believe *with* him, that they share his faith in God and His kingdom—a much more difficult task. It is not difficult to believe *in* Jesus, but to believe *with* him, to believe *what* and *as* he believed, and to work for its realization as he did, is a religious task that lays hold on the deepest sources of human life.[2]

---

[2]*See* the author's companion study, *The Religion of Jesus,* p. 264*ff.*

The Christian world has seemed possessed of a fear of studying the life of Jesus closely and carefully—a fear for itself. Such a study brings strange premonitions to its mind. May we not come too close to Jesus? May we not come to know him too well? May we not learn too much about him? There may be disturbing elements in Jesus' experience of religion, elements that might demand changes that we fear. And this fear with its submerged questionings is not without ground in Jesus himself. A careful and conscientious study of the life of Jesus may demand readjustments in our conception of Christianity and its task in the world; it may require revisions in our religious thinking, shifts in our centers of emphasis; it may necessitate a complete reorientation of the church's thought of and for itself; it may make fresh and more difficult demands upon the whole of human life. If we come to know Jesus intimately, it may mean that our conventional and confessional Christianity—a religion of respectability—will be unmasked for the empty form that it has become, and we shall see what it must become—a religion with power to recover, redeem and reconstruct the whole of our human life on the scale and scope of the kingdom of God. It will mean that our Christian experience, if it once becomes like that of Jesus in its nature and substance, must function as the governing principle and power in our human order. Our comfortable and complacent conception of Christianity will give way to a religion that actually contributes to individual character and that controls social conduct in the sense of Jesus.

Others fear for Jesus himself. Will Jesus stand the tests of careful and critical study? Is there not danger that he may lose in the process? May we with safety apply to Jesus and the New Testament records of him the same rigid historical and literary tests that we apply to the life and records of other great men of history? Here there is only one answer, and it is the answer that comes from a deep faith in Jesus. We not only *may*, we *must* so study Jesus. The exemption of Jesus and the Gospels from the most exacting critical study may come from a blind belief, but it is in reality a lack of faith. Religion is too serious a matter in human life for such *taboo*. If we may not ask and seek to answer honest questions about Jesus, if we may not approach him for the most searching study with our minds stripped for fresh and first impressions, then he can never remain a firm foundation for such a serious matter as religious faith. In such a study some of our ideas about Jesus will suffer at the hands of the New Testament itself, but we shall come closer to him than ever before. Those who have subjected Jesus and the Gospels to the most exacting and critical study find that he grows and continues to grow under such study. He is enhanced and enriched, and he becomes for them a veritable source of religious life and light.

The church's loyalty to Jesus is not a matter of extravagant claims and blind belief. Its loyalty is a deeper, more vital thing, a matter of reproducing Jesus in its own life, of remaining faithful to all that he was and represented in the way of religion. Jesus should be the sole and absolute authority in all matters pertaining to the substance of the Christian faith, for everything essentially, though not historically, Christian is to be found in his religious life and experience. The church should be for ever taking and retaking its bearings and soundings; it should be constantly testing the closeness of its life

and experience to those of Jesus himself. If Christianity
is to be true, it must take its standards of truth from
Jesus himself. In the midst of changing circumstances,
facing ever new problems, itself caught in the process of
change, the church must study Jesus more carefully and
closely than ever and press on to a better understanding
of him in the light of a changing experience and the fresh
problems that it presents.

Christianity claims Jesus as its founder, and the study
of his life and religious mind should be the chief of all
studies in the church. The church's own interest in itself
should prompt and promote this study. The church
should desire to win for itself the best and most accurate
knowledge that historical and literary research can ac-
quire.

JESUS AND THE CHRISTIAN

The Christian faith in its purity is individual and personal to a degree that is reached perhaps by no other
faith. With all of its social duties and virtues, it is pre-
eminently a religion of the spirit. The social impulse
grows out of the nature and state of the individual Christian spirit. In this the Christian is following his Master.
For Jesus religion was not only intimately but intensely
personal. The Christian, then, must study the life of
Jesus carefully and closely, that is, if his Christian conscience includes the task of following Jesus.

One of the principal problems in personal piety is that
of religious certainty. Faith is always faith, but it seeks
to be sure in spite of itself. For the Christian this certainty is to be attained only by his closeness to Jesus
himself, by the reproduction in his own life of the per-

sonal piety and religion of Jesus. But if the Christian is to follow Jesus, he must know whither and how Jesus went. The following of Jesus means the sharing of his faith. How may he know the sources, objects and issues of Jesus' faith without a constant and careful study of all that the New Testament tells us of him?

The life of Jesus is the richest single body of religious subject-matter that we possess, and the Christian must turn to it for those distinctive religious values which Jesus presents. The very exaltedness of Christian beliefs about Jesus should suggest and stimulate the most eager and earnest effort to learn to know him as he actually was. Back of these beliefs stands Jesus himself, not as their author but as their inspiration. He is all the greater because his followers claimed for him things that he did not and could not claim for himself. The Christian will always stand with reverence in the presence of the great historical expressions of the Christian faith, but when it comes to the very serious matter of living his own religious life he will exercise his native right of turning to Jesus himself that he may see him clearly and receive from him those strong and deep impulses that moved Jesus himself and which he sought to share with others. For the individual Christian, Jesus is the source of all that we mean by religious light and strength.

The faithful follower of Jesus must ask and seek to answer for himself in the light of a careful and conscientious study of the New Testament account such questions as these. What were the great religious values to which Jesus committed himself? What were the great religious truths that he lived by? What were the religious beliefs of Jesus? What was the substance of his personal faith in God? What did his personal experience of God in-

clude? What was the kingdom of God in the faith of
Jesus? What did this kingdom mean for him personally? What did he hope that it would mean for men?
Was Jesus a religious subject, an experient of religion? Did he possess a genuinely religious consciousness?
What elements did this consciousness include, if he possessed such? Did Jesus manifest religious attitudes and
aspirations? If so, what were they? What were the
sources of his personal religious convictions and certainties? What were the sources of his personal power in
religious living? What were the religious demands of
Jesus? What function did he assign to religion in the
complicated problem of living human life? What sort
of faith did he demand of his followers? Is Jesus, after
all, an authority in religion? What sort of authority
does he possess? What is the nature of the contribution he has to make to us to-day? May we live the religion of Jesus after him? Are we able, if we may?
The answers to these questions are of paramount importance for every Christian, but they are questions that
demand an intimate acquaintance with his life as it is
preserved to us in the first three Gospels.

It is the task of the preacher and teacher of religion
to know this subject-matter. It is his personal obligation to face these questions and to answer them for himself in the light of conscientious study, using all the aid
that comes from a century of research in the life of Jesus.
He must be prepared to single out the great religious
values deposited in the historical life of Jesus of Nazareth and to present them in turn to his people in the
pews, or to his students in the classroom. Whether
preacher or teacher, Jesus must live for him, and he must

bring those committed to his charge to a fresher, clearer understanding of him. He must help them to a true picture of Jesus that becomes for them, as it is for him, real and commanding.

What is the truth about Jesus? The historical truth? The religious truth? The idea that the general Christian public may not be informed and instructed regarding the truth about Jesus, any phase of his life, any feature of his personality, is a resurrection of the pre-Reformation ghost that haunted the minds of those who thought that laymen could not be trusted to hear the Scriptures read in a language they could understand. The New Testament makes it clear to us that it was among the people that Jesus belonged. He was one of them, a layman called of God from their own ranks. Not among the religious authorities, but among the people, Jesus found the readiest response. "The common people heard him gladly." (Mark 12,37b.) And to-day they will not hesitate to trust themselves to the religious truths that Jesus lived by.

A serious and careful study of the life of Jesus for minister or for layman, for teacher or for student, possesses an invincible fascination that is much more than academic. The effort of any serious-minded student to get back to Jesus as he actually was, is the most wholesome religious experience, the most stimulating religious exercise, that can come to a follower of his removed from him by nineteen centuries.

The study of the life of Jesus will not result in a uniformity of ideas and conceptions about him and, if this were possible, it would hardly be desirable. When we are once confronted by the great issues of religion presented in the life of Jesus, such becomes a minor matter.

Jesus himself did not require of his followers a conformity of conceptions about himself, an orthodoxy of religious opinion. Religion in his experience was a much more difficult matter; it involved difficulties, not for the understanding, but for the will. For Jesus religion was a matter of personal loyalty in the quest and performance of the divine will. And those followers of his who have really come to know him will feel a deeper bond than creed and confession, than doctrine and dogma can give— the common bond of loyalty to all that Jesus represents in the way of religion.

Sooner or later, we must come to a religious view and understanding of Jesus, the only view and understanding that will do him historical, personal and religious justice. Jesus was an exclusively religious personality. In him we see all that religion and God at their best may and can mean in human life and experience.

Nearly all reformations attempt a return to first things, to beginnings and original sources. It seems to be a native human conviction that primitive purity and power are to be sought in the past. This conviction is not justified in every case, but a return to the best of the past, a fresh experience of the old, often gives new life to any movement. Protestantism, the most wholesome movement within the church's history, turned again to the Bible, more particularly to the New Testament, for its source and seat of authority. Luther championed a return to the New Testament, but he got back only as far as Paul.

"The righteous shall live by faith." (Rom. 1,17.)

In the modern search for religious certainty the growing inclination, in fact, the determination, is to get back beyond John, Paul and Mark to Jesus himself, to test the whole of the Christian faith and experience, not by what has always been believed and held as true, but by Jesus' own personal faith and experience. The resolve to return to Jesus as the sole source and seat of authority springs from the deep religious conviction that true Christianity must be something more than it has been in the past. A religion worthy of the name of Jesus must find its centers of emphasis in *Jesus-like* character and conduct in the life and living of his followers.

Christianity to-day is in need less of a restatement of its faith, more of a rehabilitation of Jesus to his rightful place as the actual rather than the theoretical authority. Jesus has stated his faith and ours clearly enough. Our chief task is to expose ourselves to the immeasurable religious values perfectly expressed in his life. In his experience we find that religion possesses a richness and reality that is amazing and infinite, which in turn demands of us an unrestrained religious response. We must take less interest in heresy, more interest in apostasy. A disciple of Jesus is not to be judged by his special theory of the person of Christ, if he has such a theory. It is not necessary that he should have. All such is a matter of speculation in which each has a right to work out his own intellectual and theological salvation, if he feels that salvation lies in either of these directions.

The central issues of religion lie far deeper than the conclusions of theoretical speculation. Every follower of Jesus, no matter what his theological thinking may involve or what form it may take, must ask himself certain serious personal questions. Do I discover and discern, do I grasp, am I gripped by the infinite religious values perfectly expressed in the life of Jesus? Do I share in any appreciable measure the religious experience of Jesus? Does the religion of Jesus mean for me the elevation of my ethical ideals, the mobilization of my moral motives and powers, the leadership of my religious loyalties, the focal point of my religious feeling and faith, the kindling fire of my religious enthusiasm and devotion—in short, the polar and pivotal point of my personal piety? These are the fundamental questions of personal Christian experience that transcend all of the historical outgrowths and overgrowths of ecclesiastical traditionalism.

In this present day when the modern mind demands sincerity and solid substance, when it spurns superficialities and non-essentials, it is no time to preach theology and traditionalism, a religion of convention and confession, accepted beliefs and orthodoxy of opinion. What our modern life seeks is an enrichment of experience that will enable it to become and be what life in the past has faintly sensed but has not been. In pulpit and in pew we need a faithful sharing of the religious experience of Jesus, a reliable reproduction of his personal piety. The religion of Jesus must be preached and lived after him, given a chance to prove its authority and sufficiency in modern life. The modern mind is in a mood to see the Jesus of history, to learn to know him as he lived and worked, thought and taught, preached and prayed for the sons of men who, in his experience, are the sons of a common Father.

CHAPTER I

THE RECOVERY OF JESUS IN THE NEW TESTAMENT

THE New Testament is not a simple record of the personal religious experience of Jesus. It is rather the witness of early Christian experience which has Jesus as its principal center. Throughout the New Testament Jesus is an object, the distinctive object, of religious faith. This is true of both the writers and the original readers of the New Testament documents. The whole religious outlook of the New Testament centers exclusively on the person and work of Jesus as dying Savior and as Risen Lord. To the heavenly Christ the most devout hopes are attached, and fellowship with him is the supreme of all religious values.

Within the New Testament it is very rarely indeed that a writer calls the attention of his readers to any religious values expressed in the life of the human historical Jesus. In general, we may say that few indeed of the New Testament writers are sensitive to any such religious values. In the exigencies of their own Christian experience and that of their readers they seldom turn to the religious Jesus for consolation and comfort, elevation and encouragement, instruction and inspiration. Only three of the New Testament writers give us anything like an adequate idea of Jesus' personal religious experience, the first three Gospel writers. When we come to the epistles, it is extremely exceptional that a writer points his readers to some word of the Master or to some incident in his life. The one great event in the

20

historical life of Jesus to which they turn is his death on the cross, and even this dramatic scene they view in the light of their own Christian experience rather than in the light of what it meant for Jesus personally.

This general insensitiveness of the New Testament writers to religious values in the life of Jesus is due to the very nature of their experience. The earliest of the New Testament Christians lived in an atmosphere that was charged with the expectation of the Lord's personal return in their own generation, and the latest of them looked forward to a speedy union with him after death. The very temper of the Christian experience of the greater part of the New Testament is quite opposed to any inclination to turn to the past and seek religious values in the prosaic career that was now a matter of history.

The neglect of the religious Jesus goes back to the earliest Christian records, to the New Testament itself where only occasionally and sporadically a writer is sensitive to such and turns to his human life for the supreme religious values. This is clearly illustrated in the Christian experience of the most prolific of the New Testament writers, the Apostle Paul.

PAUL

Paul is the earliest literary witness to Christianity. His letters should furnish us with exactly the religious values which he found in the life of Jesus, for all are the spontaneous expression of his own fervent faith in him. Most of them were written at the height of the Apostle's missionary activity and zeal, and time and again in his letters we are face to face with the very pulse-beats of his deepest personal piety, at the center of which is the person of Jesus. But a lover of the Synoptic story who moves directly to the letters of Paul can not escape the feeling that he has come into a different world, into a religious experience that, both in form and in content, presents something quite distinct from the religious experience of Jesus.

Paul's neglect of the life and teachings of the historical Jesus is now a matter of common knowledge. Seldom does the Apostle cite a word he spoke or allude to an incident in his life. In I Corinthians 7,10 he quotes Jesus' word on divorce,

> "But unto the married I give charge, *yea* not I, but the Lord, That the wife depart not from her husband."[1]

In I Corinthians 9,14 he proclaims his position regarding the missionary's support as an ordination of Jesus,

> "Even so did the Lord ordain that they that proclaim the gospel should live of the gospel."[2]

Otherwise in his letters we meet only faint echoes of certain words, figures and phrases of Jesus.[3]   At times Paul

---

[1]Cf. Matt. 5,32; 19,9; Mark 10,11-12; Luke 16,18.
[2]Cf. Matt. 10,10b; Luke 10,7b.
[3]Cf. Rom. 12,14 17a 20; I Cor. 4,12; 6,7; I Thess. 5,15 with Luke 6,29-36.
I Cor. 10,21 with Matt. 6,24.
Rom. 2,1; 14,10 13 with Matt. 7,1-2.
I Cor. 5,6b-8; Gal. 5,9 with Matt. 13,33.
Rom. 14,14 20 with Mark 7,15-23.
II Thess. 1,5b; Phil. 3,13; Gal. 5,21 with Luke 9,62.
I Cor. 13,2b with Matt. 21,21-22.
Rom. 13,7 with Mark 12,17.
I Thess. 5,2 4 with Luke 12,39-40.

regrets that he has no word of Jesus to apply to special problems that arise in his mission stations (I Cor. 7,25),

"Now concerning virgins I have no commandment of the Lord: but I give my judgment, as one that hath obtained mercy of the Lord to be trustworthy."

Paul's use of the words of Jesus is very meager in proportion to the use that he might have made of them. In the greatest conflict of his career, when the whole of his work was at stake, he did not cite for the Galatians Jesus' words on the Jewish law as he might have done to advantage. The words of Jesus which Paul does cite he regards as final authority, but some of the greatest of all of Jesus' words are not even faintly echoed in the letters of Paul.

The only incident from Jesus' life which Paul narrates is the Lord's Supper. But even here the Apostle's interest is not in any sense biographical. The text of his account has a liturgical and ritualistic style. It is not just a simple narrative of something that happened in the past.

"For I received of the Lord that which I also delivered unto you, that the Lord Jesus in the night in which he was betrayed took bread; and when he had given thanks, he brake it, and said, This is my body, which is for you: this do in remembrance of me. In like manner also the cup, after supper, saying, This cup is the new covenant in my blood: this do, as often as ye drink *it*, in remembrance of me." (I Cor. 11,23-25.)

Paul alludes to Jesus' betrayal and often he speaks of the cross, but never does he approach the cross as Jesus approached it. The whole of the passion Paul views in the light of the high religious significance which it acquired in early Christian experience. Paul's piety is staurocentric; the cross of Christ stands at the top of his religious world. His gospel is the "word of the cross." (I Cor. 1,18.) It is at the cross that Paul comes into a mystical union with Christ. (Gal. 2,20.) Thus there is something deeply personal in Paul's experience of the cross. But he views the cross primarily as the climax of a scheme of salvation, the final act in the great divine drama of man's redemption.

When Paul comes to the delineation of the Christian life and to the virtues of the believer he seldom points to Jesus as an example for imitation. Often he exhorts his readers to imitate himself as he imitates Christ.

"Be ye imitators of me, even as I also am of Christ." (I Cor. 11,1.)[4]

But very seldom does he point out religious virtues in the life of Jesus to be reproduced by Christians. He speaks of the love, the law, the patience, the tender mercies, the mind, the meekness, the gentleness and the humility of Christ, but he is thinking of the heavenly Christ who emptied himself of his divine glory rather than of the human Jesus who was all of these things for his contemporaries.

Often in his letters Paul comes upon the theme of temptation, how he himself is torn in struggle, how his readers are threatened and defeated, but never once does

[4]Cf. I Cor. 4,16; Phil. 3,17; 4,9; I Thess. 1,6; II Thess. 3,9.

he turn to the temptations of Jesus and his triumph over them. To the Corinthians he writes (I Cor. 10,13),

> "There hath no temptation taken you but such as man can bear: but God is faithful, who will not suffer you to be tempted above that ye are able; but will with the temptation make also the way of escape, that ye may be able to endure it."

Paul had a remarkably rich prayer-life. He is constantly admonishing his readers to pray, but not once does he point to Jesus' words on prayer, his practise of prayer or his prayers. Paul's *Abba*-cry in Galatians 4,6 and Romans 8,15 is the only possibility of an echo from the prayer-experience of Jesus.

For Paul faith is the very foundation of the Christian life; it is faith that saves him and his readers. However, he sets Abraham as a model of faith (Rom. 4,3 9) without a single hint as to the deeply devout faith of Jesus himself.

Paul presents obedience as the great task of the Christian. He tells his readers that Jesus was "obedient unto death" (Phil. 2,8) and that "Christ pleased not himself" (Rom. 15,3), but he has in mind here the superhistorical act of a heavenly being rather than the quest of the historical Jesus for the divine will.

Paul is not sensitive to the real religiousness of Jesus, and he could not be because of his conception of his Lord's human life. Paul refers to the humanity of Jesus now and then: He was born of a woman, of the seed of Abraham and was placed under the law. But he never ascribes to Jesus more than a theoretical humanity. Jesus' historical appearance he views always *sub specie*

æternitatis. For Paul the human life of Jesus is simply
an episode in the great divine drama, simply a part of a
superhistorical plan. The historical Jesus was the incarnate Son who humbled himself to take on human
form.

> "For ye know the grace of our Lord Jesus Christ,
> that, though he was rich, yet for your sakes he be-
> came poor, that ye through his poverty might become
> rich." (II Cor. 8,9.)
> "Have this mind in you, which was also in Christ
> Jesus: who, existing in the form of God, counted not
> the being on an equality with God a thing to be
> grasped, but emptied himself, taking the form of a
> servant, being made in the likeness of men; and being
> found in fashion as a man, he humbled himself, be-
> coming obedient *even* unto death, yea, the death of
> the cross." (Phil. 2,5-8.)

In such an ethereal atmosphere the prosaic facts of Jesus'
life have no natural place.

Paul refers to Jesus as the one "who knew no sin"
(II Cor. 5,21), but the sinlessness of Jesus in the
thought of Paul is theoretical, ceremonial and ritualistic
rather than the actual accomplishment of a religious subject.

The whole tone and temper of Paul's Christian experience is away from the past. The warmest of his religious aspirations, the most fervent elements of his faith,
swing out toward the future. He lives his religious life,
not in retrospect but in prospect. He deliberately turns
his back on history.

"Wherefore we henceforth know no man after the flesh: even though we have known Christ after the flesh, yet now we know *him so* no more." (II Cor. 5,16.)

Paul lived and worked and believed in the conviction that the end of the age was at hand, that he and his readers would witness the triumphant return of the Risen Lord, that he and they would be caught up into the air to meet him. (I Thess. 4,13-18.) The whole of Paul's Christian experience is keyed up to this high hope and expectation. For Paul, Jesus was the Coming One; he does not look backward to appraise the human life of Jesus, but he looks forward in the firm conviction that he will soon be eternally with his Lord. The very height to which the whole of Paul's piety was pitched excluded any real interest in the past. Such a rare religious atmosphere is not hospitable to history. Paul may have known much more of the details of Jesus' life than his letters betray—there is no good reason why he should not—but he seeks his supreme religious values in the heavenly Christ rather than in the historical Jesus.

It is not to the Jesus of history but to the Christ of faith that Paul turns. He shows no lively interest in what Jesus, as a human personality, said or did or was. The whole of his Christian experience is centered upon the Risen Lord whom he saw on the Damascus road. The very brightness of the Damascus vision blinded Paul's eyes for ever to such a plain picture as the transmitted story of Jesus presented. What had oral tradition to communicate to one who lived in Christ and in whom Christ lived! A passionate religious personality like Paul could never be greatly interested in the earthly

Jesus once his own life had been broken in two by a
vision and commission from the heavenly Christ. Thus
the very nature of Paul's Christian experience would
conspire against his turning to the human historical
Jesus for religious values and authority.

Whether Paul set his Lord on a plane with God himself is a much-debated problem in New Testament research. There are passages in his letters which very
clearly imply that he did, and there are other passages
in which he subordinates Christ to God. The truth perhaps is not to be found in an *either-or*, but in a *both-and*.
Paul, like the majority of great religious geniuses, makes
no attempt at being consistent or systematic. He was
too passionate a religious personality to allow his fervent
feeling and faith to be regulated by logic. We can not
fit the Christian experience of Paul into any coherent
scheme of Christology. His relation to his Lord was
too deeply personal. It was the heavenly Christ who
had revealed himself in him, who had personally called
and commissioned him to his apostolic task. Consequently, all of Paul's expressions of his faith are spontaneous and free, never self-conscious. What we sift
from his letters as his theology and Christology is only
the outer garb of that great body of feeling and faith
that possessed him, purely incidental to the principal issue
that claimed him.

But it is clear enough in Paul's letters that he regarded
the Lord Jesus, as he learned to know him on the Damascus road, as a religious object worthy of worship in the
full sense of the term. To obtain Christ, to be evermore
with him, is for Paul the supreme aspiration of religious
experience. The heavenly Christ is so prominent in
Paul's personal faith and feeling that at times God is

almost obscured. Whether as equal or as subordinate, the Christ of Paul's experience is a second religious object. Without discrimination he ascribes divine predicates to God and Christ alike. Christ is the sole mediator between God and man. Through him alone may men hope for forgiveness of sins. The person of Christ is indispensable to religious redemption. Every possible relationship of the believer to God is through Christ exclusively. Paul stands in a prayer-relationship with Christ as he does with God; he prays to and through Christ. To address Christ in prayer is to address God, and Paul's personal piety is too strong in its flow to sense any compromise of his native monotheism.

In their religious experience Jesus and Paul had much in common. There were personal differences due to natural endowment, environment and training, but both were Jews with the same sacred traditions behind them. They worshiped the same God, read and revered the same Scriptures. Both were gripped by an unshakable faith in the God of Israel whom they loved and feared, to whom they prayed. They were one in the general substance of their religious attitudes and aspirations. Both approached and accomplished their tasks religiously, seeking the divine will. Both made heavy demands in the field of ethical character and moral conduct. In brief, we may say that in their personal piety Paul and Jesus have a number of important and characteristic things in common.

It is only as we strike upon the distinctive elements in the religious experience of each—those special things that made Paul, Paul and Jesus, Jesus—that we realize how far apart they really are. The strategic centers of

Paul's piety and those of Jesus do not coincide. The religious experiences of the two men are like two intersecting circles: They compass a common ground, yet the distinctive features of each lie outside and apart. What was primary for one was secondary for the other, or may not have figured at all. What was for one an abstract problem of speculative thought was for the other a pressing personal problem. In the faith of the one there appeared something new and great that was wholly absent in the faith of the other. The God of Jesus is the God of Paul. Paul hopes for and expects the appearance of the kingdom of God. But the distinctive sources and objects of Paul's faith are not identical with those of Jesus. The Apostle's faith had its birth on the Damascus road in a vision of the Risen Lord. The heavenly Christ remains the outstanding object of Paul's piety, and its principal issue is a mystical union with this exalted figure: Christ in him, and he in Christ. Faith, for Paul, is something quite distinct from the faith of Jesus. For Paul it includes a religious attitude and relationship to Christ, apart from which he knows of no real faith in God. Paul's gospel is not just of and about Christ; it is Christ: "Christ in all, and all in Christ." (Col. 3,11.)

The heavenly Christ occupies a place in the Christian faith of Paul that has no counterpart in the less involved faith of Jesus. The historical Jesus was a religious subject, but in the Christian experience of Paul he becomes a religious object apart from whom there is no hope of salvation. Between the religious experience of the two men there is a complete shift from one psychological pole to its extreme opposite. Between Paul and Jesus a development has taken place, a change so radical that the religion of the Apostle becomes a new and different religion from that experienced by his Master. In the Christian experience of Paul Jesus becomes the principal and distinctive substance of a new faith. Jesus was a Jew in his religious faith, but Paul was a Christian, that is, if we judge the two by the really distinctive elements in their personal piety. In its historical forms and appearances Christianity is the work of Paul, not that of Jesus. As Bousset writes, "With Paul the history of the complication of Christianity begins."[5]

It would be unjust to say that Paul was not a true disciple of his Lord, but he was not a follower such as Jesus had in the twelve and others with whom he sought to share his faith during his lifetime. Paul was won to the Risen Lord, not by the historical Jesus. We are not at war with Paul and his faith in the One to whom he gave his all; our task is to seek to understand him and his religious experience. Paul rendered to Christianity as a world religion the greatest service that one man could possibly render. Christianity probably owes its life to Paul, and upon the religion that has survived him by nineteen centuries the Apostle to the Gentiles has left the indelible impression and stamp of his own Christian piety and personality. In his religious experience Paul was true to himself. With the exception of Jesus, there is not in the history of religion a more fascinating, energetic and enthusiastic figure than the Apostle Paul, and it is interesting and significant to find the one in the service of the other. Paul performed the perfect feat of the religious genius: He transplanted the simple story of Jesus from Jewish to Gentile soil. The great difficulties in his way were not geographical but psychological.

---

[5] *Das Wesen der Religion,* p. 183.

With the Christian message he crossed mental frontiers and presented it in new thought-forms and idioms; he put it into the terms of an entirely different type of experience. With his theology of the cross, the soteriology of the heavenly Christ and the doctrine of the resurrection, he met the Greek mind on its own ground and won it to his faith. Thus Christianity took the first and greatest step in its history, from Galilee to Greece.

There are points of agreement and disagreement, major and minor, between Paul and Jesus. But it is quite clear in the Apostle's own letters that he in his religious life is not aiming at a reproduction of the religious experience of the human historical Jesus. Beginning with Damascus, Paul's faith was trained upon one supreme figure, and whatever picture he entertained of the Jesus of history was enveloped in the radiant haze that surrounded the heavenly Christ. Whenever Paul comes into conflict and controversy, when his message, faith or apostleship is called in question, he goes back to his experience of the heavenly Christ of the Damascus road, not to the Jesus of Galilee. It was to Damascus, not to Nazareth, that Paul turned for his highest religious values.

In the Christian experience of Paul the Christ of faith, not the Jesus of history, is the supreme religious authority. The authority of the latter is theoretical rather than actual and commanding.

OTHER NEW TESTAMENT WRITINGS

If we turn to the book of Acts, we find that the same disposition prevails which we meet in Paul's letters. The Christian messages delivered by the various speakers have as their theme the Christ of faith. In two cases the Apostle Peter turns to the human life of Jesus:

> "Jesus of Nazareth, a man approved of God unto you by mighty works and wonders and signs which God did by him in the midst of you, even as ye yourselves know." (Acts 2,22.)
>
> "Jesus of Nazareth, how God anointed him with the Holy Spirit and with power; who went about doing good, and healing all that were oppressed of the devil; for God was with him." (Acts 10,38.)

But even here there is no real recourse to the experience of Jesus for religious values. Both of Peter's allusions to the human life of Jesus are followed at once by that tremendous swing of faith to the Risen Lord:

> "Whom God raised up, having loosed the pangs of death: because it was not possible that he should be holden of it." (Acts 2,24.)
>
> "Him God raised up the third day, and gave him to be made manifest, not to all the people, but unto witnesses that were chosen before of God, *even* to us, who ate and drank with him after he rose from the dead." (Acts 10,40-41.)

In the early Christian messages of Acts the story of the human Jesus is only the paradoxical prologue to the drama of the cross, the resurrection and the exaltation. It is at these two points, the cross and the empty tomb, that the Christian experience back of Acts seeks its religious values.

There is a second character in Acts who seems strongly

under the influence even of the personal piety of Jesus, Stephen. If the charges against him in 6,14 were true, Stephen was more radical by far in his attitude toward the temple and the Mosaic law than was Jesus. In the extended address ascribed to him (7,2-53) he does not refute these charges; but the climax of the address (7,51-53), which seems to be the most genuine part of the whole, has in it a tone and temper that suggest at once Jesus' own sharp attacks on the religious-by-profession. The account of Stephen's death is certainly modeled after that of Jesus in the third Gospel. Stephen dies, as did his Master, with a prayer of forgiveness on his lips,

"Lord, lay not this sin to their charge." (Acts 7,60.)

And, like Jesus, he commends and commits his spirit—but to the Risen Lord, a prayer-object—

"Lord Jesus, receive my spirit." (Acts 7,59.)[6]

There is no real reason for doubting that Stephen and many other Christian martyrs strove to imitate the example of Jesus and in the hour of death turned to his tremendously resourceful religious experience for strength to die and courage to forgive. The present parallelism in the two accounts, however, may be only literary, for both in all probability come from the same author. But even if the parallelism is only literary, it

---

[6]The prayers of Jesus, both found only in Luke, are:
"Father, forgive them; for they know not what they do." (23,34.)
"Father, into thy hands I commend my spirit." (23,46.)

reveals very clearly on the part of the author the firm conviction that Christians should live life and surrender it in the spirit and fashion of Jesus.

There is only one other instance in the book of Acts of a resort to the life of Jesus for religious authority. In the famous farewell speech at Miletus, ascribed to Paul, the climax comes in a word of Jesus not preserved in the Gospels,

"Remember the words of the Lord Jesus, that he himself said, It is more blessed to give than to receive." (Acts 20,35b.)

Among the New Testament epistles, that of James is noteworthy in our present study, for it stands quite apart from the rest—II Peter is its nearest kin—in its religious point of view. The distinctive features of the main body of the New Testament faith do not appear in it. There is no concrete commitment to a definite Christology. The author's faith is theocentric rather than Christocentric. Christians of all generations have been sensitive to the absence in this epistle of the fundamental positions of their faith. Luther called it an "epistle of straw." The epistle is really more strongly Jewish than Christian in its feeling and faith, so much so that some scholars have pronounced it an out-and-out Jewish document. The author introduces himself as "a servant of God and of the Lord Christ" (1,1), and he seems to share most earnestly the expectation of the Lord's return (5,7-9). This latter passage is the most distinctly Christian part of the whole epistle. The Jewish character of James is unmistakable, but Jesus himself was a Jew. Even if it could be demonstrated beyond all doubt that the epistle was of Jewish origin, this fact would not sever the organic bond that binds it to Jesus and the religion he represented. But the strongest argument for James as a Christian document is the simple fact that its fundamental positions in matters of religious life and experience are those of Jesus.

There is not an epistle in the New Testament that comes nearer a reliable reproduction of the personal piety of Jesus than the epistle of James. The religious faith of its author is more closely akin to that of Jesus than the faith of any other New Testament writer outside of the first three Gospel writers, whose picture of Jesus is more strongly Christianized than is the thought of James. In fact, the author turns directly to the human historical Jesus for religious values. Of the epistle as a whole, Professor Deissmann writes: "It stands firmly on the ground of the gospel of Jesus."[7]

The author alludes to no special scenes in the life of Jesus, and he cites no particular instances of Jesus' conduct and experience as examples. His only biographical allusions are to Job and the prophets as models of suffering and patience (5,10-11), and to Elijah as a man of prevailing prayer (5,17-18). He does not point to the prayer-life of Jesus. The first major passage of the epistle (1,2-18) deals with temptation, but the author does not remind his readers of the temptation experiences of Jesus.

The author of James turns primarily to the words of Jesus for his religious authority. Not once does he cite a word of Jesus as such, but the whole of his writing is full of close reproductions, echoes and plays on words of Jesus, especially from the Sermon on the Mount. He is

---

[7]*Evangelium und Urchristentum*, p. 136.

intimately acquainted with Jesus' teaching and it is the chief formative factor in his conception and presentation of the Christian life.[8] In James we find the same moral emphasis and earnestness, the same insistence on the homely and hard tasks of religious living, the same rejection of confession and profession, the same antithesis between saying and doing, the same break with conventional religion, the same test "by fruits," the same demand that faith must function and have its issues in corresponding character and conduct, that we find in Jesus.

In brief, the epistle of James is intensely loyal to Jesus' own experience of religion, and the author conceives of the whole of the Christian life in the terms of the faithful following of Jesus. James and Jesus are the spiritual kin of the New Testament.

There is another epistolary writer of the New Testament who turns to the personal piety of Jesus for religious values, both for himself and his readers, the unknown author of Hebrews. This is really surprising, for of all the New Testament writings the epistle to the Hebrews is the most theological. The author presents the object of his faith, Jesus, as the great High Priest after the order of Melchizedek, as transcendent and above all human and historical relationships—without beginning, without end, without father or mother or genealogy. But with all of his highly speculative analogies the religious experience of the author of Hebrews is at times quite close to that of Jesus. In the

---

[8]For reproductions and echoes of words of Jesus, *see* the following passages in James: 1,6a 9-11 13-15 22-25; 2,2-4 8b 10-11 13 15-16; 3,1 10-12; 4,2b-3a 11-12 15 17; 5,1-5 12 14-15 20.

life of the human historical Jesus he discovers for himself and discloses to his readers real religious values, and he resorts to the prosaic picture of the Nazarene for the highest religious helpfulness. He is sensitive to the religiousness of Jesus, and he turns to it as a source of Christian consolation and comfort, inspiration and encouragement, light and strength.

Unlike James, the author of Hebrews turns to special scenes in the life of Jesus, to certain features of his religious personality, rather than to words of his. He points out the genuine humanity of Jesus as a source of Christian courage and comfort in 4,15-16 which is one of the finest religious statements of the humanity of Jesus in all Christian literature. He is sensitive to the prayer-life of Jesus; he speaks of his "godly fear" and of his having "learned obedience." (5,7-8.) The great aspiration of Jesus he presents as the doing of the divine will (10,7), as faithfulness to the One who appointed him (3,2).

The author of Hebrews is deeply impressed with two great scenes in the life of Jesus, the temptation and the Gethsemane struggle, and to both he points his readers for high helpfulness.

"For we have not a high priest that can not be touched with the feeling of our infirmities; but one that hath been in all points tempted like as *we are, yet* without sin. Let us therefore draw near with boldness unto the throne of grace, that we may receive mercy, and may find grace to help *us* in time of need." (4,15-16.)

"For in that he himself hath suffered being tempted, he is able to succor them that are tempted." (2,18.)

He is even more strongly impressed with the Gethsemane struggle than are the Gospel writers.

> "Who in the days of his flesh, having offered up
> prayers and supplications with strong crying and tears
> unto him that was able to save him from death, and
> having been heard for his godly fear, though he was a
> Son, yet learned obedience by the things which he
> suffered." (5,7-8.)

The author of Hebrews is firmly convinced of the
sinlessness of Jesus. Sometimes he expresses it in terms
of Jewish cult and ceremony (7,26-27), but in other
passages the sinlessness of Jesus becomes his own personal religious accomplishment, a perfection of piety
attained by godly fear and limitless loyalty to the
divine commission (5,9).

It is perfectly clear that the Christian faith of the
author of Hebrews holds the religious experience of
Jesus firmly within the compass of its supreme religious
values. In fact, he presents the Christian life as
obedience to him, and upon this obedience he makes
dependent the religious significance of Jesus,

> "And having been made perfect, he became unto
> all them that obey him the author of eternal salva-
> tion." (5,9.)

Among the other extra-Gospel books of the New
Testament we find the same lack of appreciation of the
human life of Jesus as a source of religious values, the
same insensitiveness to his religious experience, that we
found in the letters of Paul. Everywhere the distinctive

features of the Christian faith appear both for writers
and for readers. The common themes of the religious
life are treated—temptation, prayer, obedience, faith—
but there is in general no real recourse to the accomplishment of Jesus in the field of religious living. Everywhere
faith is Christocentric and Jesus is exclusively a religious
object worthy of all religious reverence. In but one outstanding passage is he presented as a religious example
that is to be copied after, the classic statement in I Peter
2,21-24:

> "For hereunto were ye called: because Christ also
> suffered for you, leaving you an example, that ye
> should follow his steps; who did no sin, neither was
> guile found in his mouth; who, when he was reviled,
> reviled not again; when he suffered, threatened not,
> but committed *himself* to him that judgeth righteously;
> who his own self bare our sins in his body upon
> the tree, that we, having died unto sins, might
> live unto righteousness; by whose stripes ye were
> healed."

THE FOURTH GOSPEL

For a century now the Gospel of John has been the
scene of endless conflict. Until the last century it was
the Gospel. It was regarded as the most authentic
account of Jesus because it came, as was supposed, from
one of his personal companions. But to-day the Fourth
Gospel, not critical prejudice, takes itself out of the
group of New Testament writings that furnish information concerning what Jesus said and did, who he was.
This first step in the recovery of the historical Jesus is

painful for many, really too painful, and relatively few have had the courage to take it. But in eliminating the Fourth Gospel from the body of reliable biographical matter concerning Jesus, we do the author and his work no religious injustice. In fact, it is only as we come to share the experience of the author and the spirit of his work that we may safely draw this conclusion. To seek to understand the Fourth Gospel as a biography of Jesus, is to misunderstand it.

This Johannine problem grew out of the feeling and recognition of the great disparity that exists between the picture of Jesus in the Fourth Gospel and that in the first three Gospels.[9]

There is a great difference in materials. There is so much that is old, so much that is new. So much that is familiar from the first three Gospels does not appear; so much that is wholly strange and different occupies the foreground. Between the Fourth Gospel and the first three there is considerable common matter, but it is presented in such a different way that open contradictions appear. The whole public life of Jesus in the Fourth Gospel is stretched over an entirely different historical framework. There are chronological conflicts concerning the date of Jesus' public appearance, the length of his ministry, the date of his death, and so forth. There are contradictions with regard to the principal scene and itinerary of his public life. There is a different account of his wonder-works, their nature and number.

The disparity between the Fourth Gospel and the Synoptics goes deeper. If these outer conflicts were the

---

[9]The most recent study of importance on this problem is that of Professor Windisch, *Johannes und die Synoptiker. Wollte der vierte Evangelist die drei aelteren Evangelien ergaenzen oder ersetzen?*

only ones, there would be no serious Johannine problem.
The only task would be one of harmonization, and the
Fourth Gospel would take its place alongside the first
three as a reliable source of information. These historical and chronological conflicts do not touch more
than the periphery of the problem. The real problem
is psychological and has to do with the picture of Jesus
as a whole. It affects the form and substance of his
thought. In the first three Gospels we have those short,
pregnant utterances of Jesus that strike straight and
true; there are seven great addresses; he speaks approximately sixty parables, and parable is the most characteristic and distinctive form of his teaching; finally, in the
first three Gospels there are those sharp, telling words
uttered by him in conflict which end the issue once for
all. But in the Fourth Gospel there are not more than a
half-dozen parallels to the sententious sayings of Jesus
in the Synoptics. There is not a single true parable,
only unclear allegory. Not one of the seven great
Synoptic addresses reappears. In contention and conflict the Johannine Jesus can give only obscure, enigmatic
and evasive replies.[10]

The words of Jesus in the first three Gospels exhibit a
resourcefulness of intellect and present an attractive
variety. But in the Fourth Gospel his utterances are
monotonous, repetitious and stereotyped, suggesting a
correspondingly restricted range of thought. In the
Fourth Gospel the theme of Jesus' thought and teaching
is wholly different. Throughout the first three Gospels

---

[10]The only exception is in John 7,53-8,11—an account which by its very
nature belongs to the Synoptic story, and in a few manuscripts it is the
concluding section of what is now the twenty-first chapter of Luke.
Originally it may have been a part of the Gospel of Mark, a theory first
advocated by Hitzig.

his thought centers upon God and His Kingdom, but in the Fourth Gospel all that he thinks and says has to do with the relation of the Father to the Son, of the Son to the Father, with his own person.

This psychological phase of the Johannine problem reaches still deeper. It strikes the very nature and substance of Jesus' experience as a human historical figure. Down to this point[11] the reader may have wondered at the consistent neglect of the Fourth Gospel, but this neglect is forced upon us by the very character and content of the account of Jesus in the Gospel of John. In the Synoptic Gospels Jesus is a religious subject with a wondrously rich religious experience. All of the characteristic elements of the religious consciousness appear as the solid substance of his personality. In the first three Gospels Jesus is, without exception, deeply and genuinely religious. But in the Fourth Gospel he ceases to be a religious subject, becomes wholly a religious object, and regards and presents himself as such. The personality of the Johannine Jesus is characterized by the poverty of its piety. The experience of the Johannine Jesus is not fundamentally religious, and wherever an element of the religious consciousness seems to appear, it is usually only empty form devoid of real substance. Judged in the light of the nature and substance of their experience, the Jesus of the first three Gospels and the Christ of the Fourth Gospel are two entirely different persons, and it is psychologically impossible to identify them. The Christ of John is Jesus only in name.

One of the finest Biblical statements concerning God is found only on the lips of the Johannine Jesus,

---

[11] Throughout the author's companion study, *The Religion of Jesus.*

"God is spirit." (4,24.)

In no New Testament writing is God more transcendent, but the experience of God as high and holy is only a formal teaching of the Johannine Jesus, and it nowhere calls forth the corresponding religious emotions on his part. The great gap which the genuinely religious subject feels between himself and his Maker never appears in the experience of the Jesus of the Fourth Gospel. Not a single expression that comes from his lips betrays the religious fear and awe that we found in certain words of his in the first three Gospels.[12] Nowhere does he manifest that native and natural sense of need, that feeling of dependence, which characterizes the Jesus of the Synoptics.

In the Fourth Gospel Jesus has no experience of God, and by the very nature of his consciousness he could not have. Instead of an experience of the Divine, God is the whole substance of his self-consciousness. He feels that he himself is God; both in public and in private he presents himself as such. The majority of his contentions with his opponents have this claim as their principal issue. He is conscious of his pre-worldly being, of having surrendered his pre-human glory, of the fact that he shall soon return to it and be with God in the glory that was his before the world was. Abraham rejoiced to see his day; he saw it and was glad.

"Before Abraham was born, I am." (8,58.)[13]

On the basis of such a cosmological consciousness,

---

[12]*See* the author's companion study, *The Religion of Jesus*, pp. 72-78.
[13]*See* 6,38a 62; 7,33; 8,14b 23; 12,41; 13,3b; 16,28; 17,5 24b.

not only the experience of God, but religious experience in any form becomes an impossibility.

The designation of God as Father is even more frequent in the Fourth Gospel than it is in the Synoptics. It is almost constant. But the Father of the Fourth Gospel is no longer the living, loving Father of the Synoptics who causes His sun to shine on the evil and the good, the rain to fall on the just and the unjust. He is no longer the impartial, true and forgiving Father of all men. The Fatherhood of God in the Fourth Gospel expresses His special relationship to Jesus who expands the thought to include the narrow circle of friends that surrounds him. All real religiousness is gone from the Father of the Fourth Gospel. This wondrous issue of Jesus' experience of God in the first three Gospels[14] has become purely theological for Jesus and mystical for his companions. The Fatherhood of God is no longer religious for Jesus personally, for he sets himself on a plane and par with Him,

"I and the Father are one." (10,30.)

In another passage (14,28b) he subordinates himself to the Father, but the solid substance of his self-consciousness is that the beholding of himself is the beholding of the Father (12,45) and that he and the Father are one in essence. Thus Jesus' relation to the Father in the Fourth Gospel approaches a metaphysical identity or oneness, and it is no longer a harmony of will with the Father such as Jesus achieves in the Synoptics.

In the first three Gospels God as Father is the solid substance of Jesus' religious faith. It is the issue of his

---

[14] *The Religion of Jesus*, pp. 78-84.

experience of God, the one key to the understanding of all that he says and does and is. In the Fourth Gospel, however, God as Father is no longer religious faith but metaphysical knowledge attained in a state of eternal existence. It is not achieved through the regular avenues of religious experience. This is clear throughout the Fourth Gospel which presents Jesus as regularly disclaiming his teaching as his own. In the Synoptics Jesus never disclaims his teaching as his own; his message of God as Father is the crystallization of his own individual experience as a human historical person, and he announces it with a conviction and certainty that give his word a peculiar authority. But in the Fourth Gospel Jesus states:

"My teaching is not mine, but his that sent me." (7,16.)
"For I speak not from myself; but the Father that sent me, he hath given me a commandment, what I should say, and what I should speak." (12,49.)[15]

He simply speaks the things which he has seen, heard and learned of the Father in his pre-human existence— pure metaphysical knowledge, not religious experience.

Along with Jesus' experience of the Divine as high and holy and as Father we found in the first three Gospels that the kingdom of God was the constant theme of his message.[16] Practically everything that he has to say is related either directly or indirectly to this great theme.

---

[15]Cf. 8,26b 28b   38b; 10,18b; 14,24b; 15,15b.
[16]See the author's companion study, *The Religion of Jesus*, pp. 105-116.

But in the Fourth Gospel the kingdom of God is gone for ever from the thought and teaching of Jesus. The expression is found only twice in the entire document (3,3 5), both times on the lips of Jesus but no longer in the sense so familiar to the reader of the first three Gospels. In the Fourth Gospel Jesus' own person, its indispensability in the scheme of salvation, has become the sole theme of all that he thinks and says.

In the first three Gospels the kingdom of God is much more than the message of Jesus. It is the principal element in his religious outlook;[17] in its immediate coming he firmly believes, and he yearns toward its appearance with a perfect passion of soul. But the Johannine Jesus has no such religious outlook. He is not expecting and praying for the appearance of the Kingdom of God among men. On the contrary, he looks forward to the renewal of the oneness with the Father that was his before the world was. He does not point men to the imminent kingdom, but sees in the future only the judgment of the world that has already begun. To the little band about him he promises an eternal oneness with himself and the Father if they will continue to believe on him as the only begotten Son of God. They are to have a Comforter to console them during the temporary separation caused by his death.

In the first three Gospels the kingdom of God is the cause to which Jesus feels himself called and commissioned; it is his great task to announce it, and to its service he commits and consecrates himself entirely.[18] The kingdom means God, and God means the kingdom. It is the highest value open to human experience and attain-

---

[17]*The Religion of Jesus,* pp. 116-128.
[18]*Ibid.,* pp. 129-137.

ment; no human sacrifice, his own or that of his followers, is too great in order to participate in it. But in the Fourth Gospel Jesus has no cause which he champions, in the service of which all thought of and for himself falls into the background. The thought-world of the Johannine Jesus is exclusively egocentric. In the first three Gospels the kingdom is an integral element, the essential issue, of Jesus' experience of God. But in the Fourth Gospel the kingdom of God is wholly supplanted by the distinctive elements of the Christian message and faith of the early second century. This neglect of the kingdom of God alone makes the Johannine Jesus and the Synoptic Jesus two different persons.

When we turn to the Fourth Gospel in quest of the religious consciousness of Jesus, which he never fails to manifest in the first three Gospels,[19] we find that it simply does not exist. The characteristic attitudes and aspirations of the religious consciousness never appear. The reason for this is clear enough: The Johannine Jesus is never really human. To be sure, he is the Word become flesh, but the humanity of Jesus in the Fourth Gospel is theological and theoretical, never religious and actual. Many Christians resort to the Fourth Gospel for the human features. Jesus is wearied by his journey, must rest, and is thirsty. (4,6-7.) He weeps at the grave of Lazarus. (11,35.) His soul is sorrowful because his little band will soon be orphaned. But these are not genuine human features at all; they are purely superficial and artificial, and can not furnish the necessary basis on which alone the religious consciousness is

---

[19] *The Religion of Jesus*, pp. 141-209.

possible. His tears at the grave of Lazarus do not start from a genuine human emotion. He weeps, not because he has lost a friend or because of the grief of the sisters, but because of the unbelief of the bystanders. The humanity of Jesus in the Fourth Gospel is only an outer garment laid on for a time but soon to be cast off. He is only a pilgrim on earth; for a while only he sojourns in human form. He is not of this world, nor can be. He is not at home in it and is out of all feeling with it. He finds nothing in the world that suggests God or the provisions of Providence. The world is essentially evil; Satan is the prince of it. It knows not God; it is hostile to him and his little band; it is to be overcome.

The Johannine Jesus goes his own way, unapproachable, majestic, unmoved by circumstances and events, all the while brooding in another world of thought and being. That human life is a boon and worth the living never occurs to him. He is not a serious sharer of our common human experience; he is not subject to the common human limitations. He is conscious of none of the native and natural human limitations out of which the religious sense of dependence springs.[20] He knows everything. On first sight he gives Peter his surname (1,42), which in Mark expresses his knowledge of this particular disciple gained only after considerable personal contact and acquaintance. (3,16.) He has only to see Nathaniel to know that he is an Israelite in whom there is no guile. (1,47-48.) He reads the past of the woman at the well (4,18) and tells her all things she ever did (4,29). From the very beginning he knows that Judas is to betray

---

[20]For a brief discussion of this consciousness of limitations on the part of the Synoptic Jesus, *see* the author's companion study, *The Religion of Jesus,* pp. 141-146.

him. (6,64 70-71.) He knows that Lazarus is dead
even before the news can reach him. (11,11-14.)

The Johannine Jesus confesses limitations of power,

"I can of myself do nothing." (5,30.)

But this again is formal rather than actual. He effects
a cure from one town (Cana) to the next (Capernaum).
(4,46-53.) He cures a man of an infirmity of thirty-
eight years standing. (5,5.) He crosses the sea of Galilee on foot from one side to the other. (6,16-21.) He
restores sight to a man born blind. (9,1.) He raises
Lazarus after he had been in the tomb four days when,
according to the popular folk-psychology of the time, he
was hopelessly dead. The Jesus of the Fourth Gospel
does not cure and heal; he performs acts of sheer omnipotence. He himself will effect the resurrection of the
believer,

"For this is the will of my Father, that every one
that beholdeth the Son, and believeth on him, should
have eternal life; and I will raise him up at the last
day." (6,40.)

In the Synoptic Gospels we found that a sense of
limitation of personal worth was one of the finest features
in Jesus' personality,

"Why callest thou me good? none is good save one,
even God." (Mark 10,18.)

Over against this natural religious recoil stands the
Johannine contrast,

"Which of you convicteth me of sin?" (8,46a.)

In the Fourth Gospel this sinlessness of Jesus is not a perfection of personal piety, an actual religious accomplishment such as it is in the Synoptics, but it is formal and theoretical because he himself is God. In the Synoptics, Jesus, in his thought of himself, remains rigidly religious. Even when he is faced with the messianic issue his thought never transcends the limits of the religious consciousness. If he is the Messiah, or is destined to be the Messiah, he is such by the divine will.[21] But in the Fourth Gospel the language and thought of Jesus concerning himself transcend all the confines of the religious consciousness. Very clearly, time after time, he sets himself as a religious value second to none, as a religious object in the absolute sense.

In the Synoptic Gospels we found that the supreme religious aspiration of Jesus was the discovery and performance of the divine will.[22] This he achieves by a terrific struggle and stress of soul that is upon him from the first day to the last. He is not always clear as to the divine will for himself, and he traverses a painful path on his way to religious certainty.

In the Fourth Gospel Jesus often speaks of the divine will as the very substance of his life-task:

"My meat is to do the will of him that sent me, and to accomplish his work." (4,34b.)

---

[21]The messianic issue in the experience of Jesus will be discussed later, see pp. 213-256.

[22]See the author's companion study, *The Religion of Jesus*, pp. 155-163.

"I seek not mine own will, but the will of him that sent me."   (5,30b.)

"For I am come down from heaven, not to do mine own will, but the will of him that sent me."   (6,38.)[23]

Finer religious characterizations of the historical Jesus are not to be found in the whole of our Christian literature. The author of these sentences gives a purely religious appraisal of Jesus and in them expresses the very essence of his life and work. It would be difficult to state more accurately in a single sentence the true mind of Jesus. But these passages do not fit the experience of the Johannine Jesus. There is no struggle for clearness and certainty; he is never in doubt of the divine will, even for a moment.

The Fourth Gospel strips all struggle from the soul of Jesus. It has no account of his temptation, for the Johannine Jesus is above temptation. The author seems to have been unable to find any real religious values in his severe personal struggles. On the contrary, they seem to have created problems for him in his conception and picture of Jesus. The Gethsemane struggle he deliberately omits. From this great Synoptic scene, where Jesus achieves his highest aspiration by submission to the divine will, the Fourth Evangelist preserves only two ragged remnants.   (12,27; 18,11b.)   The Johannine Jesus is even above suffering in the hour of death. His words from the cross reflect nothing of the terrible pain of body and agony of soul that we find in the Synoptic picture. Nowhere in the Fourth Gospel does he experience any difficulty in meeting the divine demands placed upon him. We never get the impression of moral effort

---

[23]Cf. 8,29b; 14,31b; 15,10.

and spiritual endeavor on the part of the Johannine Jesus.

The Jesus of the Fourth Gospel has no personal problems.[24] His ability to perform the most amazing feats creates no surprise on his part and gives rise to no special solicitude. His omnipotence he takes as a matter of course. He feels no personal problem in the popularity in which his wonder-works result. On the contrary, the very purpose of the Johannine miracles, for such they are, is to center interest upon and finally lead to belief in himself as the Messiah or Son of God. Of the sickness of Lazarus he says,

"This sickness is not unto death, but for the glory of God, that the Son of God may be glorified thereby." (11,4.)

In the Fourth Gospel Jesus makes no choice between cause and cures.[25] There is no growing disinclination to heal. On the contrary, the wonder-works in the Fourth Gospel move toward a super-climax which comes in the raising of Lazarus, by which Jesus demonstrates that he is the resurrection and the life. The cures of the Synoptic Jesus are acts of compassion and mercy, and they are prompted by a genuine sympathy and love for the afflicted. In the first three Gospels he refuses to give signs as his personal credentials. But in the Fourth Gospel there are few, if any, traces of tenderness. He performs his wonder-works as signs to prove his identity and to compel belief in his exalted dignity.

---

[24]*See* Chapter IV of the present study, pp. 198*ff*.
[25]Cf. pp. 202-213.

The person of the Johannine Jesus is never problematic for himself.[26]   In the Synoptics Jesus keeps his self-estimate as a deep personal secret; he guards it with a careful caution, as a sacred matter between himself and his God.   It never betrays itself in his public message, seldom in his words in private to his disciples.   If he did come to the messianic conviction, which is nowhere absolutely certain, it was only after long and hard struggle of soul.   But in the Fourth Gospel he knows who he is, all that he has ever been and is to be, from the very outset.   There is no painful climb to the messianic conviction.   He makes no effort to conceal his identity. In public and in private, before friends and foes, he openly discloses his messiahship or Sonship.   The Baptist recognizes and announces him as such.   His disciples know that he is the Messiah from the very first; it is this knowledge that wins them. (1,41   45   49.)   He discloses his messiahship to the woman at the well (4,26), his Sonship to the blind beggar to whom he has restored sight (9,37), to his enemies (10,36), and in the Fourth Gospel it is Martha, not Simon Peter, who makes the great confession (11,27).

In the first three Gospels, as we shall see, the question of his fate is one of the most pressing of the personal problems of Jesus.[27]   The prospect of a fatal outcome calls forth the strongest emotions, and Jesus finds himself in the throes of struggle.   The first forecasts of his fate come only in the last few weeks of his public life. However, in the Fourth Gospel Jesus is fully acquainted with his fate from the very outset and is

---

[26]Cf. pp. 213-256.
[27]Cf. pp. 256-264.

wholly adjusted to it. Its prospect calls forth none of
the natural and normal emotions that we should expect.
It does not throw him into a terrific stress and strain of
soul. He goes voluntarily to his end:

"Therefore doth the Father love me, because I lay
down my life, that I may take it up again. No one
taketh it away from me, but I lay it down of myself. I
have power to lay it down, and I have power to take it
again." (10,17-18.)

There is but one echo of the Synoptic forecasts of his
fate. (18,11). As he nears the end, only once does he
falter (12,17), but the feeling of fear hardly strikes
him before he recovers his stoical poise in the light of
the pre-human purpose that brings him to his fate. His
death is a part of a divinely prearranged plan into which
he fits himself. His fate is unconditioned by events and
circumstances. It is not the result of Judas' betrayal;
he is not arrested, but voluntarily surrenders himself.
Those who accomplish his end are simply irresponsible
actors in a superhuman drama which they do not understand. His death is simply a divinely appointed hour;
until it comes he is inviolable and no harm can overtake
him. This magical hour hovers over him, and when
it arrives it is simply his long-anticipated rendezvous with
death, his return to the Father from whose company he
came. His words on the cross are colorless and feelingless; they reflect nothing of the historical situation in
which he finds himself. He is simply departing from a
human life that has meant little to him. Thus the greatest of all Jesus' personal religious triumphs is gone from

the Fourth Gospel, his submission to his fate in which
he attains a religious harmony with the divine will for
himself.

When we turn to the Fourth Gospel for the distinctly
religious acts of Jesus we find that they are all but gone.
The baptism disappears as a religious step on the part of
Jesus; only a remnant of the account remains in the form
of a reminiscence of the Baptist. (1,29-34.)   The cleansing of the temple still stands, but it is no longer an
integral part of the passion story as it is in the Synoptics.
There is no choosing of the twelve, no mission of the
twelve, no journey to the north.   Although the Johannine Jesus goes often to Jerusalem, there is really no
eventful journey to the scene of his death.   The celebration of the Passover, at which time Jesus gives a final
pledge of his personal faith in the kingdom and its coming, is replaced by a private supper twenty-four hours
in advance, the washing of the disciples' feet and a long
farewell address.

In the Synoptic story we found the prayer-act to be
the supreme expression of Jesus' religious consciousness.
Over against the richness of Jesus' prayer-experience in
the first three Gospels one is impressed with its utter
poverty in the Fourth Gospel.   Prayer is a prominent
theme in the teaching of the Synoptic Jesus,[28] but in the
Fourth Gospel he says very little on prayer as a fundamental practise of piety.   About the only occasion on
which he touches on this theme is in the farewell address.
(15,14-17.)   But his words on prayer on this occasion
are simply his personal promises to the little band that

---

[28]*See* the author's companion study, *The Religion of Jesus*, pp. 183-189.

they shall be heard if they believe in him and pray in his name. Not a sentence on prayer in the Fourth Gospel leaves the impression that it is autobiographical, the fruit of Jesus' own prayer-experience. The Johannine Jesus feels no need of prayer such as we find in the Jesus of the Synoptics. When he prays it is not for himself, but for the belief of others in himself. The answer to his prayer in 12,27-28 is not for his sake but for that of the unbelieving bystanders. (12,30.) He even presents himself as a prayer-object, and personally promises to answer the prayers of his disciples. (14,13-14.)

In the Fourth Gospel there is not a single retreat to solitude for prayer, not one instance of his seeking out the seclusion of the desert to be alone with his God. The author of the Fourth Gospel seems deliberately to neglect this important factor in the religious experience of the Synoptic Jesus.[29] In fact, he seems interested in suppressing anything and everything that would suggest a real religiousness of Jesus. The practise of prayer would imply personal need on his part, but in the faith of the Fourth Evangelist Jesus is above all such need. The Johannine Jesus transcends all the situations in which he appears. Not even in the garden or on the cross does he feel the need of prayer. Three of the four Synoptic words of Jesus on the cross are prayers, but not one of the three Johannine words on the cross is a prayer.

In the first three Gospels we found seven great prayers of Jesus,[30] but of this wondrous collection not one reappears in the Fourth Gospel. Of the Gethsemane

---

[29]*The Religion of Jesus*, pp. 189-195; *also* Chapter VI of the present study, pp. 298*ff.*

[30]*Ibid.*, pp. 195-208; *also* Chapter VI of the present study, pp. 306*ff.*

prayer alone there remains a badly tattered fragment. (12,27-28a; 18,11.)   From the lips of Jesus the Fourth Evangelist has taken the most precious prayers that the history of religion knows: "Our Father who are in heaven . . . ," "Not what I will . . . ," "My God, my God . . . ,"   "Father, forgive . . . "   The Fourth Gospel reports only three prayers of Jesus: the remnant of the Gethsemane prayer (12,27-28a; 18,11), the prayer at the grave of Lazarus (11,41-42), and the highpriestly prayer (17,1-26.)[31]   The principal point to the Gethsemane prayer is gone: Jesus' submission to the divine will.   The other two prayers have no parallels in the first three Gospels. Even these two are not prayed prayers; they are not the spontaneous outbursts of a soul in petition or praise to God.   Both are public rather than private, didactic rather than devotional.   The second is literary and liturgical, even ecclesiastical. (17,1-26.)   They lack the pressing compactness and spontaneity of the prayers of Jesus in the first three Gospels.   They are the free compositions of the Fourth Evangelist, didactic discourses (especially 17,1-26), delivering the fundamentals of the Johannine faith.   Both are impossible on the lips of the historical Jesus.

In the Fourth Gospel, then, we find a virtual elimination of the prayer-experience of Jesus.   This results in a grave impoverishment of the personality of the historical Jesus at the hands of the Fourth Evangelist. On the basis of its neglect of his prayer-life alone, the Fourth Gospel takes itself out of the body of reliable biographical matter on the Jesus of history.

---

[31]The only other notice of Jesus' praying in the Fourth Gospel is in 6,11—thanksgiving at the feeding of the five thousand.

The Johannine picture of Jesus is consistent in that his demands correspond to the commanding elements of his experience.[32] His consciousness is wholly egocentric, and his demands are equally so. "Believe" is the great word of the Johannine Jesus, and the religious experience of his followers practically exhausts itself in believing in God and the One He has sent. Their reward is eternal life, a knowledge of God and the Christ. (17, 3.) The Synoptic command, "Follow me," is gone except in 1,43 and 12,26. He often speaks of the will of the Father and of keeping his own commandments, but both mean just one thing: belief in Jesus as the Son. He openly demands belief in himself.[33] Unbelief is sin. Even the Father's love for the little band is dependent upon their continued belief in him. (16,27.) Belief in the Fourth Gospel becomes doctrinal, cold and confessional. It is no longer faith, the warm personal confidence which greets Jesus unsolicited in the Synoptics. The disciples' hope of salvation depends upon exclusive attachment to his person, a thing against which the Synoptic Jesus warns as a dangerous self-delusion. The Fourth Gospel has always been famous for its "new commandment,"

"That ye love one another." (13,34.)

But when we come to investigate it, we find that it is not the great common bond of human brotherhood, but that it confines itself to the little band. It is the special

[32]For the religious demands of the Synoptic Jesus, *see* Chapter IV of the author's companion study, *The Religion of Jesus*, pp. 210-270.
[33]Cf. 3,14-15 36; 6,29 35b 40; 8,24b; 11,25-26; 14,1 6b.

insignia by which the outside world will know that they are his disciples. (13,35.)

In the Fourth Gospel the religious experience of Jesus is gone. In it the Fourth Evangelist seems to have been unable to find religious values either for himself or for his readers. In fact, the real religiousness of the Synoptic Jesus seems to have created problems for him, conflicts with his own personal faith, and consequently he neglects entirely his personal piety. For the Fourth Evangelist Jesus is exclusively a religious object, never a religious subject. Jesus has a religion only in the first three Gospels. The Johannine Jesus has no religion and needs none; in fact, in the Fourth Gospel he becomes a religion, the new and true object of religious faith. In the Fourth Gospel, then, we have to do with the Christian experience of its writer or writers, not with the personal religious experience of the human historical Jesus.

In the Gospel of John the religious experience of some early Christian or group of Christians is written back into the religious experience of Jesus himself. The Johannine Jesus is endowed with the Christian consciousness; he thinks Christian thoughts; he becomes an exponent of the Christian message; he is held by Christian convictions; Christian confessions and demands fall from his lips. The Johannine Jesus is the completely deified object of the Christian faith. The Jesus of history is gone for ever, save in name. The intensity of Christian feeling has suppressed all interest in historical fact. The Jesus of the Fourth Gospel is a figure formed and fashioned by a fervent faith, not the human Jesus with the richest religious experience of which we have any record.

The Fourth Gospel is not a biographical account of Jesus of Nazareth. It is a purely devotional document. It is the greatest of all Christian confessions. It sprang from a remarkably rich Christian life that has given to subsequent Christian experience its classic expressions. Every follower of Jesus is convinced that he is the way and the truth and the life, and with the Fourth Evangelist he confesses it with a ready and full heart. But this clear crystallization of Christian conviction is the possession of those alone who have seen in Jesus more than a center of confession, who have found in him those rich religious resources necessary for the living of life in the uninterrupted presence of God.

The Fourth Gospel is one of those rich and rare fruits of Christian piety; it is luxurious in the strict sense of the word. The values to be drawn from it belong to the upper ranges of Christian experience. They are not immediately accessible to those who feel that religion is first of all a human problem. This great document will always warm the mystical imagination and temperament, but the prosaic type of piety, confronted as it is with the pressing problem of living life religiously, will turn to the first three Gospels for the moral motives and the ethical energy necessary for its task. Into the self-consciousness of Jesus the Christian faith may pour the whole content of its convictions concerning him, just as the Fourth Evangelist has done. But when this results in the total suppression of the religious experience of Jesus himself, we may be grateful that all the Gospel writers were not Johns.

On the basis of chronological conflicts and contradictions concerning the form and content of Jesus' thought and teaching, Strauss set his famous alternative: *either Synoptic or Johannine!* But when we come to approach the two accounts on the basis of the nature and substance of Jesus' experience, the alternative is more necessary than ever. It becomes sharper than ever: *either Jesus or John!* The great psychological problem is: Why did the Fourth Evangelist choose to put his own Christian experience in a form that purports to be a life of Jesus? For this problem we have as yet no definite solution; doubtless we never shall have.

THE FIRST THREE GOSPELS

In our survey of the New Testament documents thus far we have found very little real sensitiveness to the religiousness of Jesus on the part of either writers or readers. It is only exceptionally that a New Testament writer points his readers to some religious experience of Jesus as a source of Christian light and strength. To the person of Jesus the New Testament writers attach the highest religious values. In him they see the consummation of everything that is religiously worth while. But the Jesus of New Testament piety is always a religious object—the Messiah, the Son of God, the Risen Lord, the Incarnate Word. It is not the human historical Jesus but the heavenly Christ to which the Christian hope of the New Testament attaches itself. If we possessed only the last twenty-four books of the New Testament, we should never have more than the feeble suspicion that the Jesus of history was an intensely religious personality, and of his religious experience we should know next to nothing. Outside of the first three Gospels we find not more than fragmentary and scattered data on his personal piety, and from them alone we could never reconstruct the main substance of his religious experience.

The very nature of the great body of New Testament experience conspired against a turning to the human life of Jesus for religious values. As we see in I Thessalonians 4,15-18 and in many other passages, the earliest Christian experience was keyed to the high pitch of Jesus' imminent and triumphant return. The great New Testament prayer is,

Marana tha, "Our Lord, come!"

In such an elevated and expectant atmosphere it is really surprising that any real interest in the human historical Jesus survived. How poor indeed was the prosaic story of the prophet of Nazareth in comparison with the glorious future of the Son of God! It was only later when fact contradicted faith, when the hope of the Lord's immediate return had been generally surrendered that the soberer element began to turn to the life and work of the Jesus of history. The result of this interest has deposited itself in the first three Gospels in which, as we shall see in the next chapter, we get a relatively reliable picture of Jesus as he was.

Christian tradition that goes back to Papias tells us that the story of Jesus was an integral part of the early Christian message. The main body of a prosaic account like that of Mark goes back perhaps to the memoirs of Simon Peter, and a number of passages in the second Gospel point to this intimate Petrine origin. The very existence of such an unadorned story as Mark narrates is positive proof that the beginnings in Galilee were never quite forgotten and that in certain circles there grew up a lively interest in what Jesus himself said and did. But the main body of Christian interest did not center upon the human Jesus of the past. The story of his earthly career existed simply as a concern collateral to the principal trend of early Christian feeling and faith. The story that had its scene in Galilee and that ended in Jerusalem was only the paradoxical prologue that served to set the later developments in greater relief.

Within the New Testament the first three Gospels are vi' tually our only sources of information on the religious e' perience of Jesus. In them Jesus does appear as a re-l'gious subject, as a man of tremendous religious genius, eeling and faith, who fears, loves, serves and prays to his God. But we must remember that the Synoptic authors are neither less Christian nor more biographical in their interests than Paul or John. The Synoptic writers in recounting the story of Jesus have in mind all the while the exalted object of the Christian faith to whom their own personal piety is deeply attached. Whatever of the religious experience of Jesus survives in their accounts does so by the sheer force of historical fact—because Jesus was really religious. The primary interest of the Synoptic writers is not in fact, but in the supports for faith which fact from the life of Jesus can furnish. They are interested in history only for the homiletic heart that it contains. They intend that their story of Jesus should preach the Christian message about him and prove its claims for him.

This is clear in the superscription which Mark, the earliest of the Synoptists, sets at the head of his work. (1,1.) In this title it is quite clear that Mark is not offering a life of Jesus and that his primary interest in writing his work is not biographical. He does not begin with the title: "The Biography of Jesus of Nazareth, the Son of Joseph." But at the head of his work he sets a statement that indicates its content, character and purpose:

"The Beginning of the Gospel of Jesus Christ, the Son of God."

In such a superscription we have full-fledged Christianity, pure Christian piety, not the religious experience of Jesus. But in the very next sentences Mark presents materials that justify fully our approach to Jesus as a religious subject. He opens his account with a brief notice concerning Jesus' great religious predecessor (1,2-8); at the Jordan we see Jesus taking a religious step in response to a religious message and mission, undergoing a religious rite (1,9-11); in the wilderness he passes through a religious experience and achieves some sort of religious triumph (1,12-13); he appears in public with a religious message that springs straight from his own personal religious convictions and faith, and he feels himself called and commissioned to a religious cause for God in behalf of men (1,14-15); his first followers he calls to a religious task (1,16-20); and in 1,21-38 Mark gives us one of the finest pictures of a religious personality that the history of religion knows. Thus we might go on through the whole of the Gospel of Mark, or for that matter, through Matthew and Luke.

To be sure, the Christian point of view invades the Synoptic story. A Christian color falls over various scenes, and the whole Synoptic picture is conceived and

cast from the Christian point of view with Jesus a religious object.   But the Synoptic Gospels do furnish us
with a firm foundation and abundant matter for the study
of Jesus as an experient of religion.   His personal piety
is the clearest single feature in that wonderful picture.
From the Synoptic portrait we may reconstruct the main
body of Jesus' religious experience.   If we can learn to
know this religious experience, if we can come to share
it in some appreciable measure—to the degree that it
makes us what we are and ought to be—then we have
accomplished about all that Jesus expected of his
disciples.

CHAPTER II

THE ROAD TO THE RECOVERY OF JESUS

FOR almost a century now students of the Gospels have been on the road to the recovery of Jesus as a human historical figure. In 1835 Strauss published his famous *Life of Jesus,* the first really great account to be undertaken since the early second century. Strauss set out to answer the question, Who was Jesus? entirely apart from the traditional answers of the Christian faith, on the basis of historical probability and a careful study of the best New Testament records. Down to this very day a greater modern life of Jesus has never been written. However, Strauss' *Life of Jesus* has not held its place because of the acceptability of its special conclusions. The mythical theory of the wonder-works of Jesus as modeled after Old Testament examples, and others of its particular positions, have long been abandoned. But the main lines laid down by Strauss remain intact and point the way back to Jesus as a man of our human history. The principles on which Strauss worked, the method which he employed, the objective which he set out to reach, the conscientious spirit in which he undertook and accomplished his task—all have become the great heritage of New Testament scholarship. No man of modern times has taken a longer stride in the direction of the Jesus of history than Strauss, and in the hands of his successors he placed a critical compass whose needle was trained on the richest single deposit of religious life and experience in our human history.

The work of Strauss resulted in the life-of-Jesus research, a survey of which has been made with such fascinating and brilliant bias by Albert Schweitzer.[1] The
story of the study of Jesus in the nineteenth and early
twentieth centuries is one of the most interesting chapters
in modern literary criticism, and it recounts one of the
finest feats in objective historical research. No documents of antiquity have been subjected to a more intensive
and searching study than the Gospels. Some of the finest
minds of the nineteenth century set themselves to this
task, and an almost incredible amount of labor and talent
has been expended. The life-of-Jesus research developed
into a veritable passion, not only to know him but to
possess him and make him our own. In the last three
decades the interest in the recovery of Jesus has increased
rather than diminished.

The method used by those who have been engaged in
the life-of-Jesus research has been that now universally
recognized and employed by all serious students of the
Biblical writings, that of *literary* and *historical criticism.*
Strauss was not the first to use this method. It appeared
first as a method of research in the Greek and Latin
classics. It was later carried over and applied to the
Old Testament documents. Strauss was the first to apply
it in an exacting way to the New Testament writings, in
particular to the Gospel accounts of Jesus.

------

[1]*The Quest of the Historical Jesus* (1911), translated by W. Mont-
gomery from the first German edition, *Von Reimarus zu Wrede* (1906).
It is to be regretted that the latest English edition was not revised
according to the second German edition, *Die Geschichte der Leben-Jesu-
Forschung* (1913), which is greatly enlarged over the first German
edition. Similar, yet less pretentious studies are: Weinel, *Jesus im 19.
Jahrhundert;* Pfannmueller, *Jesus im Urteile der Jahrhunderte;* Loofs,
Wer War Jesus Christus? which is the German revision of *What is the
Truth about Jesus Christ?* Leipoldt, *Vom Jesusbilde der Gegenwart.*

The word *criticism* as the name for a method and approach to the study of the Scriptures has always aroused misgivings in the lay mind, and often it has been tragically misunderstood. But *criticism* does not mean an unfavorable approach, an unfriendly attitude toward the Gospels or any other Biblical document. A critical study of the Gospels means simply a careful and conscientious study with a view to the truth and the facts. To such a method of studying Jesus' life there can be no reasonable objection on the part of an intelligent and inquiring piety.

The method of literary and historical criticism is not the mere fad or fancy of the few. It was not born, as some still suppose, of a bitter bias that was out of all feeling with its subject-matter, nor has it been employed in the field of such a sacred body of materials as the life of Jesus for the mere academic pleasure of seeing it work. The method of literary and historical criticism was born the natural child of the scientific spirit of the nineteenth century with its passion for truth and fact. In such a favorable atmosphere it grew, developed its energy and enthusiasm, and proved its worth. Now in the twentieth century it stands as the only reliable recourse of respectable research and, relative to our present problem, the only method that will bring us back within communicating distance of the historical Jesus of Nazareth.

We must remember, however, that there is nothing sacred about this method. One of its chief virtues is its recognition of its own limitations. It is neither omniscient nor omnipotent. There are questions it can not answer, problems, too, that it can not solve. There are things it can not do. Its operation is not infallible. Today there is a growing realization that it must be powerfully supplemented by the human, psychological and religious approach to Jesus. But with this consciousness of need, it does recommend itself by its fruits as the most trustworthy way of coming again as near as possible to Jesus as he actually was. Certainly it is the only method thus far that can command the respect of an intelligent piety that feels a need for an intimate knowledge of Jesus and of a reason for the faith that it entertains.

The standards by which literary and historical research has sought to distinguish the early from the late, the genuine from the ingenuine, the original from the acquired, are not the inventions of critical genius conceived apart from and forced upon the Gospels. Rather the exact reverse is true. The standards employed are those which the Gospels themselves by their very nature and substance force upon the student who reads the records reverently and who is open to observe the state of the facts. Straight through the life-of-Jesus research there runs an unmistakable spirit of loyalty and fidelity to the New Testament. The aim of those who have subjected the New Testament records to such searching study has been to acquaint themselves as reliably as possible with the facts about Jesus—to learn to know him, what he actually said and did, who he was and what it was that he aspired to accomplish. Students of the life of Jesus have sought to learn to know him as a man of history, to understand his thought and teaching, to sense his feeling and faith, to see clearly his character and personality— in short, to learn to know Jesus himself as accurately and intimately as is possible for those who are removed from him by nineteen centuries.

THE SPIRIT OF THE SEEKER

The life-of-Jesus research has been tragically misunderstood at times, grossly misrepresented, even persecuted because it failed to substantiate Christian and unchristian prejudice. Almost without exception, its best representatives have presented a fighting front against the traditional theological picture of Jesus. It has come into contention and conflict with the official organs of the faith and it has proved itself disturbing to the lay mind, but usually it has had behind it the solid substance of the New Testament. The way back to Jesus has not been a smooth path for some who have chosen to follow it to the end. For those who have made most progress it has been a rough and rugged road that has claimed its victims. But in spite of the pious prejudice that often besets the seeker's path it is a line of research that is destined to live on, indestructible, because in its heart there has always been the deep desire and determination to seek out Jesus and the religious reality he represents. For the most part, the life-of-Jesus research has been carried on in the spirit of one of Jesus' own personal confidences,

"He that seeketh findeth." (Matt. 7,8.)

So much misgiving has encountered the critical student of the life of Jesus that it is well to point out the real spirit of the quest. It is true that, for many, the quest has sprung out of a deep dissatisfaction with the traditional picture and portrayal of Jesus, out of a sense of the sharp disparity between the orthodox and official conception and the plain picture in the Gospels. For this reason the results of the life-of-Jesus research have often been negative, openly undermining not a few of the traditional positions that had been regarded as impregnable. As Schweitzer writes, some lives of Jesus, even the greatest, have been written out of hate,[2] not so much a strength of feeling against Jesus as a caustic antipathy for what traditionalism has made of him—something which he very plainly was not.

Few students in the life-of-Jesus research have pursued their study simply as a fascinating academic problem. It is indeed a rare thing to discover in them merely an intellectual interest. Every devoted student of the Gospels knows that he possesses in the life of Jesus one of the most fascinating subject-matters in the field of literary and historical criticism, but there is usually something deeper that keeps him at his task. Those who have pressed ahead in the quest have done so in the conviction that Jesus as he lived and loved, wrought and taught, is worth knowing and, with the rarest exceptions, in the great conviction that he is worth following. The quest has not been unfeelingly objective, merely asking: What did Jesus do? What did Jesus say? Often its questions have been more pressingly personal: What can Jesus do for us? What has he to say to us to-day?

Any one who has studied the results of the research of those who have been most critical in the course they have steered on their way back to Jesus knows that it is by no means impossible to be at once careful critic and conscientious confessor. The life-of-Jesus research as a whole has not been divorced from a genuine devotion to him. Its best representatives have held to the faith that we may with safety seek to see Jesus as he was without en-

---

[2]*The Quest of the Historical Jesus*, p. 4f.

dangering his real religious significance. In fact, they
have felt that it is only by this approach that he can mean
most to us. For some, faith has been able to maintain
itself only in and through such exacting criticism. For
not a few, the careful and critical approach to Jesus has
become the only way of personal religious salvation.[3]

Those who have made the greatest strides toward the
understanding of the prominent religious figures of history have been those who have pressed close to the very
pulse of these personalities, who have sensed the swing
of their faith, and who have surrendered themselves to
the sweep of their feeling. They have realized that they
are dealing with a sacred subject-matter, the understanding of which requires more than intellectual insight.
Professor Friedrich Heiler writes: "To an investigator
of religion who does not approach his subject-matter as
a sacred shrine that calls forth within him all the primitive emotions of religious reverence and awe, the won-
derland of religion will remain closed for ever."[4]
Professor Hermann Gunkel says of those who would
understand the prophets of Israel: Only he may hope to
understand them "into whose very soul a spark from
the firebrand of their spirits has fallen."[5] In the introduction to his study of Jesus, Professor Paul Wernle
writes: "How in the world shall I as a student of religion come to understand it without religion in my own
soul; how is any one to come nearer to an understanding
of a religious genius like Jesus without his own soul being
caught away by all that is pure, fine and profound in

---

[3]Alfred Loisy is a fine example. *See* his personal confessions in his
book, *My Duel with the Vatican.*
[4]*Das Gebet,* p. viii.
[5]*Die Propheten,* p. 73f.

him—things which are beyond comprehension by scientific methods? . . . There must be something Jesus-like in the investigator himself."[6]

The very mention of the name of Strauss strikes fear into the hearts of some, but his *Life of Jesus* in its first form is full of a youthful enthusiasm that is often deeply religious. In it he makes one feel keenly enough his antipathy for the church's traditional picture of Jesus, and he has no notion of sparing the timid attempts at the study of Jesus that preceded him. When his *Life of Jesus* was published (1835), it brought down an avalanche of criticism from all those who spoke in the name of the church. It practically wrecked his hope of happiness in both professional and private life. Yet twenty-five years later when he had tasted the full bitterness of his fate, he was able to write:

"I might well bear a grudge against my book, for it has done me much evil ('And rightly so!' the pious will exclaim). It has excluded me from public teaching in which I took pleasure and for which I had perhaps some talent; it has torn me from natural relationships and driven me into unnatural ones; it has made my life a lonely one. And yet when I consider what it would have meant if I had refused to utter the word which lay upon my soul, if I had suppressed the doubts that were at work in my mind—then I bless the book which has doubtless done me grievous harm outwardly, but which preserved the inward health of my mind and heart, and, I doubt not, has done the same for many others also."[7]

---

[6]*Jesus*, p. vif.
[7]Quoted by Schweitzer, *The Quest of the Historical Jesus*, p. 5.

A good representative of the liberal life-of-Jesus research to-day is Professor Wernle, of the University of Basel. His book, bearing the title *Jesus,* is as fine a product of the life-of-Jesus research as may be found. Two out of many similar passages will illustrate the religious loyalty out of which the book sprang. In the preface he writes,

"The thought that I might sometime think Jesus through and in the future might not press my way to a deeper and better understanding of him, is for me inconceivable—indeed, terrible."[8]

At a later point,

"Whoever for once has come face to face with Jesus, is awakened out of his indifference, shocked to the very soul by his presence, and is confronted directly with eternity."[9]

The most radical critic in the whole of the life-of-Jesus research from the standpoint of bringing about a substantial alteration in the modern picture of Jesus is Albert Schweitzer. His contention was not directed so much against the picture of Jesus held by the church as against the strongholds of the life-of-Jesus research itself. Schweitzer charged the liberal theologians with a false modernization of Jesus and told them plainly that their modernized Jesus never existed except as the lifeless fiction of their own imagination. The historical Jesus,

[8]*Jesus,* p. viii.
[9]*Ibid.,* p. 242.

according to Schweitzer, had just one distinctive mark, one that the liberal theologians had neglected entirely—his expectation of the immediate end of this natural world and the appearance of a new supernatural order, the kingdom of God, which was to be introduced by the superhuman Son of man with whom Jesus as the Messiah came to identify himself. This expectation of the imminent kingdom Schweitzer presented as the one key to all that Jesus was, said and did. Schweitzer's consequent eschatology came as a shock to the theological world. New Testament scholars felt that Jesus had been reduced to a man with a single mistaken idea—for the kingdom did not come as he expected. It is only slowly that Schweitzer's view is being accepted, usually with radical modifications and reservations, very seldom in its full force.[10]

But no one knows the real Albert Schweitzer unless he knows him as the medical missionary (since 1913) to the natives of the French Congo; a man who at the command of Jesus gave up one of the most promising careers as a university professor of New Testament and philosophy, as a musician and writer of unusual gift, to minister to a needy and helpless people. Among our contemporaries there is not a Christian who shares a larger measure of the spirit of Jesus than does Albert Schweitzer. Even in his most radical treatises, Schweitzer shows how firm

---

[10]The New Testament works of Schweitzer apart from his *Quest* are: *Das Messianitaets- und Leidensgeheimnis;* English translation by Walter Lowrie, *The Mystery of the Kingdom of God. Geschichte der Paulinischen Forschung;* English translation by W. Montgomery, *Paul and His Interpreters. Die psychiatrische Beurteilung Jesu.* It is understood that Doctor Schweitzer is preparing a work on the *Mysticism of St. Paul.* His great work on the *Philosophy of Civilization,* in four volumes, is as yet incomplete: *The Decay and Restoration of Civilization,* Vol. I; *Civilization and Ethics,* Vol. II.

a hold the New Testament picture of Jesus has laid upon the whole of his life and thought. It was the personal example of Jesus that set for Schweitzer the goal of his own life-work. In his memoirs of his childhood and youth he writes that it was a word of Jesus that brought to an issue his second great life-experience which determined his view of life in general and the fate of his own life in particular:

"Gradually it began to dawn on me that I had no inner right to accept my happy youth, my health and my power to work as matter-of-fact things. Out of a sense of deepest happiness I came to understand that word of Jesus to the effect that we may not withhold our lives for ourselves."[11]

The beatitudes perhaps have left a deeper impression on Schweitzer than any other utterance of Jesus. The following passage is an extract from his experience with the power of the message of Jesus:

"Never have I felt so strongly the victorious power of what is simplest in the teaching of Jesus as when, in the big schoolroom at Lambarene, which serves as a church as well, I have been explaining the Sermon on the Mount, the parables of the Master, and the sayings of St. Paul about the new life in which we live."[12]

---

[11]*Aus meiner Kindheit und Jugend*, p. 57.

[12]*On the Edge of the Primeval Forest. Experiences and Observations of a Doctor in Equatorial Africa*, p. 155f. This little book is a broken journalistic account of the first years in Africa, and it gives us the real Albert Schweitzer. It is one of the greatest Christian documents of the twentieth century. Schweitzer's account of his second period of work in Africa (spring 1924 to summer 1927) is equally inspiring (*Mitteilungen aus Lambarene*).

The fact that Schweitzer was rewarded in his quest, that he did recover and reproduce the historical Jesus in his own experience, is clear from the following account of an operation performed for a distressed human being:

"The operation is finished, and in the hardly lighted dormitory I watch for the sick man's awakening. Scarcely has he recovered consciousness when he stares about him and ejaculates again and again: 'I've no more pain! I've no more pain!' . . . His hand feels for mine and will not let it go. Then I begin to tell him and the others who are in the room that it is the Lord Jesus who has told the doctor and his wife to come to Ogowe, and that white people in Europe give them the money to live here and cure the sick negroes. Then I have to answer questions as to who these white people are, where they live, and how they know that the natives suffer so much from sickness. The African sun is shining through the coffee bushes into the dark shed, but we, black and white, sit side by side and feel that we know by experience the meaning of the words: 'And all ye are brethren.' (Matt. 23,8.) Would that my generous friends in Europe could come out here and live through one such hour!"[13]

In one of his latest works, written in the heart of his beloved primeval forest, Schweitzer confesses,

"I live my life in God, in the mysterious ethical divine personality which I can not discover in the world, but only experience in myself as a mysterious impulse."[14]

---

[13]*On the Edge of the Primeval Forest*, p. 93.
[14]*Civilization and Ethics*, p. xvi.

Such a confession comes straight and strong from a religious experience closely akin to that of Jesus.

The life-of-Jesus research has resulted in our recovery of him as a human historical figure. But this recovery, as we shall see, is more than a dull and dreary academic process. The quest requires personal elements which the crusader must launch in full and free fashion. Its success depends eventually upon the seeker's spirit, his ability to enter into the feeling and faith of the Gospel writers, to feel and believe with them. Finally, it rests upon his ability to go back beyond the Gospel writers and enter into the feeling and faith of Jesus himself, to feel and believe with him. The road to the recovery of Jesus leads straight through the first three Gospels, and it is a rough and rugged road that can not be traveled without some sort of sacrifice.

THE WAY BACK TO JESUS

The life-of-Jesus research has resulted in the realization of the limited number of reliable sources of information which we possess concerning him, and to-day the problem of our recovery of Jesus is primarily the problem of finding him in the first three Gospels.[15] The seeker may begin with the oldest and most reliable

---

[15]Strauss openly rejected the Fourth Gospel as a reliable account of the historical Jesus, a position that gradually won the favor of the great majority of New Testament scholars. To-day there is an outspoken preference for the first three Gospels, and the Fourth Gospel is set off in a class by itself. A discussion of the grounds on which the Fourth Gospel has been rejected as equally valuable with the Synoptics would require a separate volume. A special section of the preceding chapter was devoted to the bearing of the Fourth Gospel on our present problem of recovering the religious experience of Jesus.

sources in the New Testament. The restoration of the
picture of Jesus is not just a matter of stripping off all
the accumulations and accretions of the centuries that
separate us from Jesus, except so far as these accumulations and accretions have become a mental bias that
would prejudice the purity of our approach to him.
There are some, to be sure, who will never be able to see
Jesus singly and clearly as a man of history because they
are incapable of seeing him apart from all that hazy atmosphere of Christian tradition that has enveloped his
figure. The seeker who would really see Jesus must
purge his mind of all subjective bias and gird himself for
the fresh and first impressions of objective research.
Once he has accomplished this, he may begin to retrace
the road that leads to Jesus, starting back from that point
where Matthew and Mark and Luke left off.

In point of time the road to the recovery of Jesus is
not long. At most, the first three Gospels are separated
from Jesus by a period of thirty to fifty years. This
relative nearness in point of time greatly simplifies our
problem, but it remains difficult. The way back to Jesus
is beset with literary problems, and it is difficult because
we have to find our way through documents that were not
written from our modern literary point of view—namely,
the first three Gospels.

The most difficult stage of the journey, however, is
psychological. On our way back to Jesus we have to
cross a psychological terrain that is rich in its religious
feeling and faith, in its religious thought and teaching, in
its religious convictions and certainties. In brief, we have
to travel from the Christian point of view of Matthew
and Mark and Luke to the original religious point of
view of Jesus himself. This task of finding our way back

to the religious experience of Jesus through the Christian experience of the Gospel writers is by no means easy, for our own experience doubtless has more in common with that of Matthew and Mark and Luke than it has with that of Jesus.

Generations of loyal Christians have read the Gospel story of Jesus without once feeling a problem. They have not sensed the real distance that separates him from us. Nevertheless, the reader of the first three Gospels is not as immediately in the presence of Jesus as he might naively suppose. The facts of his life, even in the first three Gospels, are not as simply and plainly recounted as the uncritical reader assumes. Our recovery of him as a man of history is much more than just the simple matter of reading the New Testament records.

The life-of-Jesus research has resulted in the recognition of a profound limitation in the very nature of our best sources of information. Each of the first three Gospel writers has his own peculiarities in the selection and treatment of materials based upon his own interests, inclinations, point of view, purposes, considerations for readers and the particular stage in the development of the early Christian faith which he represents. But the question of the nature of the first three Gospels reaches deeper. In these, our best records, from which we hope to recover Jesus as he was, we do not find a single simple substance but a great body of composite matter demanding analysis into its component parts.

The serious student in the quest of the historical Jesus strikes upon three very distinct and different strains of materials in the first three Gospels: fact, faith and fiction. There is in them a solid substratum of historical fact which gives us a remarkably reliable picture of what Jesus said and did, who he was and what he sought to accomplish. Almost inextricably imbedded in this rugged bed-rock of historical fact are the discoveries, devotions, interpretations, conceptions and convictions of the early Christian faith that attached itself so enthusiastically to Jesus—in short, the findings of a firm and fervent faith as it reviewed the earthly career of its Lord. Now and again in this territory of treasures we find a deposit of the third element, fiction.

Sometimes the solid substratum of historical fact juts high above the straight line struck by faith, and in such cases we feel that we are standing face to face with Jesus as he actually was on that first day in Capernaum (Mark 1,21-38), in Gethsemane (Mark 14,32-42), or on the cross (Mark 15,33-37). But about even these purest prominences there is cast that holy haze, that radiant glow, which betrays the source of the illumination that lights them up. At other times, this solid substratum of fact is only slightly below the surface, and it is not difficult to remove the overflow of faith. Again, the depressions in this substratum are so deep that we have no hope of reaching its bottom through the mass of faith that has rushed in to fill it up. Still again, the strata run together in a solid unbroken surface and are so amalgamated that it is difficult to detect where the one leaves off and the other begins. In such cases there will be disagreement as to what is fact and what is faith.

The recovery of the historical Jesus is a difficult task. Only approximately, yet quite adequately can it be accomplished. The serious seeker must learn to distinguish between fact, faith and fiction, for all three are present. It is his task in his quest of Jesus as a man of history to recognize these three strains of materials by their characteristic ingredients and elements, to separate one from the others in order that the distinctive features of the prophet-preacher of the kingdom of God may stand out in their original relief.

The invasions of fiction into the accounts of Jesus are sporadic, easily recognized and just as easily eliminated because they are not deep-rooted. Further, their elimination in no wise detracts from the impressiveness of the Gospel picture of Jesus.

When we come to separate the findings of faith from the firm foundation of fact, we are confronted with a much more difficult and delicate task. The task is difficult because faith and fact are not only almost inextricably woven together, but they are often so welded together that each approaches the loss of its identity. The task is delicate because in this distinction between fact and faith we are treading upon holy ground, and no seeker will realize even a relative measure of success unless he remains clearly conscious of the fact that he is entering into the sacred precincts of religious experience. The deposits of faith, whether slight or extensive, are always firmly bonded to the substratum of fact by a fidelity of devotion and a strength of conviction that make a separation almost impossible without doing violence both to the faith and to the facts. The only means of loosing this bond is an attitude of reverence for all that faith finds in fact. Faith will release its hold on fact only to a sympathetic understanding and appreciation, only as research learns to share the most intimate experiences of religion itself.

The way back to Jesus leads through fiction, through

faith, to fact. Fiction and faith are to be apprehended and appreciated, not rejected. We may reject the creations of fiction and the interpretations of faith only when they are presented as historical fact. But we must learn to see that faith is the real passion that runs through the Gospels, and that everywhere fiction and fact alike are drafted into the service of faith for its own enlightenment and enrichment.

Through Fiction

It is very disconcerting to the Christian consciousness to be told that even our best accounts of Jesus, the first three Gospels, contain legendary and unhistorical matter with little or no basis of fact in the life of Jesus. Accustomed as it is to accept the Gospel accounts on their face value as so much fact, its first reaction is that of revolt. The conservative Christian feels that if one report is called fiction, then doubt falls upon the entire record. He feels that each report in the Gospels is a keystone. In fact, the whole structure of his faith is built up of inviolable keystones, and the removal of one means for him the utter ruin of his religion. In his desperation he cries out, "If I can not believe this, what am I to believe?" But such a faith can not alter the matter, and it simply betrays the fact that it lives its life in the constant fear of the repressed doubt that after all the whole of religion may be only a delusion.

Now and then in the first three Gospels we do come upon legendary materials, pure and less pure fiction that has found its way quite naturally into the story of Jesus. These invasions of fiction are not numerous, nor are they extensive. The surprising thing is not that we find legendary invasions in the Gospels; the really surprising thing is that these invasions are not more numerous and extensive than they are. It is really remarkable that we find as few pieces of fiction as we do find in the Gospels. Compared with the life-records of other great men of antiquity, particularly with those of religious personalities, the Gospel story of Jesus is relatively free from fiction.

Most of the legendary motifs that appear in the Gospels come from the characteristic habits of thought of the ancient world. The same stories in different garb are told of the great men of other ancient peoples. Such fiction as appears in the Gospels is not the conscious and deliberate creation of the Gospel writers. Behind some of it there may be a remote or more immediate basis of fact in the life of Jesus, but in it all, whether pure fiction or submerged fact with legendary accretions, we are having to do with the folk-psychology of the ancient world of which Jesus and the Gospel writers were a part. The fiction that does appear is not the work of a moment. It grew up involuntarily as the religious significance of Jesus grew and, in turn, the Gospel story grew up after him.

The Gospel writers, particularly Mark, take a special delight in recounting things which for us transcend not only the field of historical probability, but the realm of physical possibility. Mark has a very evident relish for the purely miraculous. He tells of Jesus walking on the water, stilling the storm and raising the dead daughter of Jairus in the same matter-of-fact way that he recounts the fact that Jesus entered into the house of Simon on a Sabbath day and before dawn the next morning retreated to a desert place to pray. The doubts and difficulties that beset us, the spontaneous skepticism with which we meet some of his accounts, never occurred to Mark's thought. Apart from the fact that Mark belongs to the ancient world, his whole interest in recounting the story of Jesus is fed by the force of his faith, not by any desire to confine himself to fact.

As we have said already, the invasions of fiction into the Gospel accounts are not extensive; they are easily detected on the basis of historical probability, and just as easily eliminated. But it is just at this point that we must move slowly on our way back to Jesus. We may reject such fiction as we find and declare it unhistorical and without value for our knowledge of Jesus. However, we are not permitted to eject it bodily from the Gospel accounts.

These legendary invasions usually represent deposits of faith. Sometimes this faith is not what we to-day would regard as of a very high order, for it is governed by a love for the miraculous—in some cases, the greater the miracle, the more genuine the delight of the narrator. When Matthew tells us that at the death of Jesus

"the earth did quake; and the rocks were rent; and the tombs were opened; and many bodies of the saints that had fallen asleep were raised; and coming forth out of the tombs after his resurrection they entered into the holy city and appeared unto many" (27,51b-53),

we are not deeply impressed. But in other cases, the fiction in the Gospels springs from a faith that is high and pure and strong. Consequently, it expresses valid religious convictions. When Luke tells us that

"suddenly there was with the angel a multitude of the
heavenly host praising God and saying,

> Glory to God in the highest
> And on earth peace among men
> In whom he is well pleased" (2,13-14)',

we are thrilled by the very exaltation of the theme. All
such fiction constitutes a tremendous tribute to Jesus. And
as we work our way through it in our quest of him we
must remember that we are passing through a realm of
rich religious experience that attached itself to Jesus,
and that some of this fiction represents a sacred soil into
which certain first-century souls have poured out their
best.

The most outstanding body of fiction in the first three
Gospels is to be found in the Christmas stories of
Matthew (1-2) and Luke (1,5-2,52). There is not a
section of the Synoptic story from which we may glean
such a meager amount of historical fact. In the Narratives of the Nativity there are only a few biographical
details that we might add to the general store of our information concerning Jesus, and some of these are open
to question. From them we might gather the probable
decade of Jesus' birth (4 B.C.—6 A.D.), that he was
born in Bethlehem although in later life he is connected
only with Nazareth of Galilee, that he was the son
of Joseph and Mary, perhaps also of Davidic descent.
But this meager bit constitutes the absolute maximum
of biographical matter that the Christmas stories have
to offer us.

From the literary point of view, the Narratives of
the Nativity are fiction, religious fiction. They are

without doubt early Christian legend and folk-lore. However, we as Christians may not, with right, entertain a low estimate of fiction and its function as a conductor of religious feeling and faith. Jesus himself was a master at fiction. His more than fifty parables are all pure fiction, the deliberate inventions and conscious creations of his own imagination. But in these parables, pure fiction as they are, Jesus chose to express the greatest and finest results of his religious experience. Apart from his parables, we should know very little of the kingdom of God, what it meant for Jesus himself and what he meant by it.

One of the most pernicious fallacies in popular religious thinking is the identification of *truth* and *fact*. We forget that the greatest wrongs in the world are unmistakable facts and that the greatest of all truths are the pure or partial creation of our human conception, and that as such they belong to the ideal world of the imagination and not to the real world of fact. In Christian conviction there is only one point in history where truth and fact meet—in the historical personality of Jesus.

The Narratives of the Nativity are the fruit of early Christian piety at some of its best moments and in them there is deposited some very solid substance from the living body of the early Christian faith. They confront us directly with some of the most important early Christian convictions concerning the religious significance of Jesus. In and of themselves, the Christmas stories are a tremendous tribute to Jesus, to the unique quality of his personality and character. It is of relatively few men in the world's history that such things have been told; of still fewer have such things been believed. The human race—ancient and modern, primitive and cultured—has always felt that the Divine was specially near in the life and work of its great heroes. Through the memories of such men inspired fancy has woven its fabric of fiction—fiction because it is far from fact, but true because it expresses valid convictions.

The Narratives of the Nativity, then, are the fruit and work of early Christian piety itself, the involuntary creation of the early Christian devotion and faith that attached themselves to Jesus, expressing themselves in a popular and poetic fashion. There is only one source of stimulation for the Christian imagination that is responsible for the Narratives of the Nativity, and that is Jesus himself, who he was and what these early believers discovered in him. Jesus was not their author; they were unknown to him, yet he was their inspiration. Religious literature has its prose, but it also has its poetry into which its authors pour the finest of their sentiments and spirit.

With regard to literary form the Narratives of the Nativity are fiction, early Christian folk-lore. For the critical student there can be no real doubt on this point. But when we come to approach them for their substance and content, then we see that they belong to the realm of religious faith. Their religious value is in no sense dependent upon their historical inexactness or their literary form, but upon the fundamental truths which they teach. Behind these stories, in and through them, there are operating fundamental themes that belong to the religious experience of all mankind—themes that are sacred not only in our Christianity but in all religious faiths: the natural human longing for religious salvation, its fulfillment, the joyous participation of the divine world in the redemption of men, the bringing of all to the common level of the knee, the wisest and richest along with the plainest and poorest. These are fundamental themes that are generally human in their appeal.

In the Narratives of the Nativity these great human themes receive the most exalted treatment. The star, the Wise-men, the shepherds from the hills, the heavenly host, the fond mother, the lowly born babe—all strike straight to the heart and will continue to thrill all generations of Christians. "The gospel of Christmas remains the gospel of Christmas wholly independent of the question, fact or fancy."[16]

In the Christmas stories we strike upon a solid religious substance. In their own way they say that the divine interest in the world and men is not just an empty dream; it is not just an idle promise, not just a beautiful but meaningless thought. The Narratives of the Nativity say that the divine interest in humankind amounts to a positive love and devotion that expressed itself in a gift. This gift took on the form of life actually lived—a life so striking and unique in its quality that men instinctively felt that it must have come directly from God, and in its presence they sensed the Divine.

The meagerness of historical fact and the extensiveness of fiction in the Narratives of the Nativity must not obscure our vision for this solid religious substance which they present. The Christmas stories represent some early Christian attempts at expressing the religious significance of Jesus. They were a natural and adequate expression of religious conviction concerning Jesus for the Christian circles from which they came, and they

---

[16]Bousset, *Jesus,* p. 3.

are adequate for many still. The great majority of
people who are acquainted with the Narratives of the
Nativity will never raise the question about their being
fact, faith, or fiction. In this they are right, for they
have sensed the spirit behind them. We to-day might
express our convictions concerning the religious significance of Jesus in a different way. But we must continue
to share the community of conviction out of which the
Narratives of the Nativity came and which they still
preserve. If we lose this body of conviction from which
they sprang and which expresses itself in and through
them, we have lost not only Christianity but religion
itself.

The discovery of elements of doubtful historicity in
our New Testament account of Jesus only leads us on
and back to the bed-rock of reliable historical tradition
on which he stands as the indisputable authority in all
matters of religion and religious living. But the seeker
must have an eye for the beauty and splendor of the
territory through which he finds his way. If his eye is
trained on fact only and his heart refuses to warm to
fiction, he may reach his goal but he will find a lifeless
figure at the end of his journey. The student on his way
back to Jesus who sees in the Christmas stories only a few
questionable biographical data, upon whom the flood of
feeling and faith that runs through them makes no impression, is not destined to find himself at home when
he comes into contact with that still stronger stream of
feeling and faith which the historical Jesus himself
exhibits.

Through Faith

It is highly important that the Gospels be left linked up in a vital and organic way with the rest of the New Testament, the collection of early Christian writings of which they are a part. The Gospels, as all the New Testament writings, are Christian products, ripe fruits of early Christian piety. They, with the rest of the New Testament, are the earliest literary expressions of a new, but vigorous and aggressive religious faith. The Gospels were written by men of the same faith as those who wrote the extra-Gospel books, and the same motives of evangelization and edification are behind them and were their original inspiration. Two of Paul's missionary companions, it appears, wrote Gospels (Mark and Luke), and it is difficult to conceive of their faith as differing essentially from his own. Whether authors of Gospels or of epistles, all of the New Testament writers are Christian preachers. Mark has gained a reputation for giving his readers a remarkably reliable picture of the historical Jesus, but Mark is every whit as much Christian preacher in his Gospel as is Paul in his letters. From the standpoint of initial impulse and ultimate aim the New Testament writers are one—Mark, John and Paul. If Mark gives us a more reliable picture of Jesus than John gives, it is not because Mark is any more of an historian. If one Gospel has a higher historical trustworthiness than another, this fact is an accidental product that lay entirely outside of the particular writer's centers of interest and intention.

The Gospels must be studied as a part of the religious movement from which they came, as natural and true expressions of its faith. The student who would win for himself an adequate picture of the Jesus of history must keep this point of orientation clearly and constantly in mind. It is only thus that he, approaching Jesus from the West, can learn to read and to be guided by the critical compass which not infrequently draws away from Galilee and points to Greece under the influence of deposits that penetrate to the very bed-rock of our best tradition concerning Jesus. The very existence of the Gospels is evidence enough of the important place which the story of Jesus occupied in the early Christian faith and its propagation. The four Gospels are proof positive of the fact that the story of Jesus' life and work was a principal integral element of the earliest Christian message. On the other hand, it is just as clearly evident that the *Christianity* of the Gospel writers and of the believers before them found its way into and affected the picture of Jesus that has come down to us in their writings.

The Gospels do not present just the simple and plain facts from the life of Jesus. They are not pure biography. They were written at the time of Christianity's first rapid expansion, and the fervor of its faith, the flush of its early triumphs, are cast across the figure of Jesus. The Gospels are fully as rich and important sources of information concerning the early Christian faith as they are sources disclosing the nature and substance of Jesus' own personal faith. The faith of the early Christian community in general and of the Gospel writers in particular is just as prominent in the Gospels as is fact from his life. They contain vastly more of what the early Christians thought and claimed for Jesus than they do of what he thought and claimed for himself. The facts about Jesus were reported in the interest of inter-

pretation, and the Gospels contain fully as much interpretation as they do information concerning what he
said and did, who he was. The Gospel writers fuse their
interpretations with the facts; sometimes they even suppress the facts by their interpretations. The convictions
of one of the Gospel writers often enter into his record
to the extent of obscuring the personal convictions of
Jesus himself. In the Gospels the devotion of faith is
always stronger than the desire for fact.

Wherever religious experience is deep and vital just
such takes place when faith comes into contact with history. Faith refuses to stop with mere fact. It feels
that its function is to interpret, illuminate and idealize.
The Gospels were not written to communicate historical
information but to impart religious inspiration. Even
in our best sources Jesus is not just presented; he is also
interpreted. The interpretation was the inspiration
of the presentation. Apart from the faith that attached
itself to Jesus, apart from what it found in him, there
could have been no interest in preserving a record of his
life and work. The facts about Jesus were rehearsed, reviewed and finally written in the light of what they
meant for faith. It was not the thrill of narration that
inspired and sustained the transmission of the story.
The tale was told and the story was written to present
and to preach the religious values which faith had found
in him. And just as often as not in the first three Gospels
it is the Christian experience of the Gospel writers rather
than the religious experience of Jesus that presents itself
and that would communicate itself to us. The pulse of
primitive Christian piety throbs all the way through the
Gospel story, and often it is presented as that of Jesus
himself.

We are beginning to see in the Gospels what they were and are, first of all, devotional documents. The idea of making a biographical contribution did not occur to their authors. They were neither written nor read originally as sources of information, but as sources of religious light and strength. In the Gospels the story of Jesus is drafted very simply but very surely into the service of practical Christian piety. In many cases, the Gospel writers are very indifferent toward fact when the interests of faith are concerned. In some cases, they deliberately suppress fact if it conflicts with their own faith or that of their readers. This is often the case when we compare the account of certain incidents in Mark with the account of the same incidents in Matthew and Luke.

There are scenes in Mark's Gospel which Matthew and Luke regard as unworthy and they omit them from their Gospels, or, if they retain such a scene, they eliminate the offensive elements. Mark's account at certain points is unadorned and realistic, but the accounts of Matthew and Luke at these same points are more idealistic; they deliberately remove those more realistic elements that present Jesus for them as all-too-human.

Mark allows Jesus to speak and act at the impulse of the greatest variety of natural and normal human emotions. Upon occasion Jesus is angry; he looks upon the rich young ruler and loves him; he takes the little children in his arms and blesses them. But Jesus is never angry in Luke, just once in Matthew. Both omit Mark's notice that he loved the rich young ruler and that he took the little children in his arms. Both Matthew and Luke seem to feel that the stronger as well as the more affectionate emotions in Mark's picture make Jesus too human, and they substitute a type of emotion more in harmony with their own faith. One may very properly speak of a monotony in the emotions of Jesus in the first and third Gospels; in both, his words and acts are, almost without exception, expressions of compassion. Gracious sympathy and compassion are integral and indispensable elements in the personality of the historical Jesus, but that he acted and spoke at the impulse of this type of emotion only is contrary both to historical probability and to the very nature of many of his words and acts in a number of the various situations in which he found himself. The historical student will find Mark to be the most reliable source on the emotions of Jesus, and he will discover as he moves from Mark to Matthew and Luke a progressive idealization and Christianization of Jesus' emotional life. In the treatment of Jesus' emotions by Matthew and Luke it is clear enough that, for them, fact is fitted into faith, that belief is stronger than biography, homiletics more important than history.

This is only one phase and stage in the process of Christianization that has gone on in the transmission of the story of Jesus, one that we can trace by a simple comparative study of the first three Gospels. But this process of Christianization is older than Matthew or Mark or Luke, and it left no part of the story of Jesus unaffected, no feature of his figure untouched. It was not in the power of those who first told and wrote the story of Jesus to depict his earthly life objectively, purely in the terms of historical exactness, even if such a type of treatment had occurred to them. They could not recount the things that Jesus said and did without their own faith and feeling rushing in to flood the whole story and picture of him.

One does not realize the tremendous power of this early Christian impulse until one gets a glimpse into the Christian experience of the author of the first Gospel. This writer is a Jew by native sentiment and training; his feeling and thinking are Jewish. He is the one who more than the others brings out the distinctly Jewish features of Jesus and who preserves some of his most strongly Jewish words. Yet the Christian experience of the author of the first Gospel is sufficiently strong to suppress to a great extent his natural Jewish consciousness and his Jewish training, and he preserves to us some of the sharpest of all Jesus' indictments against the Jews.[17]

This Christianization of the story and picture of Jesus was necessary and inevitable in view of the very nature and substance of the earliest Christian experience. It was natural, unconscious for the most part, and involuntary. From the very birth-hour of the Christian faith it was steadily at work. In a moment, faith flooded the whole field of fact in which Jesus appeared as a human historical figure. The whole story was permeated at once with the conceptions, convictions and confessions of the first Christians. But why was this?

Between the time of Jesus' death and the time of the first rehearsals of the Jesus-story there transpired in the experience of the disciples something that completely revolutionized their thought of him and that made it for ever impossible for them to see him again solely in the clear, cold light of history, just as he was and as he had been with them only a short time ago—the conviction that he was not dead, but alive again, and that they had seen him.

---

[17]This sort of suppression is still stronger and even more pronounced in the religious experience of the Apostle Paul.

It is not a great deal that we know or that we can say about the Easter experiences of the earliest Christians. Perhaps there is not much that we need to know or say. But they seem to have been as revolutionary for all the original experients as was Paul's vision on the Damascus road in his life. There must have been a great body of tremendously solid substance in the person of the human historical Jesus, for only such could bear up under the sheer weight of conviction and certainty which the Easter experiences called forth. At any rate, they bear tribute to the imposing impression which the Jesus of history had left with his closest companions.

The cross and the belief in the resurrection are the historical foundation stones of the earliest Christian faith. They constitute the two poles, negative and positive, of primitive Christian piety, and the two together present a fundamental paradox which was the seat of the very vitality of the new-born faith: He was dead, but is alive again, and we are witnesses. Upon this body of conviction the early Christian faith arose, and without it the story of Jesus would not have survived beyond a generation. The Easter experiences of the first disciples threw an entirely new light on the whole of Jesus' life and work. They were the great illumination points that rendered clear all that had been obscure and enigmatic.

It was in the light of the Easter experiences that the story was told and retold, written and rewritten. Our Gospels, then, present a review of the life and work of Jesus in the light of what the cross and the resurrection faith meant in primitive Christian piety. The memories recorded in the Gospels are transfigured memories, illuminated, made splendid and glorious by the Easter faith. In the progress and early development of the new faith there was often a wide departure from the prosaic past. Faith sublimated fact. The Jesus of history assumed new and strange proportions; he was engulfed in a flood of deepest feeling and faith; he began to develop miraculous, mythical, even metaphysical features.

Even in a realistic account like that of Mark the story of Jesus is not treated objectively. Mark is a Christian, and he writes as a Christian who entertains a Christian view of Jesus. The result is a Christian story of Jesus in the second Gospel. Mark's own deepest religious sentiments are bound up in his story. In depicting his hero to his readers Mark is depicting the object of his own fervent faith and the picture which he projects has an unmistakable Christian coloring, a coloring that reflects the glow of Mark's Christian convictions about Jesus and the warmth of his personal devotion to him. The Jesus of Mark, then, is not just the Jesus of history; he is the Christ of the Christian faith, the Son of God. Into his story at many points Mark introduces the findings of his own faith. The second Gospel is, first of all, a devotional document; it is the literary expression of the author's religious faith, of his Christianity. It is even more the author's confession to Christ than it is the story of Jesus as he lived, wrought and taught. The Gospel of Mark is the fine fruit of community and personal piety. Its picture of Jesus is not projected in the clear, cold light of history. In Mark, doubtless our best single source, the picture of Jesus bears the color of early Christian conviction; about his figure is cast the flush of the fervent faith that attached itself to him. Even in Mark we do not possess an impartial and unbiased story of Jesus, but the Christian story, written with full Christian partiality and prejudice, bias and color.

The Gospel picture of Jesus is not a photograph, but a portrait. It is not a plain, prosaic picture in black and white, but a portrait painted by an energetic and enthusiastic faith, and over it there falls that warmer, more inviting glow that reflects a remarkable body of Christian affection and adoration. The picture of Jesus in the Gospels is highly Christianized. Often Jesus' thought is cast in a Christian mold; he speaks, now and again, Christian words, or his own words with a clear Christian inflection; important scenes in his life exhibit a Christian cast and color; major phases of his life and work are given a Christian interpretation. Into the story of Jesus the early Christians poured the whole volume of their own rich religious experience and faith.

For this Christianization of the story of Jesus there was abundant reason. This process—the movement from the more realistic to the more idealistic, from fact to faith—sprang spontaneously and involuntarily from the Christian consciousness of the first believers. Jesus grew and continued to grow in the feeling and faith of the earliest Christians, and when they told or wrote the story of him it was not just the story of a human historical figure but the message about their own Divine Redeemer.

In the Gospels, then, there stands between us and Jesus the early Christian faith. It forms a boundary, an almost insurmountable barrier, between him and us. We do not see Jesus nor do we hear him for ourselves. We see him only through early Christian eyes; he speaks to us only over early Christian lips; we hear him only through early Christian ears.

In the course of the life-of-Jesus research relatively

few scholars have ignored entirely the strongly Christian character of the Gospels and their picture, but in the twentieth century this state of the sources has resulted for some in a complete skepticism which would need to take only a few steps in order to turn the seeker hopelessly from the quest of the historical Jesus. This skepticism had its first full expression in the work of William Wrede,[18] who cast serious doubt on the Gospel of Mark which had been the bulwark of those who had claimed to have recovered Jesus. Following directly in Wrede's steps, came Julius Wellhausen with his famous skeptical statement: "We can not get back to him, even if we would."[19] More recently Wilhelm Mundle writes: "We present-day Christians are not in a position to receive a direct impression from the Jesus of history because we have only the Gospels which do not depict the historical Jesus, but communicate to us only the disciples' testimony of faith."[20] Only two years ago Professor Rudolph Bultmann wrote: "We must frankly confess that the character of Jesus as a human personality can not be recovered by us. We can neither write a 'life of Jesus' nor present an accurate picture of his personality."[21] Still more recently (1927) Professor Bultmann writes: "Frankly I am of the opinion that we know practically nothing of the life and personality of Jesus. Our Christian sources, fragmentary and overgrown with legend as they are, were not interested in such. . . .

---

[18]*Das Messiasgeheimnis in den Evangelien* (1901).
[19]*Einleitung in die drei ersten Evangelien*, p. 104.
[20]"Der Christus des Glaubens und der historische Jesus," *Zeitschrift fuer Theologie und Kirche*, 3. und 4. Hefte (Neue Folge, 1921), p. 255.
[21]"The New Approach to the Synoptic Problem," *Journal of Religion,* VI (July, 1926), p. 359.

What these sources offer is first of all the message of the early Christian community."[22]

It is true, as Bultmann says, that we can not write a "life of Jesus." Every serious student knows that we do not possess the necessary materials. It is true, as Mundle says, that the Gospels are the "disciples' testimony of faith." The whole body of fact from the life of Jesus is communicated to us through a fervent faith. But the complete skepticism of Wellhausen and Bultmann we can not share. In fact, the sentences quoted may not in fairness be isolated from their research in the life of Jesus, for in their published works[23] they show very clearly that they have not surrendered all hope of recovering Jesus as a human historical figure.

An honest confession regarding the confused state of the sources, the mingling and merging of fact and faith, is good for the seeker's soul. But if the historical Jesus is to be found anywhere, he is to be found in the Gospels. Faith is the predominant factor in the Gospel picture, and whatever of the historical Jesus survives does so in the interest of faith, but sometimes even in spite of faith. The historical student feels that whatever of the real Jesus survives in the Gospels has done so by the sheer force of fact. He feels that the distinctive elements in the personality and experience of Jesus are still sufficiently

---

[22]*Jesus (Die Unsterblichen)*, p. 12, 15.

[23]By Wellhausen, apart from the work just quoted: *Das Evangelium Lucæ; Das Evangelium Marci; Das Evangelium Mathaei; Das Evangelium Johannis.*

By Bultmann: *Die Geschichte der synoptischen Tradition; Die Erforschung der synoptischen Evangelien.* In his *Jesus* Professor Bultmann confines himself wholly to the portrayal of Jesus' message. He writes, "Although we know little of the life and personality of Jesus, we know enough about his message to form a fairly complete conception of it," p. 15.

strong to make themselves felt even through a foreign faith and to enable us to reconstruct a fairly clear picture of him as he was.

Every seeker in his quest of the Jesus of history knows that his success at best will be only relative, never absolute; approximate, but still perhaps adequate. Jesus is worth seeking and seeing, even if we can not find and see him whole.

It is at this stage in the quest of the historical Jesus that the seeker must be especially sympathetic—the journey through the faith that preserved Jesus in its own way for us. At this point the seeker comes into the sacred precincts of a primitive piety. The faith that stands between him and Jesus is the fruit of a religious experience that possessed an almost incomparable vitality. In such a field textual criticism and exegesis will fail him. He must have an approach that sees farther, that reaches deeper than the literary surface, its form and history. Here the seeker must become a sharer, an experient rather than an experimenter.

The problem of sifting out fact from this field of faith in the first three Gospels is fundamentally a psychological problem, for in it we are confronted with two types of religious experience. This is a difficult task because the one claims the other for its own, and while the two experiences have their different and distinctive centers, they still have a great area of common ground. The one is the religious experience of the early Christians; the other, claimed as it is by the former, is the original religious experience of Jesus himself, which sometimes only shimmers through to bewilder us and again strikes us with a fulness of force that is at once comforting and disturbing.

The religious experience of Jesus and that of the early Christians have much in common. There is the great God of Israel, the future which He has in store for the faithful, His will and way as revealed in the law and the prophets, the fruits of faith in Him in the terms of character and conduct, and so forth. But then there are those distinctive elements, clear enough in our best sources, that set off the Christian experience of Jesus' followers as new and different from his own. If the New Testament makes anything clear to us, it is the fact that the early Christian faith was exclusively Christocentric. This faith focused on the person and work of Jesus as the sole hope of religious salvation. In the foreground of early Christian experience stands the person of Jesus, in, by and through whom his followers may expect exemption on the last great day. The distinctive center of religious loyalty in early Christian piety is Jesus himself as Risen Lord. But within the first three Gospels there is just as clearly reflected the personal religious experience of Jesus himself. His faith, however, is theocentric; it focuses upon God and His kingdom as the religious hope of the future. In the foreground of his faith stand God, His kingdom and its coming for which men are to prepare themselves. His own person remains wholly in the background of his thought and teaching. The distinctive center of his religious loyalty is God and His holy will.

In the experience of the early Christians Jesus as Risen Lord was a religious object, but in his own personal conviction Jesus was a religious subject, an experient of religion. Paul's apocalyptic faith (I Thess. 4,15-18) and that of the early Christians generally was the organic development of the personal faith of Jesus. But even here there is a distinct difference. In the faith of Paul it is Jesus as Risen Lord who is to come and inaugurate the new age, but in the faith of Jesus it is the Son of man, a superhuman and divine figure from whom he in certain of his words very clearly and religiously distinguishes himself. Paul and Jesus are one in I Corinthians 13 and in the Sermon on the Mount with regard to the virtues of character that are to issue from a truly religious faith. But for Paul religious faith includes a belief in Jesus as absolutely fundamental, a position that was wholly foreign to his Master's faith who set before men only God and His kingdom as objects of religious devotion. The faith of Paul as well as that of Jesus was theocentric, but Paul's faith was also Christocentric. Judged in the light of their distinctive impulses, incentives and issues, the religious experience of the early Christians and that of Jesus represent not only two different types, but two experiences of religion distinctly different both in form and in content.

In our quest of Jesus in the first three Gospels we must appraise any particular passage in the light of the nature and substance of the religious experience reflected. To what extent does a particular word or incident reflect the religious experience of Jesus? To what extent does it reflect the Christian experience of his followers? Such are the questions which we must ask. If we strike upon matter that betrays a Christocentric thought and faith, we know with what and whom we have to do. Wherever Jesus appears as a religious object we have to do with the Christian faith. But wherever he appears as a religious subject, then we are confronted with fact from his life.

This becomes a fundamental principle of all research that would find its way back to Jesus.

The Christian coloring of the picture of Jesus is not easily detected because we are fundamentally in sympathy with it and it is difficult to dissolve because our own Christian point of view readily responds to it. All will not agree as to what is Christian coloring and what belongs to the original picture, but each seeker faces the task of dispelling the Christian atmosphere that envelops Jesus and of gaining for himself the clearest possible picture. The results of this process will be painful to many, for it means the dissipation of some conceptions long held dear. If it does not result in a total dissipation, it will doubtless mean an awakening to the realization that they are not, after all, central and essential.

The Christian conscience is naturally conservative. Even when driven by a sense of historical honesty, it will undertake as few alterations as possible. Christians from the first century down to the present have loved to think that Jesus thought and spoke of himself as confessing Christians have thought and spoken of him, a fact which is clearly shown by the prevalent popularity of the Fourth Gospel. But the intent seeker must strive to gain the most unblurred picture of Jesus, even at the sacrifice of cherished sentiments. He must sympathetically remove the Christian coloring that taints, disfigures, often completely conceals the picture of the historical Jesus of Nazareth.

To classify and discuss the various types of religious experience represented in the Gospels would require a separate volume. Such a study would be extremely interesting and illuminating. We have had all sorts of learned commentaries on the Gospels, but as yet few of them have touched upon the religious experience that seeks expression in the Gospel passages. Too many of our commentaries treat the Gospels as though they were only a lifeless literature. A religio-psychological commentary that seeks to analyze the Gospel materials on the basis of the nature and substance of the religious experience that they reflect, that seeks out the impulses, incentives and issues of the religious faith from which they came, would be a real contribution to our knowledge and understanding of the religious life back of the Gospels and would bring us closer to it.

The Gospels represent a rather wide variety of religious experience. Judged in the light of their historical background and foreground, they would naturally present three main types, each with its own peculiar marks, yet the three would have much in common. In the Gospels we would naturally expect to find a distinctly Jewish type of religious experience, the personal religious experience of Jesus that was all his own, and the distinctly Christian type of religious experience that sets itself off from both that of Jesus and that of the orthodox first-century Jew. Here we can make only a few selections as illustrations.

There are passages in the Gospels that are purely neutral. They have nothing specially distinctive about them and could just as well and do appear in the religious experience of Israel, Jesus and the early Christians. A good example is the classic maxim,

"Thou shalt love thy neighbor as thyself."

To be sure, this great command had its origin in the religious experience of prophetic Israel, but it is an integral part of the personal piety of Jesus and of the early Christians after him, even though it came to both as a matter of religious heritage. It bears the stamp of Israel's religious genius, but it is an equally characteristic issue of the religious experience of Jesus and Paul. It is the gift of Israel, but Jesus and Christianity are inconceivable without it. The religious experience of Israel was the heritage of Jesus and of Christianity, and the Gospel writers ascribe words to Jesus that could just as well be on the lips of any true Jewish prophet or seer, on the lips of Paul or some other early Christian. The very Jewishness of Jesus and of earliest Christianity would naturally require just such a state of facts.

There are, however, a few passages in the Gospels that are distinctly Jewish and that cut themselves off from the religious experience of Jesus and that of the early Christians. A good example of this is the story of the Baptist's birth. (Luke 1,5-25 57-80.)[24] This story has about it nothing of the distinctive elements in the religious experience of Jesus: There is no hint of the kingdom of God and its coming. It does not contain the distinctive features of the Christian faith: There is no reference to the Messiah in general, as there might well be and still remain Jewish, nor is there any reference to Jesus in particular as the Messiah. The religious experience back of this story is purely Jewish. It is Jewish in its conception of salvation, in its religious outlook and expectation. The religious hope of the future is connected wholly with the person and work of the Baptist who is to appear in the spirit and power of Elijah to

---

[24]There are other strictly Jewish passages, all ascribed to Jesus, that reflect a special interest in Jerusalem, yet they are almost too Zionistic for him: Matt. 23,37-39; Luke 19,41-44; 21,20-22 24; 23,27-31.

turn Israel to its God. The Baptist occupies the whole
center of interest; his is the great work. He is not presented as in any sense the forerunner or advance-agent of
another, except as we read our own Christian point of
view into the angel's forecast, "He shall go before his
face." (1,17.) But when we read this passage from
the Jewish point of view, as it was originally in the experience from which it came, the Baptist is to go before the
face of the Lord God of Israel and to be great in His
sight.

The story of the Baptist's birth is fiction, but it is the
fruit of a fine Jewish faith that connects the religious
hope of Israel with the work of its prophets. Judged in
the light of the religious experience reflected, the story
of the Baptist's birth can come only from the primitive
circle of the Baptist's followers who have not yet come
into contact with Christianity and learned to view their
master in a subordinate relation to Jesus the Messiah.

The principal problem of the seeker on his way back
to Jesus is not concerned so much with the Jewish elements in the Gospels, for some of these are naturally
the common ground on which Jesus, his Jewish contemporaries and the early Christians stand. His principal
problem is that of detecting those Christian invasions
that obscure from him the original picture of Jesus. The
flood of Christian faith that has rushed in to fill up the
gaps and depressions in the transmitted facts of Jesus'
life, that sometimes sweeps fact before it into oblivion,
or that develops mists that enshroud his figure, has
wrought various changes.

Sometimes this Christian faith deposits itself in the
story of Jesus in a pure unadulterated form and ascribes
to him its own religious outlook. Into the midst of an

address in which Jesus is speaking of the immediacy of
the end, an address that exhibits a curious combination of
Jewish and Christian experience with that of Jesus
(Mark 13,3-37), a Christian outlook that is removed
from his own by two generations presents itself as a word
of his,

> "And this gospel of the kingdom shall be preached
> in the whole world for a testimony unto all the nations;
> and then shall the end come."   (Matt. 24,14.)

This religious outlook is in open conflict with that of
Jesus who expected the kingdom to come within his own
lifetime and that of his contemporaries.   (Matt. 10,23;
Mark 9,1.)   It comes from a Christian experience that
is later even than that of Paul, an experience that has
surrendered not only the hope of Jesus but that of the
earliest Christians concerning the immediate end of
things.   Such a passage can not come from the religious
experience of Jesus who reckoned in terms of days,
weeks and months, but from a Christian experience that
is girding itself for a career in the world.

Sometimes there falls from the lips of Jesus a word
that represents a primitive Christian certainty rather
than a personal religious certainty of Jesus himself.   We
meet such very often, as in Matt. 18,20:

> "For where two or three are gathered together in
> my name, there am I in the midst of them."

This passage reflects entirely the Christian point of view
according to which the person of Jesus has become the
unification point of the community, no matter how small.

It expresses a religious assurance of the early Christian consciousness rather than a personal promise of Jesus to his disciples during his lifetime.

Sometimes there comes from the lips of Jesus as his own a purely Christian conviction and confession, as in Matt. 11,27b:

> "No one knoweth the Son, save the Father; neither doth any know the Father, save the Son, and he to whomsoever the Son willeth to reveal *him*."

Here we have a purely Christian conviction and confession. It presents the findings of the early Christian faith that looks to Jesus as a religious object. It is impossible as a genuine word of Jesus, for it would mean the complete collapse of his own self-consciousness which he retains as rigidly religious.[25]

In Matthew's famous "Come-unto-me" passage (11, 28-30) we do not have to do with a challenge of Jesus, but with a Christian call to him. It is not like Jesus to recommend himself, and in this passage he is already the exalted figure of the Christian faith. The very fact that this word has been an unfailing source of comfort and consolation to all generations of Christians betrays the fact that it is the product of a rich Christian experience. It is the classic call which some early Christian evangelist issues to all alike rather than an extract from the religious message of Jesus. It is a tremendous testimony to the all-sufficiency of Jesus in early Christian experience. If we were to frame its form to fit its content, we should find that it would read in the third person rather than in the first:

---

[25]For a fuller discussion of this passage, *see* p. 310*ff.*

"Come unto *him,* all ye that labor and are heavy laden, and *he* will give you rest. Take *his* yoke upon you, and learn of *him*; for *he* is meek and lowly in heart: and ye shall find rest for your souls. For *his* yoke is easy, and *his* burden is light."

As a Christian conviction and call it loses none of its primitive persuasiveness and power.

The sifting out of such passages from the body of genuine matter concerning Jesus is for many a painful process. However, their original religious significance is not lost; in fact, it is only just recovered, for they are the crystallizations of an early Christian piety that sprang from the deepest impulses of a loyal devotion to Christ who stood at the very center of a great body of religious life. In such passages we are confronted with Christian experience rather than with the personal religious experience of Jesus himself. They are rich deposits of faith from the very depths of the Christian consciousness, anchoring themselves at suggested, favorable or necessary points in the life of Jesus. Such deposits manifest very clearly the vitality and strength of the religious life from which they came.

This Christianization process often takes on the form of a neglect of the actual situation in the life of Jesus, and certain passages show that both writer and readers are thinking, not of what happened during his lifetime, but of what is going on or is necessary in their own later day. Often the Gospel writers have the interests and needs of their readers in mind rather than a faultless reproduction of fact from Jesus' life. Genuine words of his are recast in order that they may serve more directly as inspiration for the original readers. Matthew's last beatitude has a Christian point that is shaped for his readers who find themselves in the midst of persecution,

"Blessed are ye when *men* shall reproach you, and persecute you, and say all manner of evil against you falsely, for my sake." (5,11.)

This word is a recast by Matthew to meet the situation of his own day rather than a forecast of Jesus during his lifetime.

Now and again, Jesus is represented as speaking but it is only formal, for the actual portent of particular passages shows that the writer himself is addressing his contemporary Christians through Jesus. The whole of Matthew's address to the twelve (9,35-11,1) is framed to meet the needs of the missionaries of Matthew's own day. A number of passages in this address, made up for the most part of genuine words of Jesus, are wholly remote from the actual scene between Jesus and the twelve when he sent them out. Matthew 10,17-18 reflects clearly the fates of the Christian missionaries more than a generation after Jesus' death rather than any fates that might befall the twelve in their hasty heralding of the kingdom in Israel,

"But beware of men: for they will deliver you up to councils, and in their synagogues they will scourge you; yea, and before governors and kings shall ye be brought for my sake, for a testimony to them and to the Gentiles."

Even Mark is not thinking of the actual situation in

the life of Jesus when he has him send out the twelve without giving them a message. He is thinking of missionaries of his own day who have no need of being told what to preach. When Mark permits the sandals and the staff, he is not thinking of the equipment needed by the twelve in their tour of Galilee but of the missionaries of his own day who are traversing the rough country of Syria and Asia Minor. (Mark 6,8-9.)

Often the Gospel writers lose all interest in an incident in the life of Jesus except as it lends itself to their own later faith. Incidents of grave importance for our knowledge of Jesus are often narrated from the point of view of what they meant for the early Christian faith rather than from the point of view of what they meant for Jesus personally. The story of the baptism (Mark 1,9-11) is a Christianized scene. The incident is recounted from the Christian point of view and with the Christian interest, both of which center upon the vision and the voice. The Gospel writers are interested in the homiletic heart, in the preaching possibilities, which the scene offers. Here at the Jordan they find a confirmation of the Christian faith: A vision disclosed and a voice declared Jesus to be just what Christians have believed—God's beloved Son. His baptism at the hands of John must have been an important experience in the life of Jesus himself, but the Gospel account is not presented from the angle that would show what it meant for him personally.

Often the Gospel writers will project their own faith and its findings into a particular incident. Mark and Luke take no offense at the fact that Jesus presented himself to John for baptism, nor are they disturbed by the fact that the Baptist does not recognize Jesus as the One he has been announcing. But Matthew is sensitive on both points. In 3,14-15 he introduces a special scene in which the Baptist recognizes Jesus as the One he really is and confesses that Jesus has no need of his baptism of repentance unto the remission of sins. In this scene Matthew deposits his own faith and lays down the first great Christian declaration of the sinlessness of Jesus.

Sometimes this Christianization process takes on the form of an unmistakable background that rises up behind a particular scene rather than invading the account itself. It is only as we confront certain scenes in the life of Jesus with strictly historical questions that we begin to realize how much of faith is assumed. Mark's account of the calling of the first disciples (1,16-20) is just such a scene. In and of itself, it is graphic and clear, but when we come to look for the antecedents that prepared the way for it and that led up to it, we are confronted with both historical and psychological difficulties. The scene depicts without doubt an important step both on the part of Jesus and on the part of the four fishermen. But the calling comes like a flash out of a clear sky. There are no previous contacts and acquaintanceships; Jesus calls strangers, and strangers follow a stranger. How does Jesus know that these four are just the men he wants as his permanent companions? How do these men know that Jesus is the man for whom they are ready to desert all? It is not historical fact but the faith of Mark and his readers that answers these questions or that, better perhaps, never allows these questions to arise. Mark is not recounting the story of an ordinary human person who must learn to know men through a series of contacts, common experiences and companionships. Mark is narrating boldly the earthly career of the hero and object of the Christian faith. For the Jesus of Mark's faith, to see is to know. The readiness of the fishermen to follow Jesus constitutes no problem for Mark. They respond instantly to the imposing impression of his personality. It is the One with whom they have to do that explains their promptness.

This Christianization process does not stop at particular scenes; it strikes even the major phases of Jesus' public career. According to all three Gospels, the journey to Jerusalem is a journey to death. Jesus is fully conscious of what awaits him; he forecasts his fate with complete certainty and in full detail. But this is the Christian point of view that, at a later date, surveys this eventful journey in the light of its fatal outcome. If we seek to approach Jerusalem as Jesus seems to have approached it, there are other possibilities, even probabilities. Jesus may have gone to Jerusalem with the thought of death in his mind, but he becomes certain of this only in Gethsemane on the last night of his life.[26] Or it may be that he went to Jerusalem to continue his work, for he announces his message to friend and foe with renewed vigor on arriving in the Holy City. Or it may be that he went to Jerusalem as a pious pilgrim to celebrate the most sacred of all the feasts of his people. He goes up at the time of the Passover, his disciples prepare it for him, with them he eats it on the last night of his life, and he tells them that he has looked forward to it with great desire. (Luke 22,15.)

In one respect this Christianization process strikes the whole of Jesus' public career in Matthew and Luke. For Matthew and Luke the baptism experience at the Jordan is the birth-hour and birthplace of Jesus' messianic consciousness. Beginning with the Jordan vision and voice,

---

[26]For a discussion of this problem of fate, *see* pp. 256-264.

Jesus knows that he is the Messiah, and henceforth he speaks and acts as such. Thus the whole of his public life in Matthew and Luke becomes consciously messianic. He begins his public work, accomplishes it and dies knowing all the while that he is God's chosen Messiah. But this Christianization of the career of Jesus does not appear in Mark. The baptism does not result in the messianic conviction and, as we shall see in Chapter IV, it is only relatively late in his public life that Jesus is confronted with the messianic issue.[27]

Turning again to the words of Jesus, we find that this Christianization process invades not only his religious message, but reaches down into the very depths of his own personal religious experience.

In 1,15 Mark gives us the religious message of Jesus: the kingdom of God with repentance as the reconstruction of mind and life in preparation for its coming. But Mark does not give us the religious message of Jesus in the pure form in which it came from his lips. He sets it in a Christian frame with a Christian introduction and a Christian supplement,

"*The time is fulfilled,* and the kingdom of God is at hand; repent ye, *and believe in the gospel.*"

The opening and closing statements (in italics) are clearly of Christian origin, expressions of the early Christian consciousness rather than of Jesus' own religious consciousness. *The time is fulfilled* presents the Christian point of view as it surveys human history and sees in Jesus its climax and culmination. The closing admoni-

---

[27]Cf. p. 235*f.*

tion, *Believe in the gospel,* is not found elsewhere on the lips of Jesus, and it is the later Christian call to belief in all that he represents.

Sometimes these Christianizations take on the form of quick injections of the Christian point of view into a genuine word of Jesus. In Luke 17,33 we have a genuine paradox of Jesus,

> "Whosoever shall seek to gain his life shall lose it; but whosoever shall lose *his life* shall preserve it."

But into the Markan form of this word (8,35) the Christian point of view has been inserted,

> "For whosoever would save his life shall lose it; and whosoever shall lose his life *for my sake and the gospel's* shall save it."[28]

In other words we find a simple substitution of the Christian point of view for that of Jesus. In Luke 18,29-30 we have the original point of view of Jesus,

> "There is no man that hath left house, or wife, or brethren, or parents, or children, *for the kingdom of God's sake,* who shall not receive manifold more in this time, and in the world to come eternal life."

But in Mark's parallel (10,29-30) the Christian point of view is substituted,

> "There is no man that hath left house, or brethren,

---

[28]Compare the Christianized forms of this paradox in Matt. 10,39; 16,25; Luke 9,24.

or sisters, or mother, or father, or children, or lands, *for my sake, and for the gospel's sake,* but he shall receive a hundredfold now in this time . . . and in the world to come eternal life."[29]

Such expressions as *for my sake, for my name's sake, for the gospel's sake, because of me, because ye are Christ's,* are projections of primitive Christian piety into the religious experience of Jesus. They spring from a Christocentric faith that looks to him as religious object. They constitute the religious reference of the Christian consciousness and are the Christian incentives and impulses for suffering and sacrifice.

The original religious references from the experience of Jesus are almost wholly submerged by these Christian references, but they do appear now and then in the Gospels in such expressions as *for the kingdom of God's sake, for the Son of man's sake, for righteousness' sake.* In such references we have centers of devotion wholly different from those presented in the Christian references. They are the objects of devotion which we find claiming the whole of the religious life of Jesus. For Jesus the kingdom of God, the Son of man and righteousness constitute the impulses and incentives for loyalty, sacrifice and suffering. Such expressions as *for my sake,* and so forth, are true to the Christian faith and its Christocentric convictions, but that Jesus demanded such for himself is contradicted by particular passages and by the total impression which the first three Gospels leave with us concerning his thought, feeling and faith which centered upon God and His kingdom to the exclusion of all else, even his own person.

[29]Compare Matthew's Christianized parallel in 19,29.

Before closing this section on Christianizations, two other types should be cited. In Luke 14,26-27 we have a word fresh from the religious demands of Jesus:

"If any man cometh unto me, and hateth not his own father, and mother, and wife, and children, and brethren, and sisters, yea, and his own life also, *he can not be my disciple.* Whosoever doth not bear his cross, and come after me, *can not be my disciple.*"

But in Matthew's parallel passage (10,37-38) this demand is toned down and recast in a Christian form:

"He that loveth father or mother more than me is not *worthy of me*; and he that loveth son or daughter more than me is not *worthy of me.* And he that doth not take up his cross and follow after me, is not *worthy of me.*"

The passage in Luke demands loyalty to a leader, but in Matthew it demands devotion to a religious object. From the Christian point of view men are worthy or unworthy of Christ. From Jesus' own religious point of view they are worthy or unworthy of the kingdom of God,

"No man, having put his hand to the plow, and looking back, is fit for the kingdom of God." (Luke 9,62.)

There is yet another type of Christianization of which the Gospels present a number of instances. In Matthew 10,32-33 we have a Christianized word of Jesus, if not perhaps a pure Christian confession:

"Every one therefore who shall confess me before men, him will *I* also confess before my Father who is in heaven. But whosoever shall deny me before men, him will *I* also deny before my Father who is in heaven."

In Luke's parallel passage (12,8-9) is the purer form:

"Every one who shall confess me before men, him shall *the Son of man* also confess before the angels of God: but he that denieth me in the presence of men *shall be denied* in the presence of the angels of God."

In Luke's form Jesus distinguishes himself religiously from the supernatural Son of man, but in Matthew's form he is completely identified with this divine figure and will himself be the judge on the last great day, which is the Christian point of view.[30]

The history of the Christian story of Jesus during the first century of its existence is the history of the gradual obscuration of fact from his life by faith in him as the Christ of the Easter experiences. Slowly but surely, Jesus as religious subject loses ground before Jesus as religious object. But it is the duty of the seeker on his way back to him to apprehend and appreciate the invasions of faith into the field of fact. Through these he must move with sympathetic understanding if he is to recover Jesus and his religious experience.

---

[30]Compare the other two forms of this passage (Mark 8,38; Luke 9,26) in which Jesus is still religiously distinct from the Son of man. The opening statements of all four forms are Christianized. The expressions, *confess me, deny me, ashamed of me,* are Christian both in form and content.

To Fact

Down to this point on our way back to Jesus we have tried to see the problems that confront us in our quest of him in the first three Gospels. We have found that they contain elements that do not go back to Jesus and that stand between him and us. Fiction is present, and faith is prominent, almost predominant. But it is only as we recognize the actual limitations of the first three Gospels as historical documents that we are in a position to appreciate their value and worth. The general conclusion, better perhaps conviction, that comes out of the life-of-Jesus research is that we must read our Gospels with care when we are in search of fact, but we may read them with confidence in the hope of recovering Jesus as he was.

On the nature and worth of the sources of our knowledge of Jesus as a whole we may say that we possess as much reliable information concerning him as we do of any other man of that early date. In view of the strength and vitality of the faith from which it came, it is really remarkable that the Gospel picture is as faithful to the fact as it is. Through the Gospels there runs a strong stream of personal memories that appears, disappears and reappears in the course of the story. These memories are often transfigured and glorified, but in them the Jesus of history still survives to the extent that we may be justified in hoping to see him as he was. Jesus survives in the Gospel story because he is, as Professor Deissmann says, "greater than the tradition about him. The tradition is only the last echo of his words, only a reflection of his being."[31]

---

[31]*Evangelium und Urchristentum*, p. 84.

Now and again, in fact very often, the clear light of history shines through the film of faith, through the often dense veil of Christian feeling and sentiment which later religious experience so naturally and involuntarily cast about the figure of the historical Jesus, and we see him standing before us as he stood before the Galileans who thronged his presence and trailed his steps. This primitive personal impression strikes us now and again in such a measure that it breaks through the Christian veil, and its rupture at one point helps us to detect it at other points where we may lay it gently aside in our quest of him. Once we have sensed this primitive personal impression that has preserved itself even in spite of the Christian character of the story, we have a safe guide and no great difficulty in sensing almost instinctively when this primitive impression is tempered or modified by the Christian faith and feeling of Matthew, or Mark, or Luke. The features of the historical Jesus are not completely overgrown and obscured. Where faith has touched and retouched, even distorted and disfigured, there is still hope of restoring the original, still hope of seeing Jesus in all his human and historical freshness.

It is one of the great virtues of the Gospel writers that they attempt no formal description or portrayal of Jesus' personality, no general delineation of his character. They give us something vastly better and more impressive. Their pictures of Jesus are kaleidoscopic, dramatic scenes and incidents, engaging episodes and anecdotes. Jesus speaks as one having authority; at his word demons depart; with his touch a fever subsides; witnesses are astonished beyond measure; his fame spreads like wild-fire; the crowds throng him; he retreats to solitude and seclusion for prayer. The Gospel writers' neglect of all formal description and delineation belongs to the art of their unstudied picture. Instead of laborious characterizations and portrayals they give us swift sketches, sharp clear-cut pictures of Jesus in action which enable us to sense and to share in at least some measure that primitive personal impression which he as a man of history left with his contemporaries.

The life-of-Jesus research has not resulted in a biography of Jesus. It can not, for the Gospel materials are too meager and fragmentary. Instead of a *life of Jesus* we have problems of the life of Jesus. Out of the Gospel accounts there arise many interrogation points, and many of them still await an adequate answer. We are by no means at the end of our quest. Many phases of the life and work, thought and teaching of Jesus remain problematic. The careful student ends with as many uncertainties as certainties. The outer aspects of Jesus' career, chronology, inner connections leading from one crisis to another, admit of only the most tentative reconstruction. Certain utterances of his are no longer clear to us, doubtless never will be. Not a few words are what we might call genuine but well-worn coins; they are of the real stuff, but the distinctive stamp of Jesus' thought and style has been effaced in a wide and vigorous circulation. There are many matters, major and minor, that we should like to know about Jesus, but of which there is now no real hope of learning.

The Gospels preserve only a selection of a few things from the many. We can not claim that we have every word of Jesus just as he spoke it, nor every deed just as he performed it. There are words ascribed to him which, in all probability, he never spoke, and many wondrous words that he did speak are lost to us for ever. Some of the deeds ascribed to Jesus he probably never did, but many wonderful deeds of love and kindness that he did do have not come down to us. Many of his genuine words and deeds bear a Christian cast and color. There are features of Jesus that remain enigmas for us. Not every phase of his character and personality is clear to us. But we may claim this: In the Gospels as a whole, not in every detail, we possess an account that is a reasonably reliable reproduction of Jesus as he was, did and spoke. For the Gospel picture we may claim, not an absolute but a relative genuineness.

Over against the meagerness of the materials stands the rich and distinctive character of the matter that we do possess, matter that is sufficiently rich and distinctive to enable us to see a great deal of Jesus, the greatest and grandest of that which he as an historical personality has to offer us. The outstanding matter that the seeker finds in his quest of Jesus is that he was a religious subject, an experient of religion, an exclusively religious personality. The very fact that the Gospel writers tell us that Jesus preached the kingdom of God, thought and taught of God as Father, that he passed through religious trials and struggles, that he took religious attitudes, that his aspirations and acts were religious, that he prayed to God—all give us the key to his personality. We can not know all that we should like to know, but perhaps all that we are in need of knowing. The first three Gospels do furnish us a relatively reliable body of matter with which we can effect the recovery and restoration of Jesus as *a religious personality.*

The picture of the historical Jesus as recovered by research is quite different from the traditional ecclesiastical picture and, in not a few respects, is quite opposed to it. Critical research has resulted in the disruption and dissipation of the metaphysical mists and myths that have concealed the real Jesus from our clear view. It is certainly not constructive to the theological view of Jesus; it is positively destructive of such. In not a few instances historical research has failed to find in the experience of Jesus any substantial confirmation for some of the positions which traditional Christianity has advocated most vigorously. But this presents no reason for the discontinuation of the historical approach to him. Rather it furnishes abundant reason why theological Christianity should repent itself and make a resolute return to Jesus and his simple, yet profound experience of religion.

Theologically, the results of the life-of-Jesus research have been negative; religiously, however, they have been positive and most helpful. The seeker who comes within a relative distance of realizing the recovery of Jesus experiences a sweep of mingled emotion: a feeling of relief when he beholds the utter simplicity of Jesus, yet a sense of greatly increased responsibility when he realizes the utter seriousness of Jesus. The picture recovered by the life-of-Jesus research has the virtue, not a small one by any means, of being true to the New Testament records and of presenting Jesus to our modern life in his truly religious significance. The recovery of Jesus will bring about a breach between us and some of the pious dicta of the past, but it will bind us closer to him and his pure personal piety as the only adequate approach to our common human task of living life re-

ligiously. The historical Jesus demanded courage, consecration, complete commitment—three things that seem
to be weakening in our modern Christian constitution.

The way back to Jesus is not just a path which the
trained seeker alone is prepared to pursue. The quest
of Jesus is not just the professional and academic concern of a few specialists. It is the common concern of
all who conceive of the Christian life in terms of discipleship. The layman, the uncritical student, the devotional reader, all alike may read the records for
themselves, and they may sense and seek to share with
Jesus the commanding elements of his own religious
experience. The recovery of Jesus is not a mere matter
of technical training. It requires a fundamental spiritual
sympathy with him.

The life-of-Jesus research is now meeting very definite
devotional demands. It is making a strong appeal to the
most practical type of piety. It is helping us to understand the New Testament writers as they meant to be
understood, and to see Jesus as he actually was in his own
day, among his own people, in his own experience;
further, it is teaching us to begin to take Jesus at his
word.

The life-of-Jesus research has clarified, simplified and
intensified our faith. Our faith is clarified because we
see Jesus much more distinctly. Our picture is not as
elaborate as the one which the Christian imagination has
heretofore projected, but whatever is lost in elaborate-
ness is more than replaced by a new sharpness and dis-
tinctness of feature. Our faith is simplified because
we are brought down to the real essentials. Instead of
an involved system we have to do with a simple, searching spirit. Our faith is intensified because a clear con-

ception of the meaning of God in the experience of Jesus means a radical rupture of our self-complacency and contentment. Even an approximate recovery of Jesus results in the alarming realization of how far we are from him and what he hoped of and for his faithful followers.

The life-of-Jesus research has arrived at the very positive conclusion, which amounts to a deep confession, that the life of Jesus is the richest and most resourceful body of religious subject-matter that we possess. When it comes to determine and estimate the contribution of Jesus to our human life, it is in terms of his religious experience, the most convincing thing about him. The Gospels are wonderfully rich and stimulating, and their richness and stimulation consist chiefly in what they preserve of the religious experience of Jesus.

To be sure, our best picture of Jesus will present its problems. But the presence of problems does not point to a corresponding lack of piety. In fact, the exact reverse is true. Where piety is purest, in those cases where it is the undertone and overtone of the whole life, personal problems are usually most numerous and persistent. It would be difficult to find a better example of this than the religious experience of Jesus offers, the whole of whose known life is an unbroken series of pressing personal problems that drove him to the very heart of the issue that exists between man and his Maker.

THE APPROACH TO JESUS

No man of history has been approached with such searching questions as has Jesus, yet he continues to stand as the one great inexhaustible, puzzling and paradoxical figure. He was such for his contemporaries, and we may not hope to disclose all the secrets of his person. However, it is our duty as his followers to approach him as near as we may and seek to share what he seeks to communicate to us. We trust that we are intelligent seekers of his society, and we may well ask the question: In the light of our best knowledge, what constitutes an adequate approach to Jesus?

Literary—Historical

Our approach to Jesus must be *literary*, for all the information preserved to us is deposited in written documents. To these documents we must apply the same strict literary tests that we would apply to the life-records of any other great man of the past. However, we must remember that these documents are essentially non-literary productions of non-literary men. They were written without literary ambition in the service of a commanding faith. Their remarkable literary history lay wholly outside of their original conception.

Our approach to Jesus must be *historical*. Whatever else Jesus has been, is and is to be for the Christian consciousness in the terms of religious experience and evaluation, he certainly was a very concrete fact of our human history. As an historical figure he must be approached from the discriminating historical angle. We must apply to him and to the things reported of him the same rigid biographical tests that we would apply to any other great genius of history. We must seek to get back at the actual facts, at what corresponds most closely to reality and historical probability. Not everything reported of him rests upon the same plane of fact.

It is at once clear that the historical approach to Jesus is very exacting, but behind this approach there lies a real religious reason. Religion in the life and living of his followers is too vital a concern to permit any other approach than one that promises to bring us back as near as possible to what actually took place, to Jesus as he actually appeared. Religion is always too serious a matter for any sort of side-stepping.

In making the historical approach we may not expect to learn everything that we should like to know. A century of research in the life of Jesus has demonstrated nothing but disappointment for those who expect too much. This is not a weakness of the historical method; it is rather one of its stimulating effects. It helps us to recognize the plain state of the facts, and it is often of the greatest importance and value to know that we do not know. This state of affairs is inherent in the very nature of our subject-matter. The Gospels are, in many respects, problematic documents. Jesus does not disclose to us everything that we should like to know, nor everything that we feel in need of knowing. Often we shall have to confess that we do not know. Such a confession is the only honest and honorable thing that we can do in the presence of the facts as they are, and at such points each may be left to shift for himself in the quest of a satisfactory reconstruction.

In its critical approach the life-of-Jesus research has set for itself a worthy goal, wholly independent of the prospect of actual attainment. The endeavor to reset Jesus in his own times, in his own native land, among his own people is not only commendable but positively constructive.[32] It is Jesus as he was who will mean most

---

[32]Professor S. J. Case has undertaken this in an admirable way in his *Jesus: A New Biography.*

to us, and the day is not far removed when this approach will bear rich fruit in popular piety, once it has overcome its inherited rather than natural prejudice.

But our approach to Jesus includes more than literary and historical findings. As Loisy writes, these are only "indispensable preliminaries to a deeper consideration."[33] The temptation to stop with literary and historical conclusions has been too strong for some seekers. It has often been a weakness in the life-of-Jesus research, a weakness from which it is now, however, gradually recovering.

Human—Psychological—Religious

Our approach to Jesus must be *human*. Professor Wernle writes, "The more human our approach to Jesus, the more simple and intelligible everything becomes."[34] Too many studies approach Jesus as though he had never really lived. This human approach is not heresy; it is simply elementary history. Furthermore, it is really religious. It is an approach that at least some of the New Testament writers did not neglect entirely, and it is an approach that we must make to-day in the conviction that it has an important contribution to make to faith itself. To separate Jesus from humankind and its experience is to annul its hope of high helpfulness from him.

Our approach to Jesus must be *psychological,* for in him we have to do with a living personality. Jesus was a man of remarkably rich experience. He was a man of

---

[33] *The Gospel and the Church*, p. 27. Courtesy of Charles Scribner's Sons.
[34] *Jesus*, p. 360.

resourceful mind; his teaching is the organic issue of his thinking. We see Jesus performing certain acts, passing through certain personal struggles, moved to speech and action by certain impulses and inspirations. Jesus was a man of great enthusiasm, strong emotion, possessing a wealth of will, capable of intense consecration and devotion, of certain attitudes, ambitions and aspirations. The psychological approach is not wholly new, but in making this approach mere mental mechanics and methods, professional technique and analytical apparatus will not help us much. In Jesus we have to do, not with a lifeless specimen, but with an intense personality. Not a few modern psychological approaches are disappointing because they fail to lay hold of the real source-springs of his life.

Our approach to Jesus must be *religious,* for he was an exclusively religious personality. The life-of-Jesus research has not neglected the human and psychological approach, but the religious approach has as yet hardly started, and it is really the deciding issue in the problem of our recovery of Jesus. Even to-day the theological approach is predominant in many circles of critics. Such studies seek confirmation for certain doctrinal positions and interpretations rather than Jesus as he was. Such studies are usually apologies for an unreality rather than a quest for reality itself. It is becoming increasingly difficult for the student of the life of Jesus to understand him in the terms of theology and traditional Christian thought. Dogmatism may study Jesus, but once to see him means its own death. Jesus has always been the despair of the dogmatist and doctrinaire, the whole reason for which being the fact that Jesus himself did not take a theoretical but a deeply personal view of religion. Further, the theological approach is becoming increasingly inadequate for the rigid religious demands which men are forced to face. Our modern life demands that we find in Jesus a religious resource that is sufficiently strong to cope with all of life's issues.

The recovery of Jesus as a real religious resource depends upon the human, psychological and religious approach. Such an approach requires a certain amount of detachment and historical objectivity. The seeker must disengage himself as completely as possible from the vast volume of subsequent tradition that has grown up about Jesus' figure. This does not mean an unfeeling and unsympathetic attitude. In the investigation of such a sacred subject-matter as the life and religious experience of Jesus, the seeker may not stand off at a distance as a mere observer, but he must draw near and seek to sense and to share both the purity and the power of his personal piety. At the same time he must retain a sovereign freedom and independence over against all the historical manifestations of Christianity and approach his Master as nearly as possible with his mind stripped and free for fresh and full impressions direct from him.

Vital religion, wherever and however it appears, always demands a response. The student who approaches a religious personality in a purely objective and academic way, without heart and without feeling, will find only a cold corpse for dissection. But he who approaches religion for what it means to and makes of a particular life will find a warm body and a living soul. He will feel its mighty pulse because his own heart beats.

The great danger in the way of the psychology of religion is that it may neglect, as very often it has, the more

personal and intimate aspects of religious experience. In
the interest of scientific exactness, it has often been too
objective in its treatment of subjective facts. Its gen-
eralizations, drawn as they are from a great mass and
variety of the historical manifestations of religion and
religious experience, fail to reproduce the vigorous vitality of the devoutly religious subject who feels himself
drawn and driven by great convictions which become the
commanding elements of his experience. For this reason,
we may learn from the records of Jesus, from the letters
of Paul, the confessions of St. Augustine, the autobiography of St. Teresa, more of what religion really is and
means as a promoting factor in human experience than
from many psychologies of religion. A psychology of
religion is a difficult thing, for religious experience in
its intense personal forms and appearances is more easily
communicated than described. It seeks adoption rather
than analysis.

Slowly but surely, investigators are turning to the heart
of religious experience. They are laying their hands
gently on the pulse of personal piety, listening to its heart-
beats rather than observing and judging it by the more
formal sides of its appearances and subsequent developments.   The psychology of religion is becoming, as it
must if it is to be equal to the understanding of its
subject-matter, the most intimate of all investigations.
It deals with the most sacred things in human experience.
It enters into the very depths of sensitive and super-sen-
sitive souls and beholds transactions that originally were
meant for no human eye but had their scene in that private precinct where mere man is in the presence of his
mighty Maker. Religious systems can not teach us
much about the real essence of religious experience. We

must seek out religious souls in whose experience God and all that He means reaches down and lays hold on the primary forces of personal life and becomes the commanding element in the subject's experience. We may not even approximate an understanding of religion except in the terms of what it means to the one who lives and loves it above all else. No man of history furnishes us a finer example of such religious experience than does Jesus.

The religious approach to Jesus is not new to the Christian consciousness. Christians have always approached Jesus religiously, but they have not approached him as the really religious one. Such an approach is not natural to the Christian consciousness that has always looked to Jesus as a religious object. But, sooner or later, the Christian, no matter how conservative, will have to accustom himself to this approach under the very weight of the New Testament facts. The greatest thing about the Gospels is Jesus, and the greatest thing about Jesus is his own personal piety, his intensely intimate experience of the Divine. The religious approach alone will do Jesus a fair measure of personal and historical justice. The clearest single feature in the Gospel picture is his utter and unreserved religiousness. On the basis of the New Testament itself Jesus is to be appraised and appreciated as himself religious, and only thus may his great contribution be appropriated.

In our recovery of Jesus we must heed history rather than fear heresy. The historical Jesus was *homo religiosus*. It was about Jesus the religious subject, not Jesus the religious object, that the Galileans gathered. It was Jesus the religious subject who came to them with a religious call, with a religious commission upon him, who delivered to them a religious message, who set before them a religious outlook, in whom they sensed a complete religious conviction and consecration, whom they saw wholly commanded by fervent religious feeling and faith, who retreated from them for the religious practise of prayer, whose every act and utterance sprang from a deeply religious consciousness.

The religious Jesus belongs to our human history; the Christ of faith to the realm of speculation. Therefore, we must approach Jesus as *a religious subject* rather than as *a religious object,* as a man with a religion rather than as the founder of a particular religion. We must do this in the conviction that if we miss his religiousness we miss everything that matters most. We want to know something of the meaning of God in the experience of Jesus, something of the rôle that religion played in his own life, something of the value and significance that he found religion to have for himself, and something of what he found that God and religion should mean in all human experience. Whatever else Christian conviction may see in Jesus and Christian confession may claim for him, it remains true in the light of our best effort to recover him as he was that Jesus appears first of all as a man whose genius is essentially and fundamentally religious, a man of religious beliefs and faith, of exclusively religious consciousness, making only religious demands and standing as the one great authority in all matters pertaining to the religion that is bold enough to name itself after him.

When one surveys the extensive literature, ancient and modern, that has sprung up about Jesus, one is amazed at the neglect of his religiousness. Practically every other problem in connection with his life and work, practically every other phase of his personality, has received extensive treatment. What Professor Deissmann says of the neglect of the prayer-life of Jesus, we may say of his religious experience: It is "a forgotten chapter" in the life-of-Jesus research.[35] The most adequate religious approach is Professor Wernle's *Jesus,* but even here the conventional elements are not missing.[36] But the newness and unconventionality of the religious approach in no wise compromises its real reliability.

Our modern life-of-Jesus research may review its career with a sense of pride—a century on the road to the recovery of Jesus. We may, with right, feel that we are nearer Jesus as he actually was than any generation of Christians since those first disciples who were his personal companions for a number of months. We have covered two long and difficult stages on the road to our recovery of Jesus. We have cleared the way of the most perplexing literary problems that stand between him and us. We have pressed our path to the naked bed-rock of historical fact, defining the invasions of legend and stripping off the overgrowths of faith. Jesus now stands before us as a human historical figure. But our chief task lies ahead of us yet—the task of understanding Jesus himself. This task presupposes the removal of the principal literary and historical difficulties, but the task itself can not be accomplished except in the light of the psychol-

---

[35]"Der Beter Jesus. Ein vergessenes Kapitel der neutestamentlichen Theologie," *Christliche Welt,* XIII (1899), cols. 701ff.

[36]Professor Case deals directly with the religious experience of Jesus in Chapters VII and VIII of his recent book, *Jesus: A New Biography.* Professor Bultmann in his *Jesus* treats his message as exclusively religious, yet he hesitates to venture as far as the religious personality of Jesus—a curious divorcement of a man from his message.

ogy of a living personality, the very core of whose genius and being was exclusively religious. Each scene in Jesus' life, each word of his, must be approached as the expression of an intense personal piety. The Jesus of history was a religious subject, an experient of religion, and we shall not learn to know him until we approach him as such.[37]

---

[37]This last paragraph also concludes the author's article, "The Meaning of Jesus' Baptism," *Journal of Religion*, VII (January, 1927), p. 70*f*.

CHAPTER III

THE RECOVERY OF JESUS' SOCIAL MESSAGE

THE modern mind shows a remarkable intensity of interest in Jesus. There is to-day a growing disposition to see Jesus as a human historical figure, to learn what he actually thought and believed and felt apart from all the subsequent traditions and theologies that have attached themselves to him. But when the modern mind undertakes to meet Jesus on his own ground, as it must if it is to understand him, it experiences a feeling of deep inner disquietude. The modern mind feels at once that Jesus is too thoroughgoing, too exacting, too uncompromising in some of his demands, that he is too extreme and radical, even ruthless in some of his rejections. It feels too that he is over-enthusiastic, unduly aggressive. In his presence the modern mind does not find itself wholly at home. It senses a distance that separates it from some of the most distinctive things that Jesus represented. This feeling of disquietude grows out of certain demands of Jesus which the modern mind regards as eccentric and with which it feels that it is fundamentally out of sympathy.

THE MORE DRASTIC DEMANDS OF JESUS

Some of Jesus' demands strike the modern mind as feelingless, unnecessarily unreasonable, a good example of which is his word to the three would-be disciples (Luke 9,57-62):

139

"And as they went on the way, a certain man said unto him, I will follow thee whithersoever thou goest. And Jesus said unto him, The foxes have holes, and the birds of the heaven have nests; but the Son of man hath not where to lay his head. And he said unto another, Follow me. But he said, Lord, suffer me first to go and bury my father. But he said unto him, Leave the dead to bury their own dead; but go thou and publish abroad the kingdom of God. And another also said, I will follow thee, Lord; but first suffer me to bid farewell to them that are at my house. But Jesus said unto him, No man, having put his hand to the plow, and looking back, is fit for the kingdom of God."

Others of Jesus' words strike the modern mind as impossible, even fanatical:

"And if thy hand cause thee to stumble, cut it off: it is good for thee to enter into life maimed, rather than having thy two hands to go into hell, into unquenchable fire. And if thy foot cause thee to stumble, cut it off: it is good for thee to enter into life halt, rather than having thy two feet to be cast into hell. And if thine eye cause thee to stumble, cast it out: for it is good for thee to enter into the kingdom of God with one eye, rather than having two eyes to be cast into hell." (Mark 9,43-47.)

At such words the modern mind has taken unnecessary offense because it has sought to fit them into our modern situation rather than understand them in the light of the situation in which Jesus found himself. These drastic demands are not to be isolated; they must be approached in the light of the total temper of Jesus' mind and his experience of religion. At such a point it is especially clear that we may not separate the teaching from the teacher. These words of Jesus are primarily autobiographical and in substance they amount to personal religious confessions. They spring fresh and strong from the very depths of his own personal piety. In particular they reflect more of the demands which he placed upon himself than they do of his requirements of others.

This is generally true of all those words of Jesus which strike the modern mind as eccentric. They are to be understood less in the light of what he demanded of others and more in the light of what he has already demanded of himself. Both passages cited above are clear pictures of Jesus' own complete consecration to the kingdom of God; they reflect his own utter abandonment, the depth of his own personal devotion, to the divine cause which he champions. In such passages we are not dealing with formal religious teaching but with a highly concentrated personality that deliberately tears itself from every interest, no matter how natural or how normal, in its quest of God and His kingdom. Jesus often speaks and acts as one who has burned all bridges behind him, as one for whom there is no turning back. It is this personal element, this intimate note alone that renders such drastic demands intelligible.

These drastic demands of Jesus belong to the psychology of genius. It is true of genius in whatever field of human enterprise it appears that it sets everything at stake for the one thing that means everything to it. The genius is a highly unified personality. He achieves a remarkable singleness of self that is capable of the most compact concentration upon the focus of his faith and of a total exclusion of all other things that do not bear immediately upon the goal that he has set or that interfere with its attainment. It is this high degree of concentration that enables the genius to make the great contribution he has to make in any particular field. The great genius feels that a cause has chosen him personally, he is wholly claimed by it, and to it he devotes himself with an exclusiveness that strikes plain people as an obsession. With comparative ease, apparently without feeling, he severs sacred ties because he feels that he is claimed by a higher order of values. He will break with trade, home, the nearest and dearest of kin, in order to do the thing that draws him with an irresistible force. This drastic process of severance from the usual channels of human happiness may be personally painful for him, but it seldom betrays itself in his words. His cause may take him out of the world of regular responsibilities, although the very thing he seeks to do is for the world's ultimate good. Those obligations which the general run of men hold most sacred he will set at naught, at least for himself and for any who may join him in his quest. Those natural and normal relationships which bring to most men the highest human happiness he will forego and lavish all of his repressed affection and devotion upon this more intangible thing that holds him for life. If the genius appears in a field that brings him followers, he demands of them the same undivided devotion which he himself gives in the quest in which he is engaged. He tolerates no excuses; he allows no exceptions. There are no *if's* and *and's*. He sets his followers, as he has set himself, before an unconditional *either-or*.

To accuse the genius of being anti-social is to do him personal injustice, for in reality he has humanity's happiness at heart. What the commonplace intelligence regards as his fault is in reality his great virtue: What he will not do for himself, he will do for others; what men will not do for themselves, he will do for them, even at the cost of his life. He is not often a sociable soul, but he is the least selfish of men.

Jesus belongs to the genius type of mind, and the drastic demands cited above (Luke 9,57-62; Mark 9, 43-47) spring straight from the very heart of his religious genius. Religious genius is the most exacting of all types, for it feels the call, claim and command of the More-than-human. Jesus set everything at stake for the kingdom of God. In this quest he achieved a singleness of self that is unique and which reflects itself clearly in a word like Matthew 6,22b:

"If therefore thine eye be single, thy whole body shall be full of light."

Numerous words of Jesus show the completeness of his consecration, the depth of his utter devotion. The kingdom of God claims him entirely; there is not room for anything else in his thought, feeling and faith. He broke with training and trade, with home and family. He severed every natural tie, turned aside from every usual channel of human happiness in order to devote himself without distraction to the cause of God. The natural and normal human relationships were not able to hold him. His immediate family came to Capernaum to bring him home by force, convinced that he was beside himself. (Mark 3,19b-21 30-35.) But Jesus felt a deeper kinship than that of blood and, true to the temper of genius, he responded to it. That the break with his family was painful for him never escapes his lips. His immediate family seems never to have given him its sympathy or support in his life-work; none of his family appears in his following during his lifetime in the first three Gospels. Jesus seems to have felt that he was homeless. (Luke 9,58.) His true kinsmen were his fellow-crusaders in the quest of the divine will. (Mark 3,35.)

Jesus' cause took him out of those natural and normal human relationships that men at their best regard as sacred trusts. He cut himself off from the regular pursuits of human happiness. He deserted the work of the world because he had its highest good at heart. The whole torrent of his affection and devotion he turned into higher channels that they might precipitate in a finer form for the blessing of all mankind. This required a concentration of personality that is almost inconceivable, and it was attended by a "full freedom from every sort of earthly burden."[1] Just all that this severance cost him personally we shall never know. But Jesus could not be called happy; there is a tragic element in all that he says and does. Human happiness is a relative matter, and Jesus in his strange paradoxical way could call the hungry and thirsty, the sorrowing, the persecuted and the maligned, *blessed*. It is this tragic joy that tones and tempers the whole of his personality. In sacrifice his joy is supreme. This tragic element in highest happiness is a lesson from the life of Jesus that we are slow in learning.

The demands which Jesus makes of his disciples,

---

[1]Weinel, *Biblische Theologie des Neuen Testaments*, p. 78.

especially those harsher demands, are true to the psychology of genius. He permits no dualisms of devotion. He demands limitless loyalty. There is no neutral ground. Those disciples who came to him with a *both-and* were met with an *either-or*:

> "No servant can serve two masters: for either he will hate the one, and love the other; or else he will hold to the one, and despise the other. Ye can not serve God and mammon." (Luke 16,13.)

Jesus demanded a rigorous renunciation of everything that would compromise loyalty to God and His kingdom. He permitted no excuses. As Bousset writes, "Jesus hated exceptions."[2] Both for himself and for others Jesus was absolutely uncompromising whenever the issues of the kingdom of God were at stake. His demands for discipleship often meant a break with the most sacred of human ties, and such was the experience of many first- and second-century Christians.

> "If any man cometh unto me, and hateth not his own father, and mother, and wife, and children, and brethren, and sisters, yea, and his own life also, he can not be my disciple." (Luke 14,26.)[3]

---

[2] *Jesus*, p. 66.

[3] That such words spring from the psychology of genius is clear from the fact that they have always appealed to the great geniuses of Christian history, particularly in heroic days when special issues were at stake. They have made a special appeal and have had literal fulfillment in the life of our Christian contemporary, Sadhu Sundar Singh. It is in the light of such words of Jesus that the Sadhu conceives of his life-task. *See:* Parker, *Sadhu Sundar Singh*, pp. 23, 125.

There is a strong personal note in Peter's word in Luke 18,28:

"Lo, we have left our own, and followed thee."

And Jesus' reply is true to the psychology of the religious genius who sets at naught every earthly bond for the sake of a higher order of values.

"There is no man that hath left house, or wife, or brethren, or parents, or children, for the kingdom of God's sake, who shall not receive manifold more in this time, and in the world to come eternal life." (Luke 18,29-30.)

The whole world is nothing as compared with loyalty to God and His kingdom.

"What doth it profit a man, to gain the whole world, and forfeit his life?" (Mark 8,36.)

Jesus himself was conscious of the fact that his more drastic demands were for the few rather than for all and that they had their origin in the peculiar situation in which he found himself:

"Not all men can receive this saying, but they to whom it is given. For there are eunuchs, that were so born from their mother's womb: and there are eunuchs, that were made eunuchs by men: and there are eunuchs, that made themselves eunuchs for the kingdom of heaven's sake. He that is able to receive it, let him receive it." (Matt. 19,11-12.)

At no point does Jesus seek to force the peculiarities of his own experience and situation upon all. He was not feelingless toward the sacrifices which his disciples had made (Luke 18,29-30), and his word just cited suggests an undercurrent of the personal pain which the quest of the kingdom of God must have cost him. In Jesus there is not the faintest suggestion of that splendid isolation that in so many cases leaves the genius out of all real sympathy with humankind, with those normal and natural relationships which it holds sacred. Jesus took no delight in his departures; he had no relish for rejecting. That such is the case is clear from the fact that he manifested no appetite for asceticism either in his teaching or in his conduct. With all his ruthless rejections, with all his drastic demands, there is not a trace of genuine fanaticism in Jesus. The religion of Jesus is the religion of healthy-mindedness.

We may not seek to modify the drastic demands of Jesus, to tone them down until they are made to accord with our modern temper. What Jesus said he meant; his own disciples were never in doubt on this point. But to understand these words literally down to the last implication, would be to misunderstand them. When Jesus says that the birds and the beasts are housed but that he himself is homeless, he does not mean to say that men may not seek shelter, that they may not be comfortable in life. In another connection (Matt. 6,25-34) he sees in bird and flower the proofs of the presence of Providence. When he says, "Let the dead bury their own dead," he does not mean that a man should not bury his father. The honor of father and mother was too deeply ingrained in Jesus as a Jew to permit any disrespect. In another connection he upbraids the Pharisees for making a mockery of the honor due parents. (Mark 7,10-13.) When he speaks of cutting off the hand or foot, of plucking out the eye, he is not thinking of physical mutilation such as has been practised in his name, certainly not in his spirit.   On another occasion he speaks of the hand in the secret service of the Divine (Matt. 6,3),

> "Let not thy left hand know what thy right hand doeth."

In all of those seemingly unfeeling words of Jesus there is a more subtle and finer spirit which is his very own and which he seeks to share with his followers.   In none of these passages is he demanding general disloyalty to or neglect of natural and normal human interests and obligations.   In all of them he is requiring the allegiance of the human to the More-than-human and is raising human devotion to its highest level of loyalties.

The supreme interest which Jesus sets at the center of human life is the kingdom of God.   Every other interest, personal or social, is secondary.   Man is first of all the child of his Father.   His most fundamental loyalty is due his Maker.   The one great center of his aspiration is the realization of the divine cause in human life and history.   This is the one great human quest; all other pursuits of men must find their natural but subordinate relation to it.   Men may undertake nothing without the religious reference.   All that they seek to be and to accomplish must be with the religious outlook.   Among the interests that are capable of claiming and commanding human loyalty Jesus sets the religious interest supreme.

RELIGIOUS CONVICTION AMONG HUMAN INTERESTS

It belongs to the very nature of religious conviction, wherever it is vital, to seek to command every other element of experience. Religion, wherever pure and powerful, insists on this. If the religious experience is pure, it possesses the requisite power; it becomes the passion that is capable of displacing or subordinating all others. As Professor Hocking writes: "No man has found his religion until he has found that for which he must sell his goods and his life."[4] Religion can not grow and yield fruit without "depth of earth." It must reach down to the very depths of individual and social life and lay hold on the elemental powers. It must seek out the source-springs that nourish human life in all of its responsible forms.

Religious conviction, now and again, has become this very thing in an individual life. It has been able to defeat competing interests that seek the command of an individual and to make itself supreme. If the religious experience in such cases is of a high order, the result has been the production of a personality and character that has wrought naught but good for men.

In the life of Jesus we see personal piety in its finest form. For Jesus personally religion is everything. His experience of God is the commanding element of his conscious existence. The religious interest subordinates every other interest in his experience. His every personal faculty and capacity, the whole of his individual endowment and equipment, swings with a will into the spirit and service of his experience of God. Jesus' personal

---

[4] *The Meaning of God in Human Experience*, p. 237. Courtesy of Yale University Press.

piety is primitive in that it lays hold of the elemental
forces of the human constitution and puts at the center
of life what it holds dearer than life itself. It is for
this reason that the personal piety of Jesus possesses a
peculiar purity and power. To every issue that presented
itself to him he responded with an affirmative or a negative according as it related itself to the supremacy of the
religious values that commanded him completely. As
Professor Wernle writes, "This direct path of the unconditional *'yes or no'* led straight to the cross."[5]

Religion has never yet been able to produce its finest
fruits in group life such as it has now and again in individual life. This is doubtless due to the fact that the
group seldom becomes a thinking and acting unit. The
strongest incentives and impulses are required for this.
Dangers that threaten all alike, developments that promise tangible benefits for all, will bring men together as
a thinking and an acting unit. The necessary emotional
impetus is to be found only in common fears, hopes,
ambitions and aspirations that seize all alike. Too often,
common hatreds bring men together to act as a unit. In
most cases of really concerted thinking and acting, it
is a time of some sort of crisis that concerns all in a vital
way. At the center of the group that becomes a unit
there must be a cause that is capable of claiming and
commanding the individual, a passionate concern to which
he commits himself and in the service of which he is willing to forfeit even his life. He stakes his all in
its behalf. The social solidarity of the group maintains itself in time of routine by natural bonds which
grow out of the common circumstances of its existence,

---

[5]*Jesus*, p. 31.

such as race, nation, natural resources, employment and so forth.

There are many interests that seek the command of the group, to give it its distinctive character and to control its conduct. Only rarely does the religious interest come into command. When it does appear, it is usually in an inferior form. Its cause too often is hardly more than pious prejudice, its zeal only a feverish fanaticism. Groups often act in the name of pure religion but seldom in the pure spirit of religion. Campaigns for religious causes are, more often than not, accompanied by a nastiness of mood or a questionableness of method that brands the whole movement as fundamentally irreligious because it deserts the codes and controls of ordinary morals and ethics.

The religious experience of the group, so far as it has been able to assert itself in group character and conduct, has seldom been of a high order. On many questions the group possesses a moral sense and will revolt. The religiousness of the group, better perhaps its moral sense, will assert itself in the presence of gross evil that violates the moral conventions of society. But some of our worst and most dangerous evils have become conventional, or have come to be regarded as admittedly necessary. It seems almost impossible to get concerted thinking and acting for good in the sense of a religion of righteousness. In our ordinary humdrum existence religious considerations lie, for the most part, in the theoretical background of the group mind and are by no means commanding elements in the group's actual experience, capable of creating its character and of controlling its conduct.

Our modern social order, remarkably high in religious

intelligence and just as remarkably low in religious in-
centive, is confronted with pressing problems on a scale
and of a significance that are without parallel in history.
The problems are old, but the proportions are new because of the very scale on which the modern world lives.
Peoples that once led a peaceable existence, facing and
solving their own problems in their own way, are now
caught in the whirl of the world's life. Group frictions
that formerly were local have now become irritative
along the whole social front. And the modern mind does
not yet show itself capable of dealing with its social
problems on a scale that is commensurate with their
scope and significance. The sore spots are the same old
afflictions—racial, national, economic. These are the
commanding considerations in our modern group experience, the sources of our hopes and fears, of our aspirations and apprehensions, the common interests that
bring us together to think, feel and act as groups.

Only since 1914 have we realized vividly how powerful these issues are in bringing men together and how
woefully weak our religious interest is when these other
interests are involved. Our professed religious interests
were hopelessly incapable of holding us together even
long enough to try to find a way out of armed conflict.
The only rôle that religion was able to play was to seek
to justify the human wrongs that our national and economic policies were inflicting. A Western World that
professed the discipleship of Jesus could do no more with
him, who wore no insignia to distinguish himself from the
rest of men, than strip off the seamless robe and clothe
him in khaki, horizon-blue, or service-gray. Jesus stood
on the Western Front a forlorn figure, actually deserted
by those who theoretically deified him, hearing in wordless

wonder the world's judgment against himself. In such a situation he again could do no mighty work save lay his hands on single serving and sacrificing souls who were the victims of a social order that was founded on a deep-seated unbelief.

In view of such an anomaly it is not surprising that the modern mind feels intensely ill at ease in the presence of a religious outlook such as Jesus projects. It can not help but feel that it has sinned on a tremendous scale, but it is a hopeful sign that the modern mind seeks to know Jesus at all. "Human nature's recognition of its own defects, wherever this recognition occurs, is a part of the reconstruction process that has already set in."[6]

THE "SOCIAL TEACHINGS" OF JESUS

With the growing acuteness of our modern group issues there has been an increasing interest in the social teachings of Jesus. What does Jesus expect of men as groups? What does he demand in the way of group character and conduct? In reply to these questions a whole host of studies has appeared on "JESUS AND THIS," "JESUS AND THAT." The Gospels have been literally ransacked in the effort to extract from Jesus some social program. Much of this study, however, has been little more than a pitiable pedantry that pressed special statements of Jesus into service in a way that was out of all harmony with the total temper of his mind. On the basis of a single word of his, attempts have been made to erect a whole social theory. In this process Jesus has received the gravest personal and historical injustice.

[6]Coe, *The Psychology of Religion*, p. 226. Courtesy of the University of Chicago Press.

On the basis of an utterance like Luke 6,24 we may not formulate his doctrine of wealth,

> "Woe unto you that are rich! for ye have received your reward."

Jesus had no doctrine of wealth in the sense that we to-day understand such a social theory. In historical justice, we must say that wealth in Jesus' day was usually associated with wantonness. In personal justice to Jesus, we must say that he does not portray the rich from the social view-point as profiteers, oppressors, hard-hearted and loveless, but from the religious point of view according to which wealth may stand between the rich man and the kingdom of God.

> "How hardly shall they that have riches enter into the kingdom of God! . . . It is easier for a camel to go through a needle's eye, than for a rich man to enter into the kingdom of God." (Mark 10, 23b 25.)

Jesus is not thinking of the relation of the rich man to the poor man, but of the religious hope of the rich man for participation in the kingdom of God. Jesus viewed wealth as a source of temptation, and it proves itself to be just such to-day. In his judgment he is simply true to human experience, but he is not rejecting wealth and the wealthy. Jesus viewed wealth, as he viewed every element of our human life, as a sacred trust to be discharged with a sense of religious responsibility. About the highest use of wealth in his day was for alms, a practise which the modern mind questions and rejects on

the basis that it is harmful to the recipient. The greater
and nobler uses of wealth to-day were unknown to Jesus,
and he would be as prompt now in his commendation as
then in his condemnation. We may not take his words
on wealth as formal theory, but we must approach
wealth as he did from the strictly religious point of view
as helpful or hurtful to the divine cause and human participation in it.

On the basis of a word like Luke 6,20b we may not
conclude that Jesus regarded poverty as a virtue,

> "Blessed *are* ye poor: for yours is the kingdom of
> God."

In general, the poor were the pious of Jesus' day. But
in our day poverty has become an even greater source of
temptation than wealth. In its trail lies a whole host of
human victims. Here again we must seek the total temper of Jesus' mind and view poverty from the exclusively
religious point of view. Is poverty helpful or hurtful
in the poor man's quest of the kingdom of God? Jesus'
judgment against poverty to-day would be as quick and
sharp and decisive as it was against the wealth of his day.

The same is true in our search for light from Jesus
on other social issues. We may not seek out special
statements but must strive to sense and to share the religious spirit of Jesus for the living of the whole of life.
On the basis of his word in Mark 12,17 we may not
reconstruct a theory of the separation of church and
state and ascribe it to him,

> "Render unto Cæsar the things that are Cæsar's,
> and unto God the things that are God's."

From a scene like Luke 12,13-14 we may not conclude that Jesus removes all civil life and property from the realm of religious obligation:

> "And one out of the multitude said unto him, Teacher, bid my brother divide the inheritance with me. But he said unto him, Man, who made me a judge or a divider over you?"

On the basis of Jesus' parable of the laborers who receive the same reward independent of the length of their service we may not base his promulgation of the theory of the uniform wage. (Matt. 20,1-16.) On the basis of Matthew 10,34 we may not justify the practise of war and a policy of militarism,

> "Think not that I came to send peace on earth: I came not to send peace, but a sword."

All such words are special statements made in a special situation with a special point in mind. On the basis of them we may not reconstruct wholesale social theories and programs. Things that were historically impossible for Jesus may become the solemn religious obligation of his followers who share any appreciable measure of his spirit.

When the modern mind approaches Jesus with the expectation of receiving special instructions with regard to its social issues its first reaction is that of an almost crushing disappointment. Jesus offers us no *Sozialethik*, no particular precepts for the "social mind," the "social will," the "spirit of the group." He does not address himself to the temptations and sins of the group. Most of his words are to individuals or to the narrow circle of his chosen companions. Seldom does he touch directly upon one of the social problems that are most disturbing to us to-day. About the most specific statement of Jesus on a social issue that confronts us is his word on divorce,[7] but even this utterance may not be taken apart from his general attitude toward human institutions.

Jesus gives no detailed instructions to our modern social groups such as the Baptist gave to various classes of his contemporaries (Luke 3,10-14), a series of words that sounds as much like the twentieth century as the first:

"And the multitude asked him, saying, What then must we do? And he answered and said unto them, He that hath two coats, let him impart to him that hath none; and he that hath food, let him do likewise. And there came also publicans to be baptized, and they said unto him, Teacher, what must we do? And he said unto them, Extort no more than that which is appointed you. And the soldiers also asked him, saying, And we, what must we do? And he said unto them, Extort from no man by violence, neither accuse *any one* wrongfully; and be content with your wages."

The words of Jesus that touch upon the family, property, wealth, poverty, civil affairs, politics, and so forth, are too sporadic to bear the weight of elaborate social schemes and systems. Jesus gives us no direct social message such as we find in the incisive utterances of the great sixth- and eighth-century prophets of Israel. His social teachings are hopelessly meager when compared with a

[7] Cf. Matt. 5,32; 19,9; Mark 10,11-12; Luke 16,18.

great human document like Deuteronomy. In view of the extreme meagerness of the materials, it is hardly proper to speak of the "social teachings" of Jesus. One might speak of the social significance of Jesus' religious teachings, or perhaps even better, of the social implications of his religious teachings, for his teachings are social only by implication.

A strict social ethic in our modern sense is not to be found in the scattered utterances of Jesus, for the reason that he was the spokesman of God, a true prophet, and not just a national or social reformer. In his public work Jesus appears as the champion of no social group, as the protagonist of no particular class. In this respect his consciousness of call and commission is supersocial. The tragedy of his people's fate was just as crushing in his day as in earlier centuries. Forty years after his death the Holy City was razed to the ground. (70 A. D.) While he was announcing the kingdom of God, political oppression, economic exploitation, class strife, national and racial hatred were at work in the minds of those who heard him. Yet none of these things enters into his message to alter its distinctive form or essential content. From the words of Jesus we can not even begin to piece together a picture of the social situation in the midst of which he lived and worked. In his message there are to be found not more than merely incidental allusions to the political, economic and social conditions of his day and people.

In this respect Jesus differs greatly from the prophets of Israel, the son of whose pure genius he was. Almost without exception they appeared at times of great national and social crises. They group themselves about the two great catastrophes that resulted in the end of

Israel's independent national existence, the fall of the northern kingdom in 721 B. C. and the fall of the southern kingdom in 586 B. C. The last of them appeared in connection with the restoration and return to the homeland. Israel's prophets were her greatest nationalists and patriots. Politics was a part of their piety. While they were men of real religious genius who responded to inner intuition, yet they were fully acquainted with the situation at home and abroad. Some of them, like Isaiah, were statesmen of real caliber. They spoke their mind to king and people in no uncertain terms on matters of political policies, foreign alliances, trust in military strength, revolts against oppressors, and so forth. At home they knew social, moral and religious conditions in detail. They were the confessed champions of social righteousness. They publicly condemned civil injustice, corruptness of judges and courts, the wantonness of the wealthy, public graft, class oppression, ingenuine religion and general immorality. They chose the cause of the widow, the orphan, the poor, the needy and the plain man against their lords. From the messages of the great prophets one can reconstruct a fairly accurate picture of the foreign and domestic situation in which they appeared and worked. In fact, it was often the case that just the political situation abroad or the social conditions at home, or both, brought the prophets out of private into public life.

This strong social strain in the prophetic genius that made them into reformers does not reappear in typical form in the personality of Jesus. Only occasionally do his words reflect the array of one class over against the other. (Mark 12,38-40.) Jesus preached with all the passion of the prophets, but he was never the champion of one group against another. However, we must not deceive ourselves. The social strain in Jesus is not on the surface, but it is there nevertheless like a mighty undercurrent that cuts the channel for the flood of the whole of his thought, feeling and faith.

This failure of Jesus to be explicit has exposed his teachings to a very cutting criticism from those quarters where the social issues are specially acute. Some feel that Jesus possessed a very definite disdain for the affairs of this life. He taught men to cease to care for the morrow, yet many modern men feel that this is about all that they are permitted to care about. He demanded of men that they leave family and friends, house and holdings, to become his disciples. The only rewards he had to offer were in the intangible terms of eternal life or the kingdom of God. His mind, they feel, was otherworldly. He set his values in an obscure order wholly remote from our actual existence. To great sections of the submerged thinking of our modern order the kingdom of God suggests only a beatific but highly imaginary and impossible ideal. Even enlightened men of progress in the West have felt that Jesus is the worst foe of culture and civilization, that his teachings are dangerous and destructive of the established institutions of society. The modern reaction to his teachings has often been to the effect that they are highly individual, even anti-social.

The feeling that Jesus' teachings are highly individual is an accurate reaction to the main body of his thought, but this does not mean that his teachings neglect the social interests of men or that they are anti-social. The modern social mind should reflect on the history of human advance long enough to realize that the social order does not improve apart from the appearance of good men. The clearest lesson of history is to the effect that social progress depends upon the constant introduction and intervention of personal factors and forces which come only from the purest personalities. The great social fires of the group always await the glowing spark that comes from some great soul.[8]

The modern social mind should also remember that Jesus was a prophet within, not without the social order. There is nothing anti-social in his habits of life. He felt himself specially drawn to the lower strata of the social order of his day, and his message of highest hope was addressed to them. It was upon their recovery and restoration that he was determined. The social victim may always feel that in Jesus he has more than a congenial companion; he may feel that he has in him a consecrated champion who does not condescend, but who is his own human brother. Jesus rejected no class, not even the religious-by-profession; they seem to have rejected him.

There are commanding elements in the religious experience of Jesus that will bring condemnation on our modern social order, but he is in no sense anti-social. The man who prayed and thanked God for his daily bread is not the religious dreamer who sets human life and its problems at naught, who transfers all religious values to another world out of all vital association with the exigencies of our human existence here and now. Ac-

---

[8]Albert Schweitzer writes: "Ich glaube nicht, dass man in einen Menschen Gedanken hineinbringen kann, die nicht in ihm sind. Gewoehnlich sind in den Menschen alle guten Gedanken als Brennstoffe vorhanden. Aber vieles von diesem Brennstoff entzuendet sich erst oder erst recht, wenn eine Flamme oder ein Flaemmchen von draussen, von einem andern Menschen her, in ihn hineinschlaegt." (*Aus meiner Kindheit und Jugend,* p. 63.)

cording to Jesus, it is just here and now that God is the living, loving Father of men, that His kingdom is coming, that we need our daily bread, protection against evil and constant forgiveness. A finer social expression of religious experience has never been made than that which we possess in the *Lord's Prayer*—a prayer with a social outlook and for a group to which Jesus sets no limits except those of character and conduct. The man who saw God in flower and field, who sought out eternal values in the humblest human being, can not be classed with those religionists who leave the world and men to sin, the flesh and the devil. The man who took the little children in his arms and blessed them, who looked upon the rich young ruler and loved him, who held fast to the ancient code of honor to father and mother, who coined the very essence of his experience of God in the image of the Father, may not be called feelingless and fanatical, or anti-social.

Jesus does not search out those more subtle and deadly sins of the group as we know them from experience. But the man who pronounced hatred to be murder, a lustful look to be adultery, would hardly fail to condemn the sinning on a larger scale of group against group of which the modern man excuses himself and lays to the account of the social order of which he is a part, but over which he feels that he has no control. That the individual may conduct himself toward another individual according to one standard and conduct himself as a member of a group according to another standard when his group comes into contact or conflict with another group is a contradiction, an utter corruption, of conscience that is impossible for the earnest follower of Jesus who has sensed anything of his spirit.

The piety of Jesus is personal and individual to a marked degree, but the goal of his piety by its very implications is just as strongly social. The religious experience of Jesus is not that of the ascetic or the mystic type that seeks only or first of all its own redemption. The religious experience of Jesus seeks the recovery and restoration of all mankind. The kingdom of God in his experience is not just a state of inner blessedness; it is a new humanity with God. The religion of Jesus does offer a peace and purity of personality, a cleanness of hands and heart, but it is not withdrawn from the real world of men who are caught in the struggle for survival and who face pressing problems at every turn of life. Jesus has light, plenty of livid light, to shed upon our modern social problems. In his religious approach to the whole of our human life and living there is deposited the solid substratum for our and for all social order—the religious reference.

THE RELIGIOUS REFERENCE

But what is this light? What is this solid substratum which Jesus provides for all social order? What is this religious reference? The answers to these questions involve Jesus' view of man and the world in which he lives, and they must be answered in the terms of the commanding elements of his religious experience: his experience of God as high and holy, as living and loving Father, his quest of the kingdom of God and the divine will.

For the World

Jesus' view of the world is very simply, quite unpretentiously, religious. Each religion has its view of the world, its estimate of this present order. The evaluation which any religious faith sets upon this world corresponds closely to that faith's essential content and general religious outlook. In certain faiths the world is set at the lowest possible worth; it represents no real values; it is dull, drab and dreary; it confronts men with nothing but delusion; it is essentially evil, and man's highest aspiration is permanent freedom from it. Other faiths see only an incidental value in this world. It is a sort of drill ground, a training station, for the development of religious virtues. It offers men the opportunity to compete successfully with temptation and to prepare themselves for participation in the life of the next world. It is to be endured; patience and perseverance in this process are the chief religious virtues.

The latter view of the world has appeared often in the history and biography of Christianity. We find it within the New Testament. Paul establishes a fundamental dualism between God and this world. It is under the power of sin, death and Satan. The wrath of God is upon it because it is essentially evil. It is the scene of sin, sorrow and suffering (Rom. 8,22) :

"For we know that the whole creation groaneth and travaileth in pain together until now."

Paul longs for deliverance "from this present evil world" (Gal. 1,4) because God and Christ are not in it. It is fundamentally opposed to God, and God to it. It may serve as a training ground for Christian virtue, but it offers no real values. The Christian is in the world, but not of the world. This strong strain of pessimism runs through the great majority of the New Testament epistles and on down through the main channels of Christian thought in later centuries.

Jesus' religious estimate of the world is at the very opposite extreme from that of Paul. Jesus is not blind to the world's evils, but he does not regard it as essentially evil. He establishes no dualisms between God and the world. With all of his eschatology, he never sets this present order in total depreciation. He does not turn it into a mere drill ground for developing religious virtues. He manifests no sense of superiority to it.

In the world about him Jesus discovers the Divine. The Father is in flower and field, in the humblest human life. As glorious as was the prospect of the kingdom of God, Jesus is not other-worldly. He does not long to depart this life; he surrenders it only through struggle and under protest. He does not meet the world with a flat negation; from the very depths of his religious experience he affirms the world. It is good because it is God's; it is not man's arch-enemy; it is his providential home. As such Jesus views it and loves it.

This view of Jesus was a radical departure from the prevalent pessimism of his contemporaries who had surrendered this world and its powers to Satan. This pessimism is clearly reflected in Satan's word in the threefold temptation:

"And he led him up, and showed him all the kingdoms of the world in a moment of time. And the devil said unto him, To thee will I give all this authority, and the glory of them: for it hath been delivered unto me; and to whomsoever I will I give it." (Luke 4,5-6.)

It was out of this fundamental pessimism for this world that Jewish eschatology and apocalypticism sprang. This world is hopelessly evil; it is lost. The only hopeful outlook is for the destruction of this present order and the appearance of a new order.

For Jesus' contemporaries great sections of this world, natural and human, were unclean. To come into contact with them meant contamination and defilement. There were clean and unclean animals, clean and unclean people, clean and unclean foods. The careful Jew of Jesus' day must be constantly on his guard lest he be defiled (Mark 7,3-4), and defilement through contact with unclean elements of this world meant exclusion from the presence of God. The defiled person could not approach his God until he had passed through a tedious process of cleansing.

In no passage is Jesus' affirmation of this world clearer than in his word in the contention concerning unwashed hands (Mark 7,1-23) which he turns to the issue of the sources of cleanness and uncleanness. This word was spoken in a special situation, but it reveals much more than his attitude toward washed and unwashed hands, clean and unclean foods.

"There is nothing from without the man, that going into him can defile him; but the things which proceed out of the man are those that defile the man." (Mark 7,15.)

Jesus' position here was revolutionary in his own day and is of great significance in the history of religion. He makes a complete break with a religion of externalities and seeks the sources of good and evil within men. Defilement becomes an inner matter. Mere contact with the world can not defile any man or exclude him from the divine presence. Nothing can exclude the worshiper from the divine presence except the worshiper himself.

In view of such an evaluation of this world men may well breathe a sigh of relief. Jesus lifts the burden of natural existence from men's shoulders, which is the first step in the solution of all social problems. The world is God's world; nothing in it is naturally or inherently evil. Constant contact with its roughest realities can not defile men. It is the divinely appointed scene of man's life and all that life holds highest and best. In the world men may feel that they are at home; in it they are not to lead a timid existence under the constant dread of *taboo*, but they may face the world and its problems in the clear consciousness that the heavenly Father notes even the fall of the sparrow. Man is relieved of the fear that the whole order of existence conspires against him, and he is left to face the world with the courage and confidence necessary for the conquest of all the resistance it naturally offers. The human task is not just to tolerate and endure. Man's struggle is onward and upward, a victory over all that halts and hinders his approach to his Maker. Jesus does not teach the loosest possible attachment to the world but the greatest possible devotion to all that it offers in the way of elevation and enrichment for human life.

It is of great importance that we note that Jesus' estimate of the world is purely religious. The world of fact he views wholly in the light of faith. The pressure of the harshest facts is not able to curb the passion of his faith. Thus Jesus sanctifies the world and all its concerns. In this world men are treading upon holy ground and only a keen awareness of this fact will enable them to face the world with a sense of religious responsibility.

This idealistic view of this realistic order of things is the organic issue of Jesus' experience of God. To the modern social mind that seeks the way out Jesus points the way in. Jesus' social disciple must face the world with an experience of God as high and holy that is commanding. The world is not here to set its brand upon him, the marked victim of a baneful existence. Upon the world he must set the stamp of his faith. The whole of his most elemental existence he must approach with the religious reference, with the religious outlook, if he is to maintain his claim of social being. Life in this world is a great boon; it is God's gift.

For Humankind

Jesus' view of man is just as simply and unpretentiously religious as is his view of the world in which he lives. Jesus has no theory of man, no abstract doctrine concerning human nature, its excellence or its total depravity. He approaches the human problem in the same simple way that he approaches the whole of life. He takes men without question just as they are and as he found them to be. He possessed an insight into human nature that is almost uncanny in the way in which he was able to single out the essential, the distinctive and characteristic. With all of his exalted estimate of man's worth he has just as sharp an eye for human weaknesses. His parables in which human characters appear are classical commentaries on human nature. He never pictures an ideal human character. Those characters which we usually regard as pictures of perfection he idealizes at only one point. It is characteristic of the actors in Jesus' parables that they are sketched from a single angle. His parables are silhouettes of human nature. The good Samaritan he pictures only from the angle of his natural impulse to minister to the needy. The father in the parable of the prodigal son appears in a single light, that of impartial love and forgiveness.

Jesus portrayed men just as they were and are. Sometimes he presents them in their best moments, again in their mediocrity, and still again when they are at their worst. But the men in Jesus' parables are real men, the women real women and the children real children—all a mysterious mixture of good and evil. Jesus' characters in his parables are not always moral models or ethical examples. The motives of the man who bought a field in which he had found a treasure are by no means above question. (Matt. 13,44.) The steward who is accused of swindling covers up one swindle with another. (Luke 16,1-7.) The judge who turns a deaf ear to the pleadings of a widow confirms his reputation as one who fears not God and who has no regard for men. (Luke 18,1-5.) When he avenges the widow it is not out of genuine moral motive; he simply is worn out by her continual coming. It is not the justice of the widow's cause that brings him to action. In fact, Jesus does not even say that the widow's cause against her adversary was just. The characters in Jesus' parables are not ideal, but they are always true to life. There are just such people.

Jesus thinks of men, then, just as they are—plain, unadorned human beings capable of good and of evil.

"The good man out of his good treasure bringeth forth good things: and the evil man out of his evil treasure bringeth forth evil things." (Matt. 12,35.)

Jesus approached men with no theory as to what they had been, were, or ought to have been. He knew them at first hand, as they actually appeared in the drama of human life and living.

With all the intimacy of his knowledge and understanding of men Jesus finds it in his faith to remain highly hopeful for them, perhaps for the reason that he was not thinking of human nature in general but of men in particular. He shared nothing of that Christian pessimism concerning humankind that has run like a strong stream from the thought of Paul down to the present. Such a low estimate of the human constitution as Paul holds of his own (Rom. 7,14-25) has no parallel in the thought of Jesus. Paul pictures men as under the curse and power of sin, hopelessly wretched in and of themselves. Paul surrenders men unconditionally to the misery of an abstract sinfulness that has rested upon them from the beginning. The very fact that men are human brands them as victims of a curse.

This terrible pessimism has no counterpart in the religious thinking of Jesus. He did not find men without God and without hope in the world as did the author of Ephesians. (2,12.) He shares nothing of the moral skepticism that we find in the majority of the New Testament epistles. He establishes no religious or moral dualisms; he draws no sharp divisions between the saved and the unsaved, the elect and the damned, the spiritual and the worldly, the sons of light and the sons of darkness. The desolate wretchedness of man was a favorite theme with moody souls of Israel (Psalms 14; 58; 82), but Jesus composes no *Misereres.* He gives no discourses on sin and the sinfulness of man, yet the primer prayer which he places on human lips is,

"God, be thou merciful to me a sinner." (Luke 18,13.)

Jesus' estimate of humankind is positive, not negative. His attitude is affirmative and confident. He calls and claims rather than condemns. His chief condemnations fall upon those who forget that they are human and regard themselves as secure, hopelessly saved with no chance of being lost. Jesus worked on the assumption that men are weak rather than wicked. An enthusiastic disciple vowed,

"Lord, with thee I am ready to go both to prison and to death."

But Jesus replied,

"I tell thee, Peter, the cock shall not crow this day, until thou shalt thrice deny that thou knowest me." (Luke 22,33-34.)

Jesus found men distracted and distraught rather than depraved and doomed. They are strangers to God rather than deliberate sinners against Him. They are all His children, some obedient, some disobedient, but it is not the will of the Father that any of them should perish.

Jesus had the utmost confidence in the human constitution. Often he appeals directly to the goodness and soundness of the human disposition and judgment:

"And of which of you that is a father shall his son ask a loaf, and he give him a stone? or a fish, and he for a fish give him a serpent?"   (Luke 11,11.)

"What man shall there be of you, that shall have one sheep, and if this fall into a pit on the sabbath day, will he not lay hold on it, and lift it out?"   (Matt. 12,11.)

Jesus' faith in the religious possibilities of men is limitless.   Men are capable of good and of becoming good. He believed in the changeability and transformation of men.   He gives to men not a low but a high estimate of themselves.   The sons of men may become the sons of God.

It was this exalted estimate of men that led Jesus to consume himself in the service of humankind.   The greater the need of men, the stronger the bond that drew and held him to them.   In the faith and feeling of Jesus man represents the highest value of our finite order, and he is so adjudged of the Divine.   This feeling of the infinite worth of each individual is the source of Jesus' word on love of enemies.   Men may have no enemies, for all alike are objects of divine solicitude.   It is this sense of the infinite worth of the finite that is behind Jesus' great social sentence, the *Golden Rule*.   The exalted virtues which he describes in the beatitudes (Matt. 5,3-12) are for human attainment.   The very difficulty of his demands in the Sermon on the Mount and elsewhere is a direct reflection of his firm faith in humankind.   Such demands are inconceivable from one whose view of man is clouded by the dismal doctrine of human depravity.

Jesus regarded men as perfectible, infinitely so.   To his disciples he says,

"Ye therefore shall be perfect, as your heavenly
Father is perfect." (Matt. 5,48.)

Jesus here seeks a perfection of personal life which he
did not and probably never will find in his following.
But this demand is not rendered invalid even if no follower of his ever attains it, even if we with our knowledge of ourselves know that we can not attain it. It
still stands as the religious obligation of all of his followers. Jesus with his knowledge of human weakness, without hesitation and without reservation, leads men into the
quest of perfection. It is the quest that Jesus demands
rather than perfection itself. The most hopeful portent
for its relative realization is the common human consciousness of the wide distance that separates this exalted
ideal from itself.

Jesus demanded a cultivation of human character that
corresponds to that of the Divine, for in his religious
outlook men are destined for God's society. Here again
Jesus simply staggers us with his tremendous faith in our
humankind. His faith in men overwhelms us when we
begin to realize the religious task which he sets before
us as his followers.

In Jesus' exalted estimate of men we strike upon the
second element of that solid substratum which he lays at
the foundation of a secure social structure. His view of
the world as good, of men as capable of the highest
good, seems rather remote from the social problems that
confront us, but these things bear directly upon the very
heart of our most distressing group issues. It is our
modern failure to approach the world and its humankind
religiously that explains best our modern weakness in

solving the dilemmas into which our social experience throws us. Our modern group mood is the reflection of the hard facts that surround us rather than the issue of a high faith that commands us. Unless men as individuals and as groups may meet the world in the clear conviction that it is good because it is God's, that they themselves are capable of the highest good because they are God's children, there is no hope of permanent social progress. At the very base of human experience in its social aspects Jesus lays what we have lost as a commanding conviction—the religious reference for the world and man, and the religious outlook for both.

The first step in the solution of our social problems is bringing out from the remote theoretical background of the modern mind the thought of Jesus for the world and men and placing it at the very center of our conscious existence as a conviction that creates our group character and that controls our group conduct. Our conventional Christian conception that the world is good and that men are capable of good must become a basal truth that we live by.

This attitude of unaffected affirmation of man and his world on the part of Jesus is an open optimism that defies fact and that nourishes itself in the realm of faith. Its very heart is a religious reverence quite far removed from the rationalistic mood that feeds only on raw realities. But if we are to be religious in the sense of Jesus, we may approach man and his world only in an attitude of reverence, for both are God's. This reverent attitude is the only source of a social hope that can help. It strips the world of its viciousness and relieves the human mind of the haunting fear that, after all, it may be only a victim. Jesus judged man out of the depths of his personal experience of God: He is the child of a living, loving Father.

For History

One of the finest features in the history of Israel is the close bond which its faith established between the fates and fortunes of the nation and its God. Never in the history of mankind have people and God been brought so inseparably together. Israel's history as a people began with a covenant between God and Abraham, a sacred agreement that was inviolable. From the first families, clans and tribes down to the period of national solidarity it was God who guided the affairs of His people. It was the voice of God that spoke to the whole people through its divinely appointed leaders. It was the hand of God that saved them out of the toils of the oppressor.

This belief was at first primitive and naive, and it left room for little more than narrow nationalism and racial prejudice. At every turn in his people's fates and fortunes the pious Israelite saw the hand of God. When he went to war he was conscious of divine leadership. The God of Israel fought with its armies; His strong right arm was bared on the battle-field. The tide of battle depended upon the divine favor, and the divine favor depended in turn upon Israel's loyalty to its God. A victory on the battle-field was God's own victory. A defeat was not brought about by the stronger armies of the enemy but by God who thus punished Israel for its break of faith. God used other nations as rods of oppression because of Israel's sins. It was God who made Israel's laws, who anointed its kings and in turn deposed them.

A finer expression of a people's religious responsibility would be difficult to find than appears in Solomon's prayer as he faces the task of leading God's people:

"O Jehovah my God, thou hast made thy servant king instead of David my father: and I am but a little child; I know not how to go out or come in. And thy servant is in the midst of thy people which thou hast chosen, a great people, that can not be numbered nor counted for multitude. Give thy servant therefore an understanding heart to judge thy people, that I may discern between good and evil; for who is able to judge this thy great people." (I Kings 3,7-9.)

Israel as a nation and people possessed a clear consciousness of divine call and commission; it is the most distinctive thing in its history. As a people Israel felt that it was chosen and that it had a religious mission to accomplish in the world. In the later prophets like Second Isaiah (40-66) this religious outlook rises above the earlier narrow nationalism and racial prejudice, and the God of Israel in their faith becomes the God of all nations and all peoples. He comes to guide the course of human affairs; all peoples are in the hollow of His hand; He presides over human events. In short, the God of Israel becomes the God of human history, and the cause of God and the cause of men become inseparably one.

This most distinctive feature of Israel's faith has its finest fruition in the religious experience of Jesus, in his faith in the kingdom of God. In this single expression Jesus deposited the whole of his outlook for human life and history. The course of human events, the affairs of men, have their goal and ultimate end in the kingdom of

God. This kingdom is the divine cause in human life and history. The concerns of men are the concerns of God, who has no cause, no vital concern, apart from men. The kingdom of God Jesus paints in Jewish colors, but it is devoid of all national and racial discriminations. It has no artificial boundaries; it is universally human in its scope. He sets no limits except moral character and ethical conduct. That God means everything, that He makes all the difference in human life and experience, is a fundamental truth that Jesus lived and worked by. The complete cooperation of the human and the Divine is Jesus' central conviction as expressed in the kingdom of God. The bringing of God and men together in a divine-human society is the secret source-spring that brought him into his work and that carried him through it. This society is all that Jesus knows and all that he feels as worth while to announce in the way of a religious message to men.

The social implications of Jesus' faith in the kingdom of God and its coming are simply tremendous. In his thought and feeling the kingdom of God is a social experience. In the quest of the kingdom man relates himself to a higher order, to something out beyond himself in the service of which he can forget himself, to something that is greater than himself, greater than the grandest glories of the past, more holy than the holiest of houses. A greater thing than Solomon, or Jonah, or the temple is here which calls and claims all humankind. (Matt. 12,6 41-42.) The kingdom of God is the orientation point for the human will, individual and group; it is the one great object about which human loyalties and devotions center. The kingdom of God is a social experience because it brings all men together in a common quest, with common feelings and faith, fears and hopes, with mutual intentions and interests, aspirations and ambitions. Thus the kingdom of God becomes a community consciousness, a social solidarity, in which all the elemental forces of humankind are drawn from distracting diversities into a complete cooperation with the Divine.

But the modern mind, as it turns to Jesus' picture of the future, feels that the form of his faith in the kingdom of God is too fanciful and fantastic. It takes offense at the spectacular scenery in which Jesus has cast his faith. His eschatology strikes the modern mind as too highly imaginary, as so saturated with a sheer supernaturalism that it is quite out of harmony with the modern worldview. When Jesus begins to speak of the kingdom of God as a supernatural order that is to be introduced by a superhuman agent, the Son of man, who is to come on the clouds attended by angels and surrounded by great glory, the modern mind feels that he is speaking in a language that is wholly foreign and strange to its understanding.

This reaction of the modern mind is quite correct. In this glowing picture Jesus is speaking in the idioms of the thought-world of great sections of his national contemporaries. This spectacular setting is as old as Daniel 7,14, and it survived Jesus both in Jewish and in Christian form. There is no reason why Jesus should not share this strange scenic structure which the fervent faith of his people set in the immediate or more remote future. From the point of view of historical study, it would be highly surprising if this array of future glories did not appear in the thought, faith and feeling of Jesus. It was a commanding element in the religious experience of first-century Judaism, an integral part of the historical background against and in which Jesus appeared.

The form of Jesus' faith, however, must not obscure our vision for the solid substance that gives it content. One of the gravest errors, even of students of the life of Jesus, is the rejection of his eschatology; for this may amount to the rejection of one of the most distinctive elements in his religious experience. Eschatology as a form of religious outlook is characteristic of Jesus, but it is not essential or distinctive. We may not reject the faith of the teacher on the basis of the form of his teaching. Eschatology is simply the local color cast about a great and commanding conviction of Jesus: God has a kingdom; it can and will come, and that soon.

Jesus presented this great faith of his in the thought-forms of his day, yet he himself was not committed to the form of his faith but to its essential substance. The kingdom will come when and where and how the Divine wills. This is the unbroken religious attitude of Jesus toward the fulfillment of his faith. The Son of man did not come as Jesus told his disciples when he sent them out, never expecting to see them again in this world. (Matt. 10,23.) The kingdom did not appear with power before his followers had tasted of death. (Mark 9,1.) He himself did not live to see his hope fulfilled but on the last night of his life he makes a final pledge of his personal faith to his disciples as he extends the cup (Luke 22,18), and one of his very last words in public is a firm declaration of his faith in the glorious future that is God's (Mark 14,62). With all of his eschatology, there is in Jesus none of those eccentric elements which make the visionary who is wholly committed to the form rather than to the content of his faith, noth-

ing of the fury of the fanatic whose eye is caught by a
spectacular scenery that offers no real substance.

In Jesus' view of the future there are deposited some
of the richest religious values that he represents, values
that are indispensable to any solid social structure. Human history must have a meaning, otherwise human life
becomes only haphazard existence and man ceases to be
the master of this finite order and becomes its victim.
Jesus has no teleological thesis that would prove that
there is a divine plan and purpose in the world and in
the course of human events, yet he has a religious outlook
that is deeper than all theological theory. For Jesus the
future is God's who has great things in store for men.
Human life and history move toward His kingdom. God
himself is the goal of human aspiration. Life and living
with God is the ultimate destiny of humankind. In this
personal conviction of Jesus we have to do, not with the
rationalized teleology of theology, but with one of those
irrational confidences of a living and believing personality.

It is at this point that fire flashes from the faith of
Jesus. Religious faith that possesses any measure of
power rides rough-shod over the world of fact. Faith
defies fact; it confronts fact with a confidence that is
demoralizing to the world as it is because it sees the
world as it ought to be and believes in its transformation.
Out of the political, economic and social depression of
first-century Palestine arose this fine and firm faith of
Jesus that sees in the future only the realization of the
divine plan and purpose for men.

There is also a profound ethical element in Jesus'
eschatology. Stripped of its fantastic features, taken
apart from its spectacular scenery, it offers a moral mo-

tive and an ethical enthusiasm that will carry the weight of any social structure. The future in the faith of Jesus is a source of power in the present. It is in the light of this future that the present must be lived. Jesus was not one of those dreamy seers who have no eye for the here and now. Jesus lived in the future and in the terms of the future, but this future in his faith becomes of most vital concern in all matters of the present. The future that is in store for all who believe in God was a constant spur to his present. It drove him apart for prayer; it brought him into ceaseless activity; it charged his message with a prophetic earnestness and his personality with a powerful enthusiasm, and it gave to him a calm confidence that no momentary defeat could shake or shatter.

Jesus was never completely carried away from earth by his thought of the future as were Second Isaiah and the authors of Revelation. His feet remained in the real world that is so full of pressing problems. "It was not the one bright point that glowed and glared, upon which the whole of his attention centered and toward which his acts aggressed to the ruthless rejection of all else."[9] No religious genius was ever more sensitive to the problems of the present than was Jesus. He knew the pressure of the present, the grind of routine from which men are never free. His consciousness of the relentlessness of life he coined in his famous word,

"Whosoever doth not bear his own cross, and come after me, can not be my disciple." (Luke 14,27.)

The kingdom that Jesus preaches has its transcendent

---

[9] Bundy, *The Psychic Health of Jesus*, p. 226. Courtesy of the Macmillan Company.

elements but it remains a kingdom in which men who are worthy may participate and for whose sake and perfection it is planned.   With all the supernaturalism in Jesus' view of the future, it is always the natural habitat of morally- and ethically-minded men who seek to know God, His will and way for this world and its life.   This faith in the future is fruitful for the present in that it enables faith to function here and now in every detail of human life and living.   It introduces into the present an eagerness that is unwilling to leave any human task unaccomplished.   The very nature of the future, near or far, makes men take the present seriously.   There is no outlook for the human future apart from personal character and social conduct that would prepare the way for it. It is the prospect of the future that furnishes the moral earnestness and the ethical energy for the things that are in need of being done here and now.

"The ethics of Jesus' eschatology is as reactionary as ever, and his true disciple to-day can never feel at ease as long as social and individual evils are never out of his sight.   To eliminate the eschatological element from Jesus' teaching and person is to strip him of his influence and power.   To be sure, our picture of the future will differ as widely from his as the intellectual outlook of the first century differs from that of the twentieth; but we must share his view to the effect that there is a future, that God has great and good things in store for it, and that this future demands service and sacrifice in the present.   Most of all, we must share his zeal and passion in working toward it if we are to remain his disciples."[10]

[10]Bundy, *The Psychic Health of Jesus,* p. 219.

In Jesus' day it was eschatology; in our day it is evolution. Evolution is an historically and scientifically demonstrated fact, and as a working conception of our world it has made very definite contributions to religious life. It relieves the religious mind of a pantheistic pessimism and brings God into the very stream of the world's life. It leaves God in the world, seriously interested in its welfare, working and willing His way with men. It holds to the doctrine of changing life, a doctrine that is fundamentally, even evangelically, religious. It teaches that man, whatever his primitive or present state, is improvable, that he can better his own estate, that of his fellows, and himself.

But evolution from the practical moral point of view can present very definite dangers to human progress when it is misconstrued in the popular mind. It can work in a demoralizing way when it comes to men facing the problems and pressures of the present. The person who believes that the world and man can become better is in danger of taking moral progress as merely mechanical and of falling into the fallacy that the world and men *must* and *will* become better because they can. Such a conception of evolution is positively demoralizing. Individual and social improvement are left to impersonal forces, just to things in the long rule and run, and both the individual and the group fail to cast themselves with a will into the work of the world. The evils of the present and the betterment of the future are taken all too complacently.

Such a conception of the evolutionary process in matters of human progress is absolutely false and is untrue to the evolutionary ideal at its best. The evolutionary process can impair as well as improve; it can mean elimination as well as elevation. Things can become worse just as easily as better, and, from the moral angle, they seem to grow worse more easily than they become better. Evolution teaches that the world and men improve only by survival in struggle. They survive because they are fit and strong enough to survive. If evolution means anything, it means improvement in struggle. Those who leave the improvement of the world to evolution forget its first principle—strength for struggle in the present for the sake of survival in the future. Catastrophe is at the end of the evolutionary process as well as at the end of the eschatological outlook.

There is also a strong evangelical element in the eschatology of Jesus. A God who is far removed from the affairs of men, a kingdom that does not press upon the very doors of the present, have no evangelical appeal. According to Jesus, God has a very concrete meaning in human experience. His kingdom means the realization of everything that is highest, best and most worth while in human life and history. It is Jesus' passionate personal faith that the divine cause among men will be realized, the right and the good in human life will be perfectly and permanently established, the wrong and the evil in the world will be utterly eradicated. This clear-cut conviction and confidence belongs to the very essence of a religion that can maintain itself as helpful to men and hold them to the pursuit of its values.

This great religious goal of Jesus will perhaps never be realized as a concrete fact in human society. Jesus does not lead men into the kingdom of God but into the quest of it. The quest was all that Jesus himself undertook; the kingdom itself he left to the divine will and way. But it is only in some such quest as that of the kingdom of God that men will find social salvation.

Apart from his eschatology, Jesus' understanding of the kingdom of God is very simple and is expressed in terms just as intelligible to us as they were to his own contemporaries. The kingdom of God in human experience is the quest and performance of the divine will:

"Thy kingdom come. Thy will be done, as in heaven, so on earth." (Matt. 6,10.)

The history of religion could be written as the story of the human quest of the divine will. A religion that has faltered or failed in this quest has lost its power and, if it surrenders this quest entirely, remains a religion in name only. Religious men have always felt that the Divine has a will and a way for all humanity, and the religious individual has felt himself pressed into its quest and performance. The content of the divine will in the history of religion has always reflected the high or low status of spiritual life and thinking. It varies all the way from primitive perversions to the conscientious construction of personal character and control of social conduct. In the great religions men as individuals and as groups have sought to discover and to perform the divine will for themselves. An individual or a group, even a culture or a civilization, that does not seek to know and to perform the divine will for itself can not be said to be really religious.

We have already pointed out that the supreme religious aspiration of Jesus was the discovery and performance of the divine will for himself.[11] It was the

---

[11]*See* the author's companion study, *The Religion of Jesus*, pp. 155-163; *also* the following chapter of the present study.

great task which he felt was set before him for his own
individual accomplishment. And Jesus, in turn, presents
the quest and performance of the divine will as the pure
essence of religion for his followers. Thus Jesus simplifies man's comprehension of his religious task, but in this
very simplification he has laid a heavy burden on the
moral will of the individual and the group. Jesus understood the divine will in terms of character and conduct
that correspond to that of the Divine. It is a plain,
prosaic path on which Jesus sets men, and it is a painful
path because it leads straight through the roughest
realities of human life and experience.

The social implications of this demand of Jesus have
never yet struck even the Christian world with their full
force. The very scope of the demand has hardly dawned
upon us. It includes the entire arena of human life and
history. The divine will is set as the code, course and
control of human character and conduct in all its responsible forms. It reaches out to command every ramifica-
tion of human experience. No phase of human life is
exempt. The whole of it must move in the direction of
the discovery and performance of the will of God. Every
human interest is to be governed by it; every human issue
is to be settled in its light and must mark progress toward
its accomplishment. It is to be the solid substratum, the
unbroken background, of all that men, individually and
collectively, think, or do, or seek to be. The accomplishment of the divine will Jesus understood in terms of
purity of individual and group character, and in the terms
of a corresponding purity of conduct on the part of
both—humility, love, forgiveness and the doing unto
others as we would that they should do unto us. In this
demand Jesus is absolutely uncompromising. He shows

not the slightest interest in considerations of practicability or feasibility. The human task is set in the performance of God's will.

Such is the solid substratum of all social structure as provided by Jesus in his exclusively religious approach to the whole of life. His outlook upon the world as good because it is God's, upon man as capable of good because he is God's child, upon history as culminating in the kingdom of God, upon the chief human task as the discovery and performance of the divine will, is exclusively religious.

It is very important that we note that Jesus has no social teachings except for those individuals and those groups that feel direct religious responsibility. Jesus demands that the whole of life be lived with the religious reference. The prospect of a future with God is to give human individuals and institutions their distinctive character and is to control their conduct. It is this future that is to furnish men with the strongest incentives and impulses for the problems and tasks of the present. The kingdom of God with its quest of the divine will is the great concern in human life and history that is to bring men together to think, feel and act as a unit. This, no other element in human experience, is to be the source of men's common fears and hopes, apprehensions and aspirations. The experience of God, who has a kingdom that can and will come, is to command every other element of human experience. This religious reference is to reach down to the very sources of individual and group life. In brief, human life in its every aspect is to be lived religiously.

This religious reference is the key-note that characterizes the social message of all the great prophets of religion. Amos preached social righteousness in view of the approaching day of Jehovah. John the Baptist preached a reconstruction of mind and life in view of an impending judgment. Jesus preached the same in view of the imminent kingdom of God. All great prophets of religion agree that human living without the religious reference is doomed to disaster. This outlook takes on a most striking form in one of the parables of Jesus:

"The ground of a certain rich man brought forth plentifully: and he reasoned within himself, saying, What shall I do, because I have nowhere to bestow my fruits? And he said, This will I do: I will pull down my barns, and build greater; and there will I bestow all my grain and my goods. And I will say to my soul, Soul, thou hast much goods laid up for many years; take thine ease, eat, drink, and be merry. But God said unto him, Thou foolish one, this night is thy soul required of thee; and the things which thou hast prepared, whose shall they be?" (Luke 12,16-20.)

Devotion to material goods is not the thing that Jesus condemns in this parable; fundamentally, he has no objection to these. He has a place for them, secondary to be sure, in his scale of values. He has in mind no suppression of natural and normal human interests and pursuits. The whole point to the parable is that it pictures a life absolutely devoid of the religious reference. Self is the exclusive center of devotion and the only outlook is that of an egocentric existence. The calculations of the rich man are so brutally selfish that they leave no place either for God or for man.

Over against such a self-centered consciousness Jesus sets his great maxim of service, the total dissipation of self in the behalf of God and men,

"Whosoever shall seek to gain his life shall lose it: but whosoever shall lose *his life* shall preserve it." (Luke 17,33.)

In this word of Jesus we have not to do with just a clever Oriental paradox, as the modern mind would be glad to think and dismiss it as such. Life itself is a paradox, and Jesus is here laying the solid foundation for all social living that professes to be religious in any real sense. But the modern mood of the West is not disposed to speak in paradox nor to listen long to those who put fundamental truths in such a poignant form. Paradox presses too close to where we live. It is too strong for our modest capacity for assimilation.

Jesus viewed the whole of the human problem in the light of his experience of God. This approach to life he sought to share with his followers. Men are to live always with the commanding consciousness that God is a living, loving Father and that all men are His children. Jesus demands that the whole of our experience be religious. Men must lead a God-centered existence. In the experience of Jesus, then, religion stands in a vital and organic relationship with every phase of human living. No aspect of human life is exempt, extraterritorial, from the rigid régime of reverence and righteousness. Wherever and however men may find themselves, singly or in groups, they are confronted with the task of living the whole of life religiously. Everything that men think, do and aspire to become is *sub specie æternitatis.*

Thus Jesus sublimates all of life's realities. In the light of the religious reference nothing in human life can be unimportant. A sacred significance attaches to our plainest and most prosaic pursuits. The least of services shall in no wise lose its reward,

> "For whosoever shall give you a cup of water to drink . . . he shall in no wise lose his reward." (Mark 9,41.)

"The simplest obligation thus has a cosmic outlook."[12] What can be more seriously social than Jesus' sublime thought that the simplest act of helpfulness rendered a fellow-man is a service rendered God? Tertullian ascribes to Jesus a word not found in our New Testament, but which corresponds exactly to the best of his spirit: *Vidisti fratrem tuum, vidisti Dominum tuum.*[13] Jesus' way of salvation is social; it leads through our fellow-men to God. It is in social terms that Jesus speaks of the work of the world which, with his constant religious reference, becomes the worship of God.

Jesus sets the religious interest supreme; it is to command every other natural and normal interest—racial, political, economic. Jesus teaches the neglect of none of these things but their subordination. Slowly we are learning by bitter experience, only too recent, that the predominance of any other interest sooner or later destroys the social balance, and conflict and destruction result. Jesus gives us no theory of the state, no international program, no detailed solutions for our racial and

---

[12]Professor E. S. Brightman, in the *Boston University Bulletin*, XIII, 25, p. 11.
[13]Quoted by Heiler, *Der Katholizismus*, p. 432f.

economic conflicts. True to the high order of religious experience that was his, he leaves a wide latitude for his followers in the discovery and performance of the divine will in all of these matters. He dictates no dogmatic documents that specify each detail. Jesus simply directs men toward the kingdom of God as the superlative hope of social experience. Every human enterprise must have its more-than-human goal. Every social problem, major or minor, must be faced and solved in the light of the religious reference. Ahead of the social structure there must rise up the religious outlook. In it there must be the fervent faith that furnishes nerve and fiber for the social body, rendering it both sensitive and strong.

Personal piety in its purity is always as simple and single as life itself. It invades every phase of the individual personality. It requires an undivided devotion, an unrestrained response of the whole life. It is the completeness of religion's command of an individual that gives a life its richness and unmistakable reality. The same is true of religion's claim upon group life. Jesus views the whole of human life as single, absolutely undepartmental.[14] He does not divide human society according to the various directions of its interests and concerns. He does not separate one activity from another. He does not classify men according to race, nationality, economic or other activity, not even according to their religious beliefs. The usual distinction between the secular and sacred spheres he rejects. All life and living is sacred, independent of race, nation, or economic employment—a sanctified obligation of the human to the Divine. Everywhere, in each relationship, Jesus

---

[14]"Only in the measure in which society takes on the character of an ethical personality does its ethic become that of a truly ethical community." (Schweitzer, *Civilization and Ethics*, p. 236f.)

sets man directly in the presence of his Maker whose will is his chief concern and task.

In his teaching Jesus conducted no separate department of social ethics. In the popular sense, he has no social teachings. Our modern distinction between individual and group religion, morals and ethics did not exist in the mind of Jesus. Human life and living for Jesus is a single, indivisible whole, as undepartmental as the living self. It is true that some of his words have a predominantly individual emphasis, others more of a social point. But even the most social of his statements presuppose an indispensable background of individual character, as the *Golden Rule*. The most individual of his instructions,

"Ye therefore shall be perfect,"

is not a selfish anti-social subjectivism, as it has often been construed in the life of the mystic and ascetic, but has its very definite social implication. There is not a major utterance of Jesus but that throws upon the individual the most exacting demands in the creation of character and at the same time draws its logical and inevitable social duties and responsibilities after it. In the personal experience of Jesus religion strikes life as a whole with no thought of a distinction between the individual and the social such as our modern point of view makes.

It belongs to the greatness of Jesus that he did not coin his fundamental demands into particular precepts. If he had done this, he would have anchored his spirit for ever in the bed-rock of the first century. The true prophets of humanity are never pedant enough to note all exceptions, to define all details. It belongs to the very essence of their genius to lay down fundamental principles for the living of life as a whole. Jesus does not provide a definite program for the improvement of the social order; he calls men to a higher order. His attitude on any particular social problem must be described as objective. He approaches it from the outside and views it in the light of something else. Jesus did not dictate how each of his followers should act each day, upon each occasion, in each concrete circumstance. Personal and social piety, as we see it in Jesus' own experience, pursues a problematic path. Each day and each generation has its own evils to overcome. The morrow must take care of itself. We need not fear the future if it has in it the elements of hope and strength that enable us to meet the present and its problems.

Our modern world has accomplished an almost exaggerated development of group-consciousness which has not been attended by a corresponding development of group-conscience. It is this latter fact that renders our modern social situation serious. Men are grouped about all of our major social interests—racial, political, economic. Common fears coming from the pursuit of these interests have generated a strength of feeling that determines our group attitudes and aspirations. This strength of group feeling is accompanied by a corresponding weakness of group faith. Moral motives and considerations of conscience are for the most part absent from the attitudes and conduct of one group toward another. On the surface our modern groups seek to keep up the appearance of respectability and reason, but they make no concerted effort to be religious in the solving of social issues. In reality, we have to-day no commanding group-experience of religion—men brought together by a universal sense of need, by common fears and hopes, acting, thinking and feeling as a religious unit. Our modern group-experience has different centers of interest, and the religious interest, if it appears at all, is only sporadic and conventional, lying on the periphery of our group life unable to command the controlling centers that give our modern group life its distinctive character. We seek to solve our social problems without the religious reference.

The modern mind seems to feel that the solution of its social problems is a matter of ways and means, of mechanical methods. The very complexity of our modern culture and civilization, the very scale on which the modern world lives, will require a technique that will tax the ingenuity of our experts in the field of the social sciences. From this quarter we need have no fear, for we possess the necessary intelligence. Our weakness will not be in the ability to produce the technical apparatus; it will be rather in the flabbiness of our moral fiber. The centers of our spiritual courage seem to be disrupted. We lack the simplicity and sincerity of spirit necessary for the successful operation of any social system. The social aspects of our faith are not strong enough to function. We hardly possess the moral disposition that would lead as far even as mutual understanding. Our modern social need is not so much of light as of strength; we know, but we seem unable to do. We are not commanded by that high order of moral and religious convictions which gives strength to the group will. Such religion as we possess we restrict for the most part to individual life and forget that a religion worthy of the name must cut its regular course in the central currents of group life. The contribution of Jesus to the solution of any of our major social problems will not be in the terms of method and technique but in the terms of a simple, searching spirit for the living of life as a whole.

We live in a very different world from that of Jesus. A whole new order of civilization and culture has appeared since his day. The centers of the world's life have shifted to the north and west, and this shift has brought with it some of our special and peculiar problems. These problems never confronted Jesus in their modern form. Their solutions he naturally left unformulated. He did not prescribe all the details of conduct for any particular situation for the world since his time and for all time to come. But he did lay down certain religious principles for the living of life, both as individuals and as groups, and he has left the individual and the group, as the case may be, to determine the type of conduct that is in harmony with his spirit for the living of life in all its aspects.

Jesus has really very little to say to our modern day in the way of specific instructions, but he has a great deal to communicate. His contribution to the solution of our social problems is not a program or theory, a set scheme or system, but the gift of a spirit. Men are to live together in all the aspects of human life, not according to formal rule and regulation, but they shall live life naturally and freely at the impulse of a deeply religious spirit which springs from the commanding elements of their experience—the world is good because it is God's, men are capable of good because they are God's children, human history is to move toward His kingdom in which

His will is sought and performed, as in heaven, so on earth.

On detailed solutions of modern social problems Jesus is silent for clear historical reasons. Standards in the social scale, wage adjustments, profits of group production, rights and responsibilities of capital and labor, ownership of natural resources, world markets, class strifes, racial hatreds, political policies, and so forth, are problems that did not cross the mind of Jesus in our modern sense. In view of this fact we may not modernize Jesus and force him to speak our language and to think our thoughts after us. We must leave him in his own historical setting. He was born in Bethlehem of Judea in the days of Herod the king, not in the twentieth century. We must leave him to think his own thoughts and to express them in the idioms of his own native provincial dialect in his own individual way. Often Jesus does not say just what we would like to have him say, but we may not, in historical and personal justice to him, compel him to speak otherwise. We must learn to understand him in the light of his own first-century and Judaistic background. Thereby we shall find that much in Jesus that strikes us as foreign and strange to our modern world-view belongs simply to the local color of his day.

We have not discharged our duty toward Jesus when we have sought to understand just his thought and teaching and to translate both into the idioms of our own day and thought. Our great task, if we feel that any bond at all holds us to him, is to press our way down to the bedrock of the whole of his experience, to sense, to seek and to share in such measure as we may the richness and reality of his exclusively religious reactions to the sum total of all that our human life offers. Here we shall strike upon that solid substratum on which we may erect the entire human structure with a feeling of assurance and complete confidence.[15]

---

[15]These last three paragraphs are a restatement of materials found in the author's book, *The Psychic Health of Jesus*, p. 145f.

CHAPTER IV

The Personal Problems of Jesus

WHEN we begin to seek out the personal problems that Jesus faced and fought his way through, we come close to the very pulse of his piety. These problems— their origin, rise, persistence and solution—are not as clear to us in the Gospels as we might wish. The writers of the first three Gospels furnish us the materials for our knowledge of these problems, but they do not feel them as keenly as does the careful student of Jesus' life. No account of Jesus furnishes us a clearer insight into his pressing personal problems than does Mark, whose picture in this respect is much richer than that of Matthew and Luke.[1] But even Mark leaves the majority of these problems unsolved, and his materials are often too meager and inadequate to help us toward a satisfactory solution. In many cases Mark does not seem to feel these problems, nor does he seem to sense that they are problems for his readers. But if Mark had felt all of the personal problems of Jesus which we feel, I doubt very much if he could have solved them for his own thought or for ours, for the simple reason that their solution, in many cases, lay deep in the mind and consciousness of Jesus who did not choose to disclose his deepest decisions or to reveal his real reasons for this

---

[1] A casual comparison of Mark with Matthew and Luke will show that the two later Evangelists have a tendency to eliminate the pressing personal element so prominent in the second Gospel. In the Fourth Gospel, as we saw in Chapter I, all real struggle is stripped from the soul of Jesus.

198

or that important move or step which he took in his unreserved obedience to the divine will, the performance of
which was the supreme passion of his life.

Only rarely do the personal problems of Jesus come
to the surface. But now and again their pressure is so
strong that they escape over the usual reserve of his lips
in words to his trusted group, never, it seems, in public
utterance. We cite only two instances, both of which
will figure presently in our discussion:

> "I came to cast fire upon the earth; and what do I
> desire, if it is already kindled? But I have a baptism
> to be baptized with; and how am I straitened till it
> be accomplished." (Luke 12,49-50.)
>
> "My soul is exceeding sorrowful even unto death:
> abide ye here, and watch." (Mark 14,34.)

These spontaneous outbursts do not tell us a great deal
about Jesus' personal problems except that they were
present and persistent in his experience. In many cases
we have no word from him to give us a clue to these
problems. Often we have only a critical situation and a
statement of his reaction, a retreat from public to private,
a night or a period of seclusion and solitude, an eventful
series of experiences culminating in a crisis, the development of a dilemma, a clear choice and a determined decision, a change in conduct or attitude, or a setting-out
on a new course of action.

From such meager and sporadic materials we seek to
learn as much as we can, which is not a great deal that
is certain, about the personal problems of Jesus. All
that they involved for him personally we are not in a
position to say, but we do know that he faced such and

that they pressed upon him persistently. Their general nature, however, is quite clear: They were exclusively religious, involving his discovery and personal loyalty to the divine will, without exception problems of the genuinely religious consciousness.

The reader of the first three Gospels is hardly under way when he comes upon a scene that depicts Jesus confronted with the most vital issues that could concern him, the temptation scene. In Matthew (4,1-11) and Luke (4,1-13) Jesus is brought face to face with three specific temptations which demand very definite decisions. His replies to the tempter are so decisive, his choices are so deliberate and determined, his rejections of the suggestions of Satan have a tone of such finality about them that the Christian imagination has been led to think that Jesus here, once for all, before entering upon his public work, settles these issues for ever. These three temptations, however, do not belong to the immediate prepublic life of Jesus but to the very fiber of his experience in public. Mark has no such temptations prior to Jesus' appearance in public; in 1,12-13 he gives only the most uncommunicative notice concerning this initial period of temptation. The historical student, on the basis of Mark and later representations of Matthew and Luke, will find that the personal problems which were certainly involved in the three temptations arose and confronted Jesus at both earlier and later stages of his public work.[2]

Jesus can not have solved problems before they presented themselves to him, as Matthew and Luke represent. These issues sprang from the nature of his experience in public, and this is one of Mark's virtues

---

[2]*See* the author's companion study, *The Religion of Jesus*, pp. 19-24.

from the standpoint of historical and psychological fact over against Matthew and Luke. Mark has Jesus face and solve his personal problems only as they actually confront him, and in his account these problems arise naturally out of particular situations in which he finds himself. In Mark we get our first insight into the fact that Jesus had personal problems only at the close of his first day in public where he faces an issue that is the natural outcome of the events and experiences of this first day. (1,21-38.) Other personal problems of Jesus assume definite form only relatively late in his Galilean ministry, problems which he did not and could not have solved in advance of his appearance in public. All three temptations of Matthew and Luke reflect situations in the public life of Jesus; all three presuppose experience in public, and at least two of the three have behind them months of public work.

The idea that Jesus solved his problems in advance must be abandoned for ever, not only on the basis of the nature of the three temptations in Matthew and Luke, but because the public life of Jesus is too full of stress and strain of soul from beginning to end. There are too many retreats for prayer, too many critical situations, too many turns in the course of events, to suppose that Jesus battled but once, in the initial wilderness retreat. Any one who is doubtful on this point should study such words of inner conflict as were quoted above, the dire distress of Jesus in Gethsemane and his only utterance on the cross in Mark. Jesus' philosophy was simple and prosaic on this point,

"Sufficient unto the day is the evil thereof." (Matt. 6,34b.)

We shall see Jesus facing the most critical issues of religious experience in the order and form in which they presented themselves to him. We never find Jesus unprepared or off his guard, but he never anticipates. He never crosses his bridges before he comes to them.

We have no way of knowing all the personal problems that Jesus was forced to face and to solve. The Gospels give us all too few glimpses into the inner life of Jesus who was all too reticent in these purely personal matters that now concern us. In the selection and discussion of these problems we shall confine ourselves to those issues that are clearest in the records and that seem to have been most pressing and persistent in the mind of Jesus himself. We single out three problems that are clear and unmistakable: the problem which Jesus' cures created for him, the messianic issue and the problem of his fate. It is important in our study of Jesus as a religious subject that we gain an insight into these problems, for they are fundamentally religious and reveal to us very clearly the deeply religious character and content of his consciousness.

CURES AND CAUSE

In our discussion of the cures of Jesus we are interested in them from only one point of view, the personal religious problem which they seem to have created for him. A philosophical treatise on the subject of what traditional Christianity has defended as the Biblical miracles we leave to those interested in such. The historical student has no interest in such abstract questions; he never speaks of the miracles of Jesus, only of his cures. That Jesus did cure and heal is no longer open to serious question. Modern science and historical criticism openly reject some of the wonder-works ascribed to him, and in the interest of religion itself. But with the majority of the cures ascribed to Jesus the historian and the scientist have no quarrel. The progress of science in the last quarter-century has increased rather than decreased our confidence in this phase of Jesus' public activity. The majority of his cures are quite intelligible in the light of our modern psychotherapy. They were effected through suggestion and auto-suggestion; they were cures of functional disturbances, especially those of a nervous origin. The student must leave a healing ministry of Jesus if he intends to find any historical matter at all in the Gospels. His healing activity was one of the two principal phases of his public work (Matt. 4,23-25), more prominent, it seems, than Jesus himself desired that it should be. All that we know of Jesus is bound up too organically with his cures for them to be declared unhistorical in a wholesale fashion.

The Gospel picture of the healing ministry of Jesus is really an important contribution to our knowledge of him. There is a remarkable dignity about his cures. There is no parade or show and, with two exceptions, both of which are later legendary accretions (Mark 7,32-37; 8,22-26), there is nothing that suggests the trappings that belonged to the professional healers of his day. Jesus uses no charm words, no weird formulas, no magical objects, no mysterious manipulations. He heals by word, simple command and touch. Healing, as teaching and preaching, was not an art learned by him; it was a personal gift and endowment. Under the imposing impression and influence of his presence—charged as it was with an extraordinary but natural strength and force of personality which stimulated a complete confidence and effected a mobilization of dispersed powers in others, together with his own clear consciousness of high call and commission—deranged minds were restored to their normal functioning, deaf heard, blind received their sight and the lame walked. The whole secret of the power of Jesus' personality seems to have been an actual ability to generate in others a confidence in themselves which became a motive power that resulted in moral and religious recovery, and for some, in cure.

Jesus' healing ministry was not a planned part of his public work. The prevalent Christian idea that he entered upon his public work with this question settled once for all is based upon the first temptation of Matthew (4,3-4) and Luke (4,3-4), which has as its principal point the proper place and legitimate employment of his extraordinary personal powers. This temptation presupposes Jesus' full consciousness of his power to cure and, as is clear in the taunts at the cross, it threw him into that paradoxical position in which he was able to save others but himself he could not save. The discovery of the presence of these unusual personal powers created for Jesus just such a serious personal problem as Matthew and Luke here represent. But historical and psychological fact is against their representation, according to which Jesus fought his way to clearness and certainty on this point prior to his appearance in public and before he had performed a single cure.

According to Mark, Jesus' extraordinary personal powers became a problem for him only when he came into the full swing of his public work. In Mark Jesus effects his first cures during his first day in public (1,21-34), at the close of which he is driven apart for petition and prayer (1,35-38). The appearance of these powers on this first day seems to strike Jesus as something new in his experience. Their unexpected appearance creates for him a pressing personal problem. There is too much of surprise and solicitude in Jesus' mind and attitude at the success of his word and touch on this first day to suppose that the whole question had been settled once for all by a struggle in self and solitude prior to his appearance in public.

Mark's account of the appearance of this initial personal problem of Jesus has virtues of its own. (Mark 1,21-38.) Mark's narrative of this first day in public is unadorned and realistic. It has no unnatural atmosphere about it; quite simply, yet quite naturally, Mark brings Jesus into active engagement in his public work. The course and character of the day's events, the attitude of the people as well as the state of his mind during and at the close of the day, make it clear that this Sabbath in Capernaum marks a beginning, something new both in the experience of the Capernaum crowds and in the experience of Jesus himself. The state of his mind at the close (1,35-38) shows that the experiences of the day are initial and introductory for Jesus himself. During the day he is confronted with new experiences that, at its close, force him to face certain problems with regard to his work and to make certain decisions of an order that belong at the very beginning of his public activity.

Mark's first day of Jesus in public is primarily a day of cures: the cure of the demoniac in the synagogue (1,21-28), the cure of Simon's wife's mother (29-31) and the cures of the sick at sunset (32-34). The fourth incident comes on the following morning (1,35-38), and it is this closing scene that makes a day of the group, for it is the culmination of the first three incidents. Without this closing scene the first three incidents would tell us little of Jesus, but now as Mark reports the fourth incident a new and glorious light falls on Jesus' person. According to Mark, Jesus rises early in the morning, "a great while before day," retreats from the house of Simon to a desert place apart, and there engages in prayer. The early hour makes it clear that Jesus is facing problems of a critical character, problems which confront him as the result of his first day in the presence of the people and which bring him from his rest in Simon's house to his knees in a desert place apart. Mark's early hour might lead us to conclude that Jesus has spent a troubled night in the midst of struggles of soul which drive him to solitude and seclusion for petition and prayer. Luke omits these pressing psychic elements. He neglects Mark's early hour for the notice, "when it was day"; he omits the notice that Jesus "there prayed," and thus the chief point to the incident as well as the climax of the whole day is gone. (Luke 4,42-43.)

According to Mark, Simon and his companions seek Jesus out, and when they find him, he has already passed his struggle of soul and has reached his decision. To the word of Simon and his companions, "All are seeking thee," Jesus replies,

"Let us go elsewhere into the next towns, that I may preach there also; for to this end came I forth." (Mark 1,38.)

Jesus' reply conceals rather than reveals the struggle through which he has passed, but it presents an important decision that throws an interesting and instructive light on him and his conception of his public work. His word, "That I may preach . . . for to this end came I forth," confirms our conclusion to the effect that it was the message of the kingdom of God that brought Jesus out of private into public life. He regards his real work as that of preaching; he seeks to avoid personal popularity and desires first of all the opportunity to announce his message. He feels himself called to champion a cause, not to effect cures. Message, not miracle, is the real essence of his mission. Thus Jesus faced a crisis at the very outset of his ministry; he passed through a severe struggle of soul for clearness and certainty; he reached an important decision; he deliberately chose a certain course of conduct in harmony with what he felt as the divine will for himself. At the close of his first day in public, according to Mark, Jesus achieves a religious triumph.

Mark's little picture in 1,35-38 is one of the finest that has come down to us from the whole life of Jesus. We feel ourselves almost as immediately in his presence as did Simon and his companions; we feel that we have brushed sleeves with Jesus as he actually was. Mark's account is so full of those pressing personal elements— the early hour, the period of prayer, the clear choice, the deliberate decision—that we are about as close to Jesus historically this one time as we can hope to come.

Thus the opening day in Capernaum becomes eventful for Jesus personally. This first appearance of his power to heal and to cure throws him into the midst of serious problems which are the result of the events and experiences of this first day in the presence of the people. Within a brief day Jesus attains fame and great popularity, both of which he feels as a serious handicap. He seems to have felt that his cures draw attention and devotion to himself and threaten the cause which his message presents and which he regards as the very heart of his mission.

Jesus' problem here, in one form or another, is common in the experience of the great champions of religion: the popularity of the prophet growing at the expense of the thing that he seeks to accomplish. The closest parallel we find in our Christian contemporary, Sadhu Sundar Singh, who writes from his experience:

"I found that, however much I impressed upon the people that it was not my personal power that had effected the cure, but the power of Christ in answer to prayer, they insisted on looking upon me as a wonder-worker; and I saw that I must not do this again, as it would encourage superstition and distract attention from the Gospel I have to preach."[3]

"Years ago it became clear to the Sadhu that 'miracles' detracted from instead of aiding his gospel message. Hence in 1918, when he was making his great tour through the South of India, he took the utmost care to prevent adding fuel to a fire whose burning could serve no true purpose."[4]

Every great cause needs its consecrated champion. In order to succeed it must win for itself a leader who completely forgets himself in its service. Increase in following must not produce in the leader any sort of self-sat-

[3]Streeter, *The Message of Sadhu Sundar Singh*, p. 33. Courtesy of the Macmillan Company.
[4]Parker, *Sadhu Sundar Singh*, p. 169. Courtesy of Fleming H. Revell Company.

isfaction; otherwise, it is at the very head that the cause is threatened and endangered. Instances in history of leaders whose heads have been turned from their causes to themselves and their leadership are not unknown, and the result has always been the appearance of a new leader or the miserable defeat of the cause. Great leaders make great contributions to great causes. Without a champion there is no cause; it is only as the champion appears that the cause appears. The cause presents itself because the champion has made it his very own. When the cause has claimed him, then he can help it to claim others.

Popularity is dangerous to the leader of any cause and to the cause itself, and the popularity of the leader may impair the popularity of the cause. Jesus seems to have feared popularity for this very reason. His own popularity becomes problematic for him, a psychological state that rarely exists except in the minds of the truly great. He feels that the fame, resulting from his cures, endangers his cause of the kingdom of God. It is this that explains best his repeated retreats from cure-curious crowds and his growing inclination to be away from the people in the later stages of his Galilean work.

The day in Capernaum closes with a lack of success for Jesus' cause. He seems to have regarded his work in Capernaum as a failure. Upon the Galilean cities that witnessed his "mighty works" he lets fall his woes because they repented not in view of the coming of the kingdom of God. And the wonder-loving city of Capernaum he singles out for special denunciation:

"And thou, Capernaum, shalt thou be exalted unto heaven? thou shalt go down unto Hades: for if the mighty works had been done in Sodom which were done in thee, it would have remained until this day. But I say unto you that it shall be more tolerable for the land of Sodom in the day of judgment, than for thee." (Matt. 11,23-24.)

There is a pessimistic undertone in Mark's account of Jesus' first day in public. At the very outset Jesus seems to meet with disappointment; he does not receive the response he desires; the people see the prophet and his cures rather than the cause which he champions. The eager crowds and enthusiastic followers seem to have been attracted and held by his person rather than by his cause.

This focusing of attention upon the person of Jesus which began with this first day has never left him. Even down to the present day Christian interest centers upon the person of Jesus rather than upon the cause for which he set all at stake. At this point Jesus stands in open conflict with the course and development of Christian thought. His own person he forced into the background; the cause of God, His kingdom, he held for ever in the foreground.

Nowhere in the first three Gospels does Jesus perform cures as a support for the work which he undertakes. Although he entertains a religious attitude toward his cures and ascribes them to God, he nevertheless does not ascribe to them the importance in his faith and cause that miracle has had as a support and proof in the history of the Christian faith. In Jesus we see more or less of an antipathy for wonder-works. He feels that he and his work are hampered and hindered rather than helped by the fact that he can, and at times is practically compelled, to cure. The one thing that forces Jesus to cure is an irresistible confidence in his ability to help. Some of his contemporaries were well aware of his disinclination to heal. The leper in Mark 1,40-45 is sure of Jesus' ability, but he is skeptical concerning his willingness to cure,

"If thou wilt, thou canst make me clean."

Jesus was forced to curb this phase of his work because of the general public attitude which was inclined to center upon himself as a wonder-worker rather than upon the cause which he represented. For Jesus cures and the crowds brought by them stood in direct antithesis to the divine cause. This attitude is clearly reflected in his state of mind in the first temptation of Matthew (4,3-4) and Luke (4,3-4) and in a scene like Mark 1,35-38.

An additional factor that was inextricably interwoven in this personal problem of Jesus was his natural sympathy and compassion for the afflicted and needy, and this natural feeling came into conflict with his personal devotion and consecration to the cause he championed. This dilemma is pictured in a pertinent way in the temptation to turn stone into bread, food for the hungry. But the fundamental religiousness of Jesus asserts itself,

"Man shall not live by bread alone, but by every word that proceedeth out of the mouth of God." (Matt. 4,4.)

Jesus' decision at the close of the day in Capernaum is permanent and makes itself felt through the whole of

212 OUR RECOVERY OF JESUS

his public work. In the first three Gospels, beginning
with Mark 1,35-38, we may observe quite unmistakably
a growing disinclination of Jesus to heal. The greater
part of his healing activity comes in the early Galilean
months. As his work progresses, his cures become less
and less frequent. In Mark all of Jesus' cures are confined to Galilee with one exception, the cure of the blind
man at the gates of Jericho on the way to Jerusalem.
(Mark 10,46-52.) There are no Jerusalem cures in
Mark, only a general mention of cures in Matthew
(21,14), and in Luke only the later legend of the healing of the severed ear (22,51).

We have no specific occasion on which Jesus refused
to cure, but as the Galilean movement gains momentum
he begins to avoid the multitudes and when he does
effect a cure he almost invariably commands silence. As
early as Mark 1,35-38 Jesus rejects healing as the essence of his mission, yet he does not reject this type of
ministry entirely. During the remainder of his public
life, with the exception of the brief week in Jerusalem,
we find him effecting cures, particularly in the earlier
Galilean days, whenever he is confronted with dire
human need and unreserved personal confidence. Jesus
viewed and performed this phase as he viewed and
accomplished the whole of his mission—religiously.

Jesus' cures in particular and his ability to cure at all
brought him face to face with one of the fundamental
problems of the religious consciousness—the temptation
of cause and calling to it, which is especially the temptation of the prophet and religious genius.[5] In his facing

---

[5] A clear parallel we see to-day in Sadhu Sundar Singh. *See* Heiler,
Sadhu Sundar Singh, pp. 48-49.

and solving this personal issue we see the genuineness of Jesus' religious consciousness: He seeks the divine will for himself, and once he is clear and certain of it he acts accordingly in a spirit of unflinching and limitless loyalty.

THE MESSIANIC ISSUE

When we come to the messianic question we strike upon one of the most puzzling problems in the life of Jesus. However, the origin of this problem is relatively recent. Christian thought and faith from the very first regarded Jesus as the Messiah, and in this Christians felt that they were only sharing Jesus' own thought and belief concerning himself. The Gospels were read and his words were expounded in this light. Even the older lives of Jesus in the nineteenth century never questioned seriously the fact that Jesus regarded himself as the Messiah. The messianic question was debated, but from only one angle: In what sense did Jesus regard himself as the Messiah, political or spiritual?

The older lives of Jesus devoted a great deal of attention to his growing messianic consciousness. They traced a development within Jesus from a political or national to a purely spiritual conception of his messiahship. In the threefold temptation they saw him defeating a messianic nationalism in favor of a spiritual Messiah whose kingdom is not of this world. Others, like Renan, traced a degeneration in Jesus: In Galilee, particularly in the Sermon on the Mount, he is a religious sage uttering spiritual truths clothed in a sunny optimism; but toward the close he becomes pessimistic, his thought turns to the fantastic realm of the Son of man, and he dies as a mo-

rose stormer who fails to capture the Holy City. Other
lives of Jesus left the messianic conviction constant and
unchanged from beginning to end. Jesus' chief problem
was one of pedagogy: He spent the greater part of his
time disabusing the disciples' minds of their nationalistic
notions in favor of his own spiritual conception of his
messiahship and messianic task. The general public had
a false conception of his messiahship, and the people who
hailed him as he entered into the Holy City allowed him
to die because he had disappointed their messianic ex-
pectations.

But late in the nineteenth century the messianic question took on a new form, a form less dominated by the
traditional positions of the Christian faith on this point
and one more in accord with the confused character of
the messianic materials within the Gospels themselves.
In the twentieth century the question has been raised and
vigorously debated: Did Jesus regard himself as the
Messiah in any sense whatever? The answers have been
radical, the affirmative as well as the negative. The
two extremes are represented by William Wrede[6] and
Albert Schweitzer.[7]

In 1901 William Wrede, in a work of remarkable
brilliancy, maintained that Jesus never gave himself out
to be the Messiah and, what is more startling to traditional Christian thought, that he never held himself to
be the Messiah. The messianic conviction concerning
Jesus did not exist during his lifetime, either in his own
mind or in the mind of his followers and contemporaries.
The messiahship of Jesus was of purely Christian origin,
the work of early Christian faith as the result of the

---

[6]*Das Messiasgeheimnis in den Evangelien* (1901).
[7]*Das Messianitaets- und Leidensgeheimnis* (1901).

Easter experiences. "It is only with the resurrection that Jesus becomes the Messiah."[8]

The traditional position that the disciples had no difficulty in believing in Jesus' resurrection because they were already convinced that he was the Messiah, Wrede reversed to read: The disciples came to the belief in Jesus' messiahship because they were already religiously convinced that he had been raised from the dead, was alive again and that they had seen him.

In support of his reversal of these two great convictions of the earliest Christians, Wrede could point to the religious experience of Paul for whom the great wonder in connection with the person of Jesus was that "God raised him from the dead," a theme that runs like an unbroken thread through the Apostle's letters. This same conception has deposited itself in the book of Acts in two extracts from the most primitive Christian preaching. Both messages are credited to the Apostle Peter.

The first is from his Pentecost address:

"Ye men of Israel, hear these words: Jesus of Nazareth, a man approved of God unto you by mighty works and wonders and signs which God did by him in the midst of you, even as ye yourselves know; him, being delivered up by the determinate counsel and foreknowledge of God, ye by the hand of lawless men did crucify and slay: whom God raised up, having loosed the pangs of death: because it was not possible that he should be holden of it." (2,22-24.)

The second is a part of Peter's message in the home of Cornelius in Cæsarea:

---

[8]*Das Messiasgeheimnis in den Evangelien*, p. 213.

"Jesus of Nazareth, how God anointed him with the Holy Spirit and with power; who went about doing good, and healing all that were oppressed of the devil; for God was with him. And we are witnesses of all things which he did both in the country of the Jews, and in Jerusalem; whom also they slew, hanging him on a tree. Him God raised up the third day, and gave him to be made manifest, not to all the people, but unto witnesses that were chosen before of God, *even* to us, who ate and drank with him after he rose from the dead. And he charged us to preach unto the people, and to testify that this is he who is ordained of God *to be* the Judge of the living and the dead." (10,38-42.)

Such passages in Acts are very important in the history of Christology. The earliest conception seems to have been that it was only with the resurrection that Jesus came to the messianic dignity in Christian conviction. During his lifetime he was a prophet, teaching and healing, for God was with him; as such he came to his death. Then comes the great Christian adversative: Nevertheless, he was raised from the dead as God's Messiah, the Judge of the living and the dead.

It is from this point of view that Wrede turns his cutting criticism upon the messianic materials within the Gospels. All such matter he declares to be unhistorical: the messianic conviction on Jesus' own part or on the part of his contemporaries and intimate disciples, the messianic confessions of the demoniacs with Jesus' commands for silence, and the famous scene at Cæsarea Philippi in which Simon Peter confesses, "Thou art the Christ." (Mark 8,27-30.)

In the same year (1901) Albert Schweitzer startled the theological world with his reconstruction of the messianic question. He presented the consciousness and career of Jesus as exclusively messianic. Jesus knew that he was the Messiah from the very first. This conviction was so intense that it dominated the whole of his public life, all that he said and did. But Jesus kept his messiahship his own personal secret. At first only the demoniacs recognize him for the One he really is. Later in the Galilean months the twelve come to the messianic conviction. But all confessions of his messiahship Jesus meets with the commands for silence and secrecy. It is only toward the close that his secret is wrung from him by the pressure of events, and the disclosure results in his death.

The utter radicalism of Schweitzer's reconstruction is in his extreme eschatological emphasis, for he resolves the whole of Jesus' public life into a series of eschatological words, deeds and sacraments. Jesus becomes the herald of a purely supernatural order which he himself expects to see displace the old order. His teachings, as in the Sermon on the Mount, are not permanent but probationary. They hold true only for the brief interval until the Son of man shall come with power. The new supernatural order will have its own codes and controls for character and conduct. But the kingdom did not come as Jesus expected and announced, and he goes to Jerusalem to die, thus to force it to come. Toward the close he comes to the conviction that he, the Messiah, is destined to become the supernatural Son of man, and in his thought he for the first time completes the identification of these two figures, hitherto separate and distinct in Jewish thought and history.

Both Wrede and Schweitzer have made important contributions toward our understanding of Jesus; however, contributions of a very different character. The former has shown the thoroughly Christian character of our best source, Mark, and how the whole story of Jesus was told and written in the interest and service of the early Christian faith and its predominant ideas. Wrede's work created a commotion among a few New Testament specialists who rejected rather than refuted his position. Among his contemporary colleagues Wellhausen alone took him seriously and shared much of his general position.[9] But to-day Wrede is destined to come into his own with respect to his principal position, namely: Our best sources of information concerning Jesus, the first three Gospels, are strongly Christianized and their authors have written into them fully as much of their own faith as they have of fact from the life of Jesus.[10]

Schweitzer, on the other hand, called attention to the neglect of one of the integral elements in the life and teaching of Jesus, the eschatological element. Since the appearance of Schweitzer's works, his open-minded colleagues in the field of New Testament research have had to revise their understanding of Jesus in favor of a promi-

---

[9]*Einleitung in die drei ersten Evangelien* (1911).

[10]Professor Rudolf Bultmann, of the University of Marburg, manifests a strong influence from Wrede. *See* his *Geschichte der synoptischen Tradition* (1921) and his article, "The New Approach to the Synoptic Problem," *Journal of Religion*, VI, (July, 1926). In his *Jesus* (1927) Professor Bultmann writes, "Personally I am of the opinion that Jesus did not regard himself as the Messiah," p. 12. Professor S. J. Case is highly skeptical about the messianic conviction as an element in the personal religious experience of Jesus and locates its origin in the resurrection faith of the earliest Christians; *see* his *Jesus*, p. 372*ff*; *also* his article, "The Alleged Messianic Consciousness of Jesus," *Journal of Biblical Literature*, XLVI (1927), pp. 1-19.

nent eschatological element, even if they rejected his extreme eschatological emphasis.

The weakness of both Wrede and Schweitzer is the extreme to which each has carried his own thesis. Each seeks in the sources a set system that is not there. They approach the messianic issue with an *either-or*, while the facts seem to point to a *both-and*. For Wrede, the messianic secret is the dogma of Mark's faith without basis in fact in the life of Jesus. For Schweitzer, it is an historical fact of Jesus' own self-consciousness which furnishes the sole key to the understanding of him. To strip the Gospels of all messianic elements as Wrede does involves an almost terrible devastation of our best sources, but with Wrede we shall have to admit that the great body of the messianic elements in the Gospels are of Christian origin and that we can say very little that is definite regarding the messianic issue in Jesus' own mind. To resolve the whole life of Jesus into an unbroken series of messianic words and acts, as Schweitzer does, results in a dreary dogmatization of the mind of Jesus that does violence to our New Testament accounts by its utter neglect of the fundamental religiousness of Jesus' mind. But to Schweitzer we shall have to concede that his criticism has restored one of the clearest but most neglected features in the Gospel picture. Wrede has brought us nearer the Gospels and the Gospel writers that we may understand them better. Schweitzer has brought us nearer the Jesus of history with the result that we see him more clearly and accurately.

The Messianic Matter in the First Three Gospels

It may seem strange that both Wrede and Schweitzer

turn to the New Testament and find materials sufficient
for the support of their diametrically opposed positions
with regard to the messianic issue. But in reality this
is not at all strange, for our best sources present a confused mass of matter on the messianic question that is
almost hopelessly inextricable. It is positively depress-
ing for the student of the life of Jesus that he can not
assure himself of the facts, and he might drop the issue
were it not for the inescapable pressure which drives
him to do his best in the effort to see Jesus as he really
was.

In the discussion that follows we shall present the
messianic matter in four natural groupings. First: Did
the general public regard Jesus as the Messiah? Second:
What of the messianic confessions of the demoniacs?
Third: Did the disciples come to the messianic conviction concerning their Master during his lifetime? Fourth:
Did Jesus come to regard himself as the Messiah; what
was his attitude toward the messianic issue? Our interest here is not in settling the messianic question either for
Jesus or for ourselves. Our interest is in something
deeper—the religious experience of Jesus involved in it.
If Jesus did come to regard himself as the Messiah, we
may say with certainty that this consciousness was fundamentally religious, expressing itself in genuine religious
attitudes and aspirations.

I

The first three Gospels nowhere report that the general
public in contact with Jesus regarded him as the Messiah.
With all the startling elements in Jesus' personality and
ministry, elements that drew great crowds and that held

them spellbound and amazed, the general public does not stumble on to the idea that he is the Messiah. Jesus' fame spreads like wild-fire and all sorts of rumors are current concerning him, but the messianic rumor, the first to arise and the easiest to spread, never seems to occur to the eager multitudes. The general tenor of public opinion concerning Jesus was to the effect that he was a prophet. This is the regular attitude of the Galilean crowds with whom Jesus enjoyed his greatest popularity. Twice in their Galilean accounts the writers of the first three Gospels take occasion to quote public opinion concerning Jesus.

"And king Herod heard *thereof;* for his name had become known: and he said, John the Baptizer is risen from the dead, and therefore do these powers work in him. But others said, It is Elijah. And others said, *It is* a prophet, *even* as one of the old prophets."[11]

Later, toward the very close of the Galilean days, in the villages of Cæsarea Philippi, Jesus puts the question to his disciples, who were in closer touch with public sentiment on this point than he was:

"Who do men say that I am? And they told him, saying, John the Baptist; and others, Elijah; but others, One of the prophets."[12]

These rumors are wild enough—John the Baptist risen from the dead, the reincarnation of Elijah, Jeremiah, or of one of the old prophets—but the messianic

---

[11]Mark 6,14-15; compare Matt. 14,1-2; Luke 9,7-8.
[12]Mark 8,27-28; compare Matt. 16,13-14; Luke 9,18-19.

idea does not appear. For the general public, then, the career of Jesus is unmessianic. The older lives of Jesus that presented his contemporaries as disappointed in the type of messiahship represented by him drew their materials from the realm of imagination, not from the Synoptic sources.

The one great public incident in the life of Jesus that has been regarded almost without exception as messianic is the triumphal entry into the Holy City.[13] This is, to be sure, the greatest public ovation and demonstration ever accorded Jesus, but that it was messianic either for Jesus or for the crowds is not at all certain on the basis of the Gospel accounts themselves. The common conception that Jesus is here acclaimed as the Messiah by the Galilean Passover pilgrims is not at all clear in the story itself. How is it that these Galileans did not recognize Jesus as the Messiah before? How is it that they come to this idea so late and only when they are off their native soil? How is it that they acclaim Jesus as the Messiah on the first day of the passion week and never raise a voice in his behalf when he is caught in the coils of the death-process only five days later? The time between this ovation and Jesus' death is too short to permit the development of a general public disappointment. There is nothing in the character of Jesus' three days of public work in Jerusalem to bring about a complete reversal of popular sentiment against him.

The first thing that strikes the historical student in the account of the incident itself is that Jesus is represented as setting the stage for the demonstration by sending two of his disciples ahead to secure a colt, and the historical student finds it difficult to imagine Jesus staging anything,

---

[13]Matt. 21,1-9; Mark 11,1-10; Luke 19,29-38.

especially a demonstration in his own honor. The only
messianic element in the incident is the singing of extracts
from messianic Psalms. The original incident may not
have been in honor of Jesus at all. He and the crowds
with him were Galilean pilgrims to the greatest of all
Jewish feasts, and as they neared the Holy City and first
caught sight of its sacred walls, they may have burst out
in messianic Psalms, as was the usual custom of pilgrims
approaching the Zion of their God. Or it may be that
the usual demonstration that took place when the Holy
City first came into view developed into an unpremedi-
tated ovation in honor of Jesus. At any rate, the account
in its present form pictures a spontaneous outburst of
provincial Galilean pride, which is especially clear in
Matthew 21,10-11:

"And when he was come into Jerusalem, all the city
was stirred, saying,
WHO IS THIS?
And the multitude said,
THIS IS THE PROPHET, JESUS, FROM NAZARETH OF
GALILEE.

II

The encounters between Jesus and the demoniacs
constitute one of the most unintelligible situations in the
whole of the Gospel account. The folk-psychology involved in them is wholly foreign to our experience, and
it is only by sustained effort that the trained historical
imagination can orient itself in these strange situations.
Further, these scenes present an almost inextricable tangle
of conflicting elements: Faith and fact are so smoothly

merged that even the careful student is never sure where the one leaves off and the other begins.

In Mark the demoniacs constitute a special class of cure to which attaches a special significance and which present one of the outstanding peculiarities of Mark's early Galilean account. In Mark only the demoniacs recognize Jesus as the Messiah from the very first. This they do because they are inhabited by demons who, according to the folk-psychology of the day, possess more-than-human insight. They see in Jesus what his responsible contemporaries do not see, the Messiah, whose appearance means their own destruction. Publicly they confess his messiahship; Jesus regularly commands silence and orders the demons to depart. The first cure in Mark is that of a demoniac (1,21-28), who gives the typical messianic confession of his kind:

"What have we to do with thee, Jesus thou Nazarene? are thou come to destroy us? I know thee who thou art, the Holy One of God." (1,24.)

Then follows Jesus' command for silence which results in the cure. Such scenes appear often in the earlier Galilean days,[14] to which Mark gives the following general characterization:

"And the unclean spirits, whensoever they beheld him, fell down before him and cried, saying, Thou art the Son of God. And he charged them much that they should not make him known." (3,11-12.)

[14]Mark's confessions of the demoniacs appear in 1,23-24 34; 3,11; 5,6-7; Jesus' commands for silence in 1,25 34; 3,12; 5,8.

These encounters between Jesus and the demoniacs have been a never-ending source of debate, the two extreme wings being represented again by Wrede and Schweitzer. Wrede declares both the confessions of the demoniacs and Jesus' commands for silence to be unhistorical. ".These features must be stricken from the historical account of Jesus. It is exactly the systematic regularity of their appearance that renders them suspicious and that betrays their origin."[15] They are expressions of Mark's Christology in particular, of early Christian theological theory in general, both being read back into the life of Jesus. They are Christianizations of Jesus' historical career, deposits of Markan and early Christian faith. They are simply one phase of Mark's means of messianizing Jesus' unmessianic career.

Schweitzer's view is just the opposite: The confessions of the demoniacs are very strange, but they are historical. "We shall perhaps never succeed in explaining the peculiar apprehensions and actions of the demoniacs; but there is no reason for doubting the facts as they are reported."[16] These confessions of the demoniacs Schweitzer fits into his thesis of the messianic secret: By their statements the demoniacs threaten Jesus with the betrayal of his secret, and he issues his sharp commands for silence in order to preserve his incognito.

That there is a prominent faith element in these encounters between Jesus and the demoniacs is perfectly clear in the accounts themselves. For Mark, these scenes involve much more than a meeting between Jesus and certain distressed human beings. They are not just cures; they are much more—conflicts between the Mes-

---

[15]*Das Messiasgeheimnis in den Evangelien*, p. 31.
[16]*Die Geschichte der Leben-Jesu-Forschung*, p. 339f.

siah and the kingdom of Satan. For Mark's faith, and from his supernaturalistic point of view, these scenes present concrete cases of the defeat and destruction of Satan's reign and power in the world. It is not the human victim but the demons that inhabit him who recognize Jesus for the One he really is and utter a cry of dismay with a messianic ring to it. The human victims hardly figure in these scenes. In such encounters it is the Christ of Mark's faith with whom the demons have to do and to deal; in the presence of the Messiah they must surrender their hold on men.

The historical fact seems to be that Jesus did cure just such deranged persons as Mark represents in the case of the demoniacs. As we may conclude from analogous cases in modern psychotherapy, these cures were effected by the power of Jesus' personal presence to which such afflicted individuals would be most sensitive, susceptible and suggestible. Under the imposing impression of Jesus' personality they may have indulged in strange statements, even extravagant outbursts. In encounters with this type of afflicted, Jesus must quite naturally resort to decisive, even drastic procedure.

Into these facts Mark has introduced the findings of his faith, for which they have a special significance. Here Mark finds in the life of Jesus a concrete substantiation for his own personal faith in Jesus' messiahship, as it also probably was for the early Christian faith in general even before Mark undertook the writing of his account. Mark has the demoniacs make Christian confessions; as contemporaries of more-than-human insight, they see in Jesus what the general public did not see and what his personal followers, even Jesus himself, did not at first appear to think that he was or was to be. Thus, for

Mark, these encounters between Jesus and the demoniacs transcend the realm of fact and have their scene and significance in the realm of faith. It is because of their significance for Mark's own personal faith and for the Christian faith in general that he takes a special interest in them.

That these scenes as messianic moments in the life of Jesus can not be taken as literal history is clear from the fact that Mark does not represent them as messianic for the witnesses—the general public and the personal followers of Jesus. In spite of such scenes which are messianic for his faith, Mark nevertheless portrays Jesus' public career as essentially unmessianic. It is this general tenor of Mark's narrative that probably brings us nearest the historical facts. It is this unmessianic undercurrent that carries the whole body of Mark's narrative along, and its survival in his story as a whole, in spite of his own messianic faith and the messianic elements in his depiction of the demoniac encounters, increases our confidence in the trustworthiness of his account of Jesus.

These messianic aspects of the demoniac encounters belong to the realm of the earliest Christian faith and not to the body of fact from the life of Jesus. If Jesus had been in possession of the messianic secret, it would have been betrayed by the Capernaum demoniac on his very first day in public. (Mark 1,21-28.) Here Wrede, it seems, brings us nearer both truth and fact than Schweitzer. Mark's faith sees in Jesus what his contemporaries, the general public in contact with him, did not see. From Mark's Christian point of view, Jesus was what his public life and work did not reveal him to be. Faith discovered, fact did not disclose, the messiahship of Jesus.

There is also an important literary element in Mark's demoniac scenes. In each case one gets the impression that the real point is reserved for Mark's readers and that the confessions of the demoniacs are primarily for the readers' benefit. The general public, the disciples and Jesus himself remain unimpressed by what the demoniacs say. Mark's demoniacs are really speaking to the readers of the second Gospel. Mark intends that his readers shall see in Jesus what his contemporaries did not see and what the disciples and Jesus himself realized only later.

III

The Gospel materials on the messianic conviction of the twelve disciples are very meager, much more so than the casual reader supposes. It is only as we begin to single out definitely messianic incidents in the experience of Jesus' chosen companions that we realize fully how meager these materials are. There are a number of situations in the life of Jesus in which the Christian point of view involuntarily sees the messianic conviction of the twelve expressing itself, if not openly, at least as an undercurrent. But when we come to reset ourselves in the actual situation of the disciples, then we realize that nothing necessarily messianic is involved in what is said or done.

The common Christian idea that the personally chosen companions of Jesus were convinced of his messiahship from the very first and that the chief problem in their experience in his company was the overcoming of false conceptions of his messiahship in favor of his own true understanding, has no basis in the first three Gospels.[17] In the first three Gospels it is not the messianic conviction that wins the first followers, the two sets of fisher brothers. In Matthew (4,18-22) and Mark (1,16-20) Jesus calls these men and they follow at the very first meeting. Mark's abrupt account of this important step both on the part of Jesus and on the part of these fishermen creates serious historical and psychological problems. Luke felt these very problems, and he delays the calling of these men until they have been in the company of Jesus throughout the eventful day in Capernaum (4, 31-43), hearing Jesus preach and witnessing his cures, until he has preached from their own boat and they have witnessed the miraculous draught of fishes. (5, 1-11.) But in none of the first three Gospels is the messianic moment even hinted at as an element in the early experience of any of the disciples in Jesus' company.

In the first three Gospels it is a puzzling problem how the disciples came to entertain the messianic conviction at all. We never see them struggling with erroneous conceptions of his messiahship, succeeding or failing, a state of the disciples' mind of which the older lives of Jesus made so much. The one principal problem of the twelve seems to have been to reconcile themselves, if sooner, to the prospect, if later, to the fact of Jesus' tragic fate.

It is only toward the very close of the Galilean days that the messianic conviction is expressed for the first

---

[17]This common Christian idea has its basis in the Fourth Gospel alone, in which it is the messianic conviction that wins the disciples to Jesus in the first place. A good illustration of this is found in Andrew's winning word to Simon, "We have found the Messiah." (1,41.) Consult the whole of the Fourth Gospel's section on the recruiting of the first followers. (1,35-51.)

time within the circle of the twelve. It is the famous
scene at Cæsarea Philippi, the confession of Simon Peter,
which Mark recounts as follows:

"And Jesus went forth, and his disciples, into the
villages of Cæsarea Philippi: and on the way he asked
his disciples, saying unto them, Who do men say that
I am? And they told him, saying, John the Baptist;
and others, Elijah; but others, One of the prophets.
And he asked them, But who say ye that I am? Peter
answereth and saith unto him, Thou art the Christ.
And he charged them that they should tell no man
of him."[18]

This confession comes from the lips of Simon Peter,
but he appears as the spokesman of the twelve, uttering
the common conviction of the group. All three Gospel
writers regard the incident as closing with the twelve
convinced of the messianic dignity of their Master. All
three treat the scene as a turning-point in their narratives.
Henceforth they picture a new intimacy between Jesus
and the twelve; there is less publicity, more privacy,
more intimate scenes, greater sharing of confidences, and
Jesus' words to the twelve become more personal.

The confession scene at Cæsarea Philippi, however,
stands practically isolated in the Gospel narrative. The
source of this messianic conviction on the part of the
twelve we do not know. How long they have been of this
conviction, how they came to it in the first place, we are
not told. There are no special elements in the experience
of the twelve down to this point that would furnish the
psychological antecedents out of which such a conviction

---

[18]Mark 8,27-30; *see* parallels in Matt. 16,13-20; Luke 9,18-21.

would naturally grow. They have not learned of Jesus' messiahship from the general public, for their own private conviction is set in sharp contrast with the current contemporary opinions to the effect that Jesus is a prophet. The disciples have heard the confessions of the demoniacs from the very first day in Jesus' company and have remained unimpressed by them. They have not learned it from him, for this is the first time that the messianic issue has come up between Jesus and his intimate followers.

Wrede declares the confession scene at Cæsarea Philippi to be unhistorical: It is simply another phase of the process of the messianization of Jesus' unmessianic career, and the command for silence which is Jesus' prompt response puts the scene in the same class with the demoniac encounters. Wrede's daring at this point requires a critical courage that very few students of the life of Jesus have cared to possess, and the consequences are too far-reaching, resulting in an almost complete source-skepticism. The fact that the Gospel writers provide no psychological preparation for this messianic conviction and confession is not to be taken too seriously, for they seldom show any interest in the underlying motives that lead up to important incidents which they depict. The twelve may have been of the messianic conviction and Simon Peter may have confessed it at Cæsarea Philippi, but that the scene was messianic for Jesus himself is a very different question. At this point, as we shall see, we may share some of Wrede's skepticism in the interest of discovering the original facts.

There is another incident in which the messianic conviction of the twelve is fully as clear as it is in Peter's confession at Cæsarea Philippi, the request of James and

John on the way to Jerusalem (Mark 10,35-40):

"And there come near unto him James and John,
the sons of Zebedee, saying unto him, Teacher, we
would that thou shouldest do for us whatsoever we
shall ask of thee.   And he said unto them, What would
ye that I should do for you?   And they said unto him,
Grant unto us that we may sit, one on thy right hand,
and one on *thy* left hand, in thy glory."

This account has all the marks of historical reliability.
It is highly uncomplimentary to the two disciples involved
and there is no good reason why it should be reported
unless it comes straight from the life of Jesus.[19]   In it
is embedded a word of Jesus that is as reliable as any
that has come down to us—the figures of the cup and
the baptism. (Mark 10,38.)   Further, the incident has
behind it wholly natural antecedents.   In the request we
see that the disciples share Jesus' faith concerning the
kingdom and its coming.   As psychological preparation
we have the constant theme of Jesus' message from the
very outset. (Mark 1,15; Matt. 10,23; Mark 9,1.)
There is no reason why the disciples should not share the
eschatological expectation of Jesus.   The only new element in their point of view is their identification of Jesus
with the apocalyptic Son of man, which, as we shall see,
was not the point of view of Jesus himself.   But as the
incident stands it testifies to the existence of the mes-

---

[19]Both Matthew and Luke feel the uncomplimentary character of the
incident.   Luke omits the Markan form entirely and preserves the heart
of the passage from another source (12,50), in which it has no connection with a request of these two disciples.   Matthew modifies the setting
and has the mother of James and John present this selfish request.
(20,20-21.)

sianic conviction concerning Jesus among his most intimate disciples.

We may review the messianic materials presented thus far as follows. If the messianic conviction concerning Jesus existed at all among his contemporaries, it was the private conviction of the twelve. If the messianic conviction was an element in the experience of the twelve, it was of relatively late origin, inconstant and short-lived. It seems to have appeared only at specially enthusiastic moments when the disciples' feeling and faith rose high above the usual level of their thought concerning Jesus, and it seems to have found only sporadic expression. It was not sufficiently strong to carry them through the tragic events of the passion week. The mental state of the disciples in the resurrection reports—disappointment, depression, skepticism—shows clearly that, if they did come to Jerusalem believing in Jesus' messiahship, they had surrendered this faith in the face of cruel fact. It is only in connection with the rise of the Easter faith that the messiahship of Jesus appears as a firm and an irrepressible conviction of the disciples. In its best form the messianic element in the experience of the disciples during Jesus' lifetime seems to have been more of a high hope than a strong and stable conviction,

"We hoped that it was he who should redeem Israel." (Luke 24,21.)

IV

It is only as we come to the question, Did Jesus regard himself as the Messiah? that we realize how

puzzling a problem it presents because of the utter con-
fusion of materials even in our best sources, where faith
and fact meet and merge almost beyond hope of identification. The uncritical reader of the Gospels will
hardly sense the problem, for his picture of Jesus is
composite, made up of details from all four Gospels.
This popular composite picture is somewhat as follows.
Jesus was aware of his messianic dignity from the first.
He received the messianic consecration at the Jordan
(Matt. and Luke) ; at once in the wilderness he settled
the issue as to the kind of Messiah he would be by rejecting the materialistic conceptions in favor of a spiritual
messiahship (Matt. and Luke) ; he appeared in public
as the Messiah, as such he began and accomplished his
work (Matt., Luke and John) ; as the Messiah he was
rejected and condemned to death (all four Gospels).

It is an easy matter for the Christian with his Christian point of view to read the Gospel story and to see in
it the messianic career of the Son of God. This is an
easy matter because the Gospels were written from this
very point of view by men who were religiously convinced that Jesus was the Messiah and that, in reality,
he had never been anything else.

But when we begin to compare the Gospel accounts
on this point, to study them separately and seek to reset
ourselves in the situations which they present, we discover that the matter is not so simple. When we begin
to confront the positions of faith with the propositions
of fact, the certainty of the messianic conviction on the
part of Jesus becomes extremely problematic.[20] Did the

---

[20]In the Fourth Gospel there is no messianic problem. Jesus is always
the Messiah—for himself, for the Baptist, for his disciples and for the
general public, both friends and foes.

messianic issue present itself to Jesus in any form whatever? If so, When, where and how did Jesus come to
the messianic conviction? Did it really constitute the
principal content of his self-consciousness? What was
his own personal attitude toward the messianic issue?
In answer to these questions we meet with a variety of
voices from the Gospels.

As we pointed out in Chapter II, Matthew and Luke
regard the baptism as the birth-hour and birthplace of
Jesus' messianic consciousness. It comes to him by divine declaration. (Matt. 3,13-17; Luke 3,21-22.) This
is not so clear in the incident itself as in what follows
immediately,[21] the three temptations in the wilderness,
all of which are presented as directly or indirectly messianic. Here in self and solitude Jesus settles the issue
for himself, and henceforth he is the Messiah in his own
chosen sense. (Matt. 4,1-11; Luke 4,1-13.)

There remain but two other messianic steps in his
career. Late in the Galilean days his intimate followers
recognize him for the One he has known himself to be
from the very beginning. (Matt. 16,13-20; Luke 9,18-
21.) At the very close the messianic issue becomes public
and Jesus is condemned to death by the Jewish authorities for blasphemy. (Matt. 26,59-66; Luke 22,66-71.)

Thus, in Matthew and Luke, the whole of Jesus' public career becomes messianic. He begins his work, accomplishes it and dies, knowing all the while that he is
God's chosen Messiah. He may have succeeded in
keeping his messianic consciousness a secret even from
his most intimate disciples until the very close of the

---

[21]In Matthew (3,14-15) Jesus not only arrives at the Jordan fully
aware of his messianic dignity, but he is recognized as such by the
Baptist.

Galilean ministry, he may have kept it from the general public until the last night of his life, but beginning with the Jordan incident and experience Jesus knows that he is henceforth the Messiah, and he speaks and acts as such. The great majority of modern students of the life of Jesus have shared, and many still share, this Matthew-Lukan presentation of the messianic issue in the experience of Jesus.

As we saw in Chapter II also, the Jordan incident in Mark is not necessarily messianic in character. The baptism (1,9-11) is followed immediately by a period of temptation (1,12-13), but Mark gives us no hint as to the nature of the temptations through which Jesus passed. He gives only the most general kind of notice concerning this initial retreat: Jesus "was in the wilderness forty days tempted of Satan." In Mark the messianic conviction is not the result of a moment's revelation at the Jordan; it is not at once subjected to severe test prior to Jesus' public appearance; it is not the chief promoting factor that brings him out of private into public life. In Mark the whole of Jesus' public career does not appear as messianic. In brief, it is impossible to regard these prepublic experiences of Jesus as messianic without making a radical revision of the whole of Mark's Galilean account that would destroy its principal point and climax.

In this conflicting picture, presented by Matthew and Luke on the one hand and by Mark on the other, the historical student is forced to make a choice, and he chooses to part company with Matthew and Luke, and to follow Mark. His reasons for this choice are primarily psychological. The threefold temptation of Matthew and Luke presupposes two things. In the first place, it presupposes that Jesus is fully aware of his extraordinary personal powers to cure and heal, and, as we saw in an earlier connection in this chapter, this is a psychological anticipation. In Mark this problem confronts Jesus only in connection with his first cures, which cause him great solicitude. In the second place, the threefold temptation presupposes that Jesus is in full possession of the messianic conviction prior to his appearance in public. But in Mark the first definite and distinct messianic moment on which we can lay a finger is the scene at Cæsarea Philippi (8,27-30), where Simon for the first time from any of his responsible contemporaries confronts Jesus with the messianic issue. By assigning the messianic issue to the immediate prepublic life of Jesus, Matthew and Luke have accomplished another psychological anticipation. By placing the threefold temptation with its tests of such definite and distinctive character in the prepublic period Matthew and Luke have brought about an extreme alteration in Mark's picture of Jesus. With these three specific tests at this early point Matthew and Luke have Jesus solve problems even in advance of their appearance in Mark. In self and in solitude he defeats temptations prior to his public appearance which, according to Mark, present themselves to him only when he comes into the full swinging stride of his public work, during which in Mark he is forced to battle with these very temptations in the stress and strain of severe religious struggle.

All three tests belong to the very nerve and fiber of Jesus' experience in public. Mark does not have these three temptations in the figurative form which they assume in Matthew and Luke, but he has them none the less. In Mark these three temptations do not assume the highly fantastic form of dramatic dialogues with Satan; they are actual historical situations in which Jesus finds himself. In his Galilean account we see Jesus in these very situations, confronted with these same problems and making identical decisions. All three tests have their historical parallels and psychological points of contact in the later public life of Jesus.[22] All three fit vitally and organically into Jesus' experience in public where they are out of all historical and psychological association with the initial retreat to the wilderness following upon the Jordan experience. The threefold temptation, assigned as it is to the prepublic experience of Jesus, represents a Christianization of the story at this point. Matthew and Luke have Jesus face and defeat specific temptations prior to the possibility of their appearance, when in reality all three are the natural issue of his experience in public.

Regarding the nature and importance of Jesus' experience in the wilderness during this first retreat (Mark 1,12-13), the historical student must confess that he knows and can say but little. Mark's notice is too brief, too general in character, too uncommunicative in content, to enable one to conclude very much. Mark does attach to the incident considerable importance for he gives it a place among the promoting factors that brought Jesus out of private into public life. But the historical student can say that, in Mark, this initial retreat does not result for Jesus in the solution of such fundamental problems as Matthew and Luke represent, for in Mark's account we see Jesus facing these problems only later when the full pressure of his public work is upon him. Jesus' atti-

---

[22]Mark's historical parallels are 1,35-38; 8,11-12; 8,32b-33. *See* the author's companion study, *The Religion of Jesus*, pp. 19-24.

tude is never that of one who has solved these things far in advance and who has nothing left to do but give them a formal dismissal. Thus the historical student is forced to feel that Mark's representation is nearer the facts as they were in the life and experience of Jesus.

It is difficult to say what the temptation meant for the Christian thought and faith of Mark. At best, it throws only a neutral light on the baptism. But in Mark these two initial experiences of Jesus contain no distinctly messianic elements. The temptation remains for us a problem, but that Mark considers it of importance for Jesus and his appearance in public is clear from the fact that he reports it at all and in the particular place in which he reports it.

It is still more difficult to say what this first wilderness retreat meant in the experience of Jesus himself. Our best recourse perhaps is to draw analogies from the field of comparative religious psychology. The most that we can say with any measure of certainty is that it appears as a period of orientation and adjustment such as other great religious figures have experienced prior to their public work. In its brevity, general character and uncommunicativeness Mark's notice of the temptation of Jesus is quite similiar to Paul's retreat into Arabia (Gal. 1,17), a period in Paul's life passed over entirely by the author of Acts and mentioned by the Apostle himself in only the most cursory way.

The messianic issue, according to Mark, presents itself to Jesus only during the course of his career in public. The first specific personal problem that confronts Jesus in Mark comes at the close of his first day in the presence of the people, the problem of cures and cause. (1,35-38.) It is at this point that Jesus' specific personal problems begin in Mark, but they assume a definite messianic aspect only in 8,27-30.   In Mark the messianic issue confronts Jesus as the result of eventful experiences, unforeseen and unescapable, during active engagement in his public work.

According to Mark, Jesus is confronted with the messianic issue in three different ways and from three different sources: by the demoniacs, by the twelve at Cæsarea Philippi and by the Jewish authorities on the last night of his life.

On the first public occasion, in the synagogue in Capernaum, Jesus is met with the messianic confession of the demoniac, and similiar scenes with the demoniacs continue through the earlier part of the Galilean period.[23] In each case Jesus' command for silence results in cure.[24] We have already questioned the historicity of these confessions on the ground that the general public and the disciples remain unimpressed by them, a situation plausible enough for faith, but quite out of the question as a matter of historical fact.   We can not imagine a scene that would be messianic for the demoniacs and for Jesus, and unmessianic for the other witnesses.   These messianic features in the encounters with the demoniacs are really foreign to the actual situation, and they have a natural place only for the writer and readers of the second Gospel who review these scenes from the standpoint of later Christian conviction.

The whole undertone of Mark's narrative speaks against these scenes as definitely messianic for Jesus himself.   If Jesus had been in possession of the messianic

---

[23]Mark 1,23-24; 1,34; 3,11; 5,6-7.
[24]Mark 1,25; 1,34; 3,12; 5,8.

secret, a bit of tact would have stood him in good stead in the face of such confessions. His sharp commands would confirm rather than refute the statements of the demoniacs. Further, when we review Jesus' healing ministry as a whole, we find that his commands for silence are not messianic admissions which in turn order strict secrecy. He just as often commands silence in other cases of cure that are not attended by messianic confessions.[25] His commands for silence, confined as they are not to the demoniacs, are to be understood in the more personal light of his own loyalty to the divine cause which he has chosen and which he champions.

The whole temper of Mark's narrative is to the effect that it was not the demoniacs in particular, but Jesus' healing activity in general that threw him into the midst of pressing personal problems. The outcome of his first day in public, in which his power to cure and heal strikes him as something new, shows that Jesus' problem is not just that of guarding a personal secret. This is clear from the fact that his decision in Mark 1,38 does not have to do with the demoniacs in particular but with his ability to cure in general. Jesus' choice on this occasion is not for a messianic or unmessianic career; it is not a choice of one type of messianism to the rejection of others. It is clear enough that his choice has to do with the essence of his mission—the effecting of cures or the preaching of cause. On the basis of Mark, in whose narrative these demoniac confessions amount practically to a dogma, we are not able to say that they helped Jesus to the messianic conviction for himself. If they did contribute to his arrival at the messianic conviction, it was not on the basis of their own merit alone but be-

---

[25]Mark 1,43-44; 5,43; 7,36; 8,26.

cause they were simply a part of the whole of Jesus' ministry of healing. But there is no reason for supposing that Jesus' ability to effect cures led him to the idea that he was the Messiah. Healers were too common. In the Beelzebub contention, Jesus says,

"If I by Beelzebub cast out demons, by whom do your sons cast them out." (Matt. 12,27.)

The second time that Jesus is confronted with the messianic issue in Mark is at Cæsarea Philippi where for the first time he hears a messianic confession from the lips of one of his most intimate disciples. (8,27-30.) We have already approached this incident from the standpoint of the disciples and, if it is historical, it is certainly a messianic moment in their experience. But that it was messianic for Jesus is open to question.

In the first place, the questions of Jesus on this occasion are surprising to any careful student of his life.[26] Up to this point Jesus has never manifested any interest in the opinions of others concerning himself. This is the only point in the whole of the Synoptic narrative where he inquires concerning either public or private opinion with regard to his identity. With the exception of this one scene, all other expressions concerning his identity come unsolicited on his part. All other such utterances are spontaneous on the part of the speakers. Jesus otherwise never encourages such expressions; on the contrary, he discourages them. Rather than soliciting them, he regularly suppresses any such suggestions. The cries of the demoniacs he silences, and when the disciples

[26]"Who do men say that I am?"   (Mark 8,27.)
"But who say ye that I am?"   (Mark 8,29.)

are witnesses of any incidents that might center their attention exclusively on himself,[27] he commands secrecy. Jesus seemed to fear an attention that centered exclusively upon himself, a fear that is wholly natural in the experience of any great religious figure who is completely consecrated to his cause and who sees defeat in any movement among his following that would exalt himself at the expense of what he is seeking to accomplish.

What it was that prompted Jesus to solicit both public and private opinion on this occasion we can not say, but in this respect the Cæsarea Philippi scene is unlike anything that precedes or follows. This double inquiry is so thoroughly uncharacteristic of Jesus, his interest here in the opinion of others is so unusual and isolated, that one might well doubt the historicity of the whole scene on the basis of this consideration alone.

In the second place, Jesus' reaction to Simon's confession is not at all certain. In Mark and Luke he commands silence.[28] If the disciples are of the conviction that he is the Messiah, they are to keep it to themselves and are not to speak of it, even to him. Of a man who was so completely consecrated to his cause as was Jesus, it is difficult to believe that he found any sort of gratification in the disclosure of the messianic conviction within the group of his personally chosen followers. In Matthew only does Jesus greet Simon's confession with open approval. (16,17-19.) In Matthew Jesus' response is even more than an admission; it amounts to a celebration; he acclaims the confession of Simon as of divine origin. But it is doubtful if there is a passage in all of the first three Gospels that is of later origin than

[27]The transfiguration (Mark 9,2-10) is such an incident.
[28]Cf. Mark 8,30; Luke 9,21.

just this passage of Matthew. It is historically impossible on the lips of Jesus. It comes from the period of nascent Catholicism and represents an official Christian theory that Matthew carries back in the mind of Jesus.

Critical scholarship is forced to favor Mark and Luke, according to whom Jesus' reaction is uncertain. He meets the confession of Peter with neither an affirmative nor a negative; he is wholly noncommittal and, judged in the light of the confessions of the demoniacs and the hearing before the Jewish authorities, Mark and Luke seem to give us the facts: All messianic suggestions, whatever their origin, Jesus meets in a noncommittal way. The confession of Simon he greets as he greeted the confessions of the demoniacs, with a command for silence.

On the basis of the scene at Cæsarea Philippi we are not in a position to say that Jesus did or did not regard himself as the Messiah. If he did, his reticence and reserve remain unbroken. That the incident at Cæsarea Philippi was messianic for Jesus personally, we may neither affirm nor deny with certainty.

The third time that Jesus is confronted with the messianic issue in Mark is on the last night of his life at his trial before the Jewish authorities.[29] Here the question is put to Jesus in the most unequivocal form by the high priest (Mark 14,61),

"Art thou the Christ, the Son of the Blessed?"

According to Luke, who has an account of the Jewish hearing that varies greatly from that of Matthew and Mark, Jesus is evasive, and the question is put to him

---

[29] Cf. Matt. 26,59-66; Mark 14,55-64; Luke 22,66-71.

twice. His second answer is noncommittal, "Ye say that I am." Jesus' answer in Matthew is not a pure affirmative, "Thou hast said." In Mark, however, Jesus seems to give a clear affirmative, "I am."

In spite of the wording of Jesus' reply all of the first three Gospel writers regard it as an admission. In Matthew and Mark the high priest rends his garments as traditionally prescribed that he should do in the presence of blasphemy, and in all three Gospels Jesus is condemned to die by the Jewish authorities for this chief of all religious offenses. Down to this point everything seems to indicate clearly that Jesus on the last night of his life confessed publicly that he was the Messiah or that he was destined to be the Messiah.

But in Mark, Jesus' "I am" is followed by a strongly adversative statement which compromises the purity of the affirmative,

"I am: and ye shall see the Son of man sitting at the right hand of Power, and coming with the clouds of heaven." (Mark 14,62.)

In connection with his "I am" Jesus speaks of a divine agent from whom he distinguishes himself religiously, and this final statement seems to be simply a re-declaration of the faith that has held him from the beginning. The messianic issue is the crux of the Jewish trial and the Gospel writers depict him as put to death because he regarded himself as the Messiah. But we shall have to say that Jesus does not give an unqualified affirmative and that on the last night of his life he is practically as reserved and reticent as ever on the messianic question.

A sifting of the Gospel of Mark[30] for the messianic issue in the experience of Jesus results in a paradoxical picture. In spite of Mark's faith to the effect that Jesus was the Messiah and in spite of the cues he gives his readers on this point, he nevertheless presents Jesus' public career as essentially unmessianic for Jesus himself. When we turn to Mark seeking Jesus' own attitude on the messianic question, we strike a puzzling problem for which neither Jesus nor Mark gives us a satisfactory solution. With regard to his great message Jesus is explicit enough, but when we come to seek statements and attitudes of his on the question of the messiahship for himself we are met with a reserve and reticence that leave us completely in the dark. Jesus acts and speaks as the called prophet, as the commissioned preacher, of the kingdom of God. This consciousness of high call and holy commission is clear in every word and act. But his words and acts never betray the messianic conviction as the driving force out of which he speaks and acts.

In Mark the messiahship is not a necessary or even an evident element in Jesus' consciousness of call and commission to a public career. If the messianic issue did confront him at an early date, it was not in the initial retreat to the wilderness, but only when he came into the full swinging stride of his work in public as the result of

---

[30]With the exception of the threefold temptation which presents the messianic issue as the principal problem in the immediate prepublic period, Matthew and Luke treat the messianic issue in the experience of Jesus in practically the same way as does Mark. Matthew anticipates the Cæsarea Philippi scene by having the first messianic confession provoked by the walking on the water (14,33) ; however, he still reserves his climax for Cæsarea Philippi where Jesus gives his festal confirmation to Peter's confession. The only additional messianic matter in Matthew (11,2-19) and Luke (7,18-35) is the question of the Baptist through his disciples and Jesus' enigmatic reply—a scene that complicates rather than clarifies our problem.

experiences through which he passed. If the messianic issue presented itself to Jesus, it was a problem with which he struggled in the very depths of his soul, his own purely personal problem which did not betray itself in his public words, acts or attitudes. Only occasionally toward the close is there an undertone and hint of its presence in his words and moments alone with his disciples. Jesus, in the first three Gospels, never claims to be the Messiah, nor does he give himself out as such; in fact, it is nowhere perfectly clear that he regarded himself as the Messiah at all.

The thesis that Jesus never regarded himself as the Messiah can be defended on the basis of Mark, as Wrede has so brilliantly done. In the earlier and major part of his public life, during practically the whole of his Galilean work, his thought is purely objective, centering upon the divine cause which he champions. It is only toward the close of the Galilean days that we find any hint in Mark to the effect that his thought is taking on a messianic form, and, *if* it is taking on a messianic form, we can not be at all sure as to its exact content. Whether from our Christian point of view we think to discover it or not, it is at best only a hardly distinguishable element in the background of his mind. If Jesus in his own thought was convinced that he was the Messiah, he practised an unbroken reserve and reticence. Mark never has Jesus make a clear, unequivocal statement on the messianic issue as it concerns him personally unless it is on the last night of his life. (14,62.)[31]

In Mark the messianic conviction is not the result of

---

[31]"Although the primitive Christian community firmly believed in the messiahship of Jesus, its tradition almost never allows him to answer questions relative to his messiahship with a full affirmative." Johannes Weiss, *Die Schriften des Neuen Testaments*, I, 303.

a moment's revelation at the Jordan; prior to his appearance in public Jesus does not gain clearness and certainty on this point. In Mark, *if* he ever achieves it at all, he must make a painful climb to the messianic conviction. It is the outcome and issue of a long stress and struggle of soul that runs through practically the whole of his public life, a stress and struggle of soul that drives him apart for prayer and petition for clearness and certainty concerning the divine will for himself. If Jesus did arrive at the conviction that he was or was to be the Messiah, it came only out of a fierce inner conflict, the details of which we shall never know, that forced him to face the messianic issue as the will of God for himself.

The Religiousness of Jesus' Reactions

In recent times the self-consciousness of Jesus has been discussed almost without exception as an historico-critical, linguistic, or *religionsgeschichtliches* problem. The approach of Wrede, that of his few followers and many opponents, was historico-critical, denying and defending the genuineness of the messianic passages in the Gospels. The linguistic problem has hinged upon Jesus' use of the term *Son of man,* its relation to the messianic idea in general and to Jesus' messianic conviction in particular.[32]   Albert Schweitzer presents the *religionsgeschichtliche* form of the problem, seeking to determine the content of Jesus' self-consciousness in the

---

[32]The most radical study on this question of the *Son of man* is that of Hans Lietzmann, *Der Menschensohn* (1896), who maintains that Jesus never used this term as a self-designation because it was linguistically impossible in Aramaic, Jesus' mother-tongue. The most recent study of this problem is that of Georges Dupont, *Le Fils de l'Homme* (1924).

light of the religious background in which he appeared
and finding in him a merger of two religious outlooks,
the traditional-messianic with the eschatological-apoc-
alyptic.

The importance of such study from such angles is
known and appreciated by all serious students of the
life of Jesus, but they do not exhaust the approaches
and they really neglect the one approach that comes nearest doing Jesus historical and personal justice. Almost
without exception they neglect the religious approach,
which in the writer's mind is the only way back to Jesus
as he really was. A less academic approach to our best
sources reveals to us very clearly that Jesus' self-consciousness was exclusively religious and that the messianic
issue, in whatever form or sense it presented itself to
him, was for him simply a problem in personal religion.

A whole group of modern New Testament critics has
developed what we may call a *liberal theological traditionalism* in dealing with the messianic issue as it concerned Jesus personally. Here Bousset is representative:
"It was only in the messianic idea that Jesus found the
expression that fitted his self-consciousness of peculiar
position and super-prophetic significance."[33] This rather
widely held position is, it seems to me, historically and
psychologically false. Bousset deals with the messianic
issue in the mind of Jesus as though it were for him only
a linguistic matter, a problem of vocabulary, when in
reality it confronted him with one of the deepest and
most characteristic problems of the genuinely religious
consciousness. Nowhere do we see Jesus laboring under
a linguistic difficulty. He exercises no careful choice
in the existing titles; he offers no criticisms and makes no

---

[33] *Jesus*, p. 90.

corrections. He expresses no reservations and makes no revisions. The idea that Jesus accepted the messianic title with the suffering reservation, which at an early date deposited itself in the prophecies of the passion, is of Christian origin and belongs to early Christian apologetics. Jesus forecasts his fate, but nowhere do we see him grounding his disciples in a new, or training them away from an old, terminology.

As we shall see presently, Jesus' fate brought him face to face with the most critical problem of the religious consciousness and it became a still more serious problem for his followers, but nowhere do we see him seeking to adjust a traditional faith to meet the fact of his fate, an adjustment that would have amounted to cancellation. We see no conscious effort on his part to fill an old term with a new meaning that better fitted the state of his own feeling with regard to himself. We never see him searching for terms adequate to express his conception of himself. The adequacy or inadequacy of the messianic title very probably never occurred to Jesus. We never see him rejecting one type of messianism in favor of another. Even in the threefold temptation Jesus is not refusing proposed courses of messianic conduct so much as he is seeking, choosing and obeying the divine will for himself.

If we could establish beyond all question the messiahship of Jesus in his own thought and conviction, if we could locate its origin, trace its development and determine its exact content, we should still be quite far from the heart of his innermost consciousness in this matter. The solution of the messianic problem could give us at best only the form which Jesus' thought for himself assumed, only the historical background against which his figure towers aloft. Even if we give the messianic conviction full and free sway in the experience of Jesus, it still remains secondary and subservient to that deeper element in his nature which he never fails to manifest—the religious consciousness. In every feature of the picture that has come down to us, Jesus' consciousness—in its character and in its content, in its control and in its confession—is fundamentally, once for all and for ever, religious.

Independent of the question of the messianic conviction existing in the mind of Jesus or in the minds of any of his contemporaries, independent of the historicity of the messianic scenes, the self-consciousness of Jesus is not to be described as messianic. If Jesus did regard himself as the Messiah or as destined to be the Messiah, this conviction was for him the divine will. Whatever he was to be or to do, he was to be and to do according to the divine will. The messianic consciousness, if Jesus possessed such, he always subordinated to that deeper element in his nature, the religious consciousness.

Without exception, Jesus' reactions to the messianic issue are deeply religious. Nowhere is this clearer than in the temptation scene where messianic questions receive the answers of a pure piety. In spite of its Christian cast and color, in spite of the anticipation of Jesus' personal problems involved in it, we are deeply indebted to Matthew and Luke for preserving to us the threefold temptation in the form that they have. Their account of the state of Jesus' mind constitutes a very important contribution to our understanding of him. In this threefold test, misplaced as it is by Matthew and Luke, we secure an invaluable insight into the utter religiousness of Jesus' mind that is not furnished us by Mark in his historical parallels to these three struggles. All three temptations sprang organically from the innermost life of Jesus, and they throw an interesting and instructive light on his religious thinking and feeling. In them we witness a range of religious reflection, a clearness of ethical conception, a purity of moral principle, a soundness of judgment, a directness and effectiveness of dialetic, a deliberateness of decision, a decided and determined devotion to duty as interpreted and understood, a carefulness of choice, a volume of wholesome volition, a code of conduct, all conspiring to discover and completely controlled by the divine will—in brief, a perfection of personal piety that stands unique in the history of religious experience.

The threefold temptation belongs to the religion of Jesus; in it the real religiousness of his self-consciousness appears with special clearness. It is a religious experience, or series of religious experiences, from the very depths of his soul. Here we come unusually near the very pulse of his personal piety. We see that the whole of his life and thought is dominated by just one thing— loyalty and obedience to the divine will. Throughout the threefold test we see Jesus deliberately choosing the will and way of God, controlling his conduct in accordance with this choice. All three temptations seem to be distinctly messianic, raising Jesus' thought for himself to the highest heights. Yet in and through such an exalted experience Jesus remains religious. His thoughts and attitudes never transcend the limitations of the religious consciousness. Even when faced with the possibilities of his person in the divine plan and purpose, he still seeks the divine will for himself and acts according to the fundamental principles of the purest piety. The threefold temptation is a religious triumph, or series of religious triumphs, achieved by Jesus. In fact, such is the principal point to the whole of the account in Matthew and Luke. This profound religiousness of Jesus must have had its roots in the firm bed-rock of historical fact, for even in such a highly Christianized scene as Matthew and Luke depict, the fundamentals of Jesus' personal piety break through upon us like a great light from another world.

This religiousness of Jesus' reactions is clearest in the threefold temptation, but it is also unmistakable in the messianic matter of Mark. Jesus' commands for silence, whether to demoniacs or to disciples, rested upon a broader basis than public or private messianic confessions. If these confessions are historical, the commands for silence have a deeper source than a dogma of Mark or a personal caution of Jesus. They sprang spontaneously from the depths of his religious consciousness. If we accept all the messianic confessions as historical just as Mark reports them, which we may without introducing a dogma, we meet in Jesus' commands for silence that spontaneous revolt, that instinctive recoil, of the really religious consciousness that has committed itself without reserve to the quest and performance of the divine will.

Jesus' reaction to the request of the sons of Zebedee is religious. In reply to their request for reservations on his right and left we meet with one of the finest expressions that can come from the religious consciousness,

"To sit on my right hand or on *my* left hand is not mine to give; but *it is for them* for whom it hath been prepared." (Mark 10,40.)

Jesus' reaction to the question of the high priest is just as deeply religious. If we regard his "I am" as an open affirmative, we are still confronted with the deeply religious view which he takes of his own person. His word,

"Ye shall see the Son of man sitting at the right hand of Power, and coming with the clouds of heaven" (Mark 14,62b),

is a final declaration of the apocalyptic faith that has held him from the first and it lays bare the heart of the personal religious hope that held him to the last.

If we inquire into Jesus' estimate of himself, we shall have to say that, like all great prophets and preachers of religion, his own person remains completely in the background. In the foreground of his thought stands the divine cause which he champions and which consumes him so completely that he has no thought for himself except as facts which he is forced to face and as experiences through which he passes compel him to reckon with the divine plan for his own person.

"Jesus' messianic consciousness, *if* he possessed such, was his own private and personal problem. Its solution and issue never altered substantially the content of his message, although it greatly increased the divine demands upon himself. The prominence of the part that he was to play in the final realization of the kingdom of God never caused him to parade his person and to neglect his cause and calling as a preacher and prophet of that kingdom . . . It was only most rarely, reluctantly and reservedly that he spoke of himself. Even the highest pretentions regarding the personal rôle that was destined for him in the future were subjected and subordinated to the divine will. Whatever may have been its content, Jesus subjects his self-consciousness to the most conscientious control. He seems to have felt restricted and restrained rather than refreshed and rejuvenated by any such possibilities. It pressed him apart for prayer and petition rather than encouraged him to elusive enterprises and augmented aggressiveness. He did not rush ruthlessly ahead, but moved with caution, seeking clearness and certainty, awaiting the divine direction . . . Jesus' self-consciousness, *if* messianic, appears less in the form of a claim for himself, more in the form of a concession to the divine will."[34]

With all the exalted elevation which such a conviction involved we see that Jesus kept it strictly on the level of religion; with great care and caution he never allows it to transcend or to destroy his deeply religious consciousness. For a weaker nature, the messianic possibility would have resulted in the complete collapse of the religious consciousness.

Jesus' self-estimate never comes clearly to view. It remains, as he chose that it should, his own private matter. The sense in which he held himself to be the Messiah is nowhere exactly clear, whether present or future, now or then. In fact, we are not sure that Jesus came to regard himself as the Messiah at all.[35] If he did face

[34]Bundy, *The Psychic Health of Jesus*, p. 221f., 223.

[35]The more I study the messianic possibility in the experience of Jesus, the more I am convinced that he was faced with this issue. Perhaps the twelve confronted him with it. (Mark 8,27-30.) Judas may have betrayed the messianic conviction of the twelve. (Mark

the messianic issue for himself, as it seems to me that he must have, we are not in a position to say how he solved it; the sources are too vacillating. However, we may say that the messianic issue, in whatever form it presented itself to Jesus, was not for him a general problem of calling and career. It was a purely personal problem of his innermost life which he fought out in that *sanctum sanctorum* where man stands alone in the presence of his Maker. Into this private precinct we may not press our way, but we are permitted to know that Jesus, in the messianic issue as in all other issues, did bare his soul to God in simple, yet sublime submission and self-surrender. And this is enough, all that we are in need of knowing.

In conclusion on the messianic issue, we may say that it is just at this point that the genuine religiousness of Jesus' consciousness strikes us with full force. Jesus was all that he was by religious conviction. He took a strictly religious attitude toward his own person. His supreme aspiration is religious—the discovery and performance of the divine will.

THE PASSION PATH

The problem of his personal fate is the last of the three problems that we have singled out, and it was the last to confront Jesus. The issue of cures or cause set upon him as the outcome of his first day in public, and

14,10-11.) In all probability the Jewish trial hinged upon it. (Mark 14,55-64.) Certainly, on the basis of the threefold temptation, we may say that the messianic issue must have torn at the very roots of his soul. (Matt. 4,1-11; Luke 4,1-13.) But I am also equally convinced for myself that, whatever the source of this strange suggestion, Jesus rejected the messiahship outright—a rejection that preserved the health of his mind and the integrity of his relation to his God.

the messianic issue became critical for him only toward the close of the Galilean days. The Synoptic writers begin to give full and sustained attention to Jesus' fate only after Simon's confession at Cæsarea Philippi. (Mark 8,27-30.) However, there is an early passage in Mark which many students regard as a sort of veiled prophecy of the passion; it comes in the midst of one of Jesus' contentions with his Galilean opponents:

"And John's disciples and the Pharisees were fasting: and they come and say unto him, Why do John's disciples and the disciples of the Pharisees fast, but thy disciples fast not? 19 And Jesus said unto them, Can the sons of the bridechamber fast, while the bridegroom is with them? as long as they have the bridegroom with them, they can not fast. 20 But the days will come, when the bridegroom shall be taken away from them, and then will they fast in that day." (Mark 2,18-20.)

This is a clear allusion to Jesus' death; however, there is no real reason for regarding it as genuine. The issue is really settled in Mark 2,19a where Jesus' question leaves nothing more to be said, and this genuine parable is too much to the point to require the exposition in 2,19b-20. Verse 19b is a later Christian elaboration of this parable, to which Matthew and Luke have no parallel.[36] Verse 20 is not from the lips of Jesus but is a later Christian exposition of his parable in 19a, written in the light of the deep depression that possessed the disciples at his death.

[36]Cf. Matt. 9,14-15; Luke 5,33-35.

Jesus' Forecasts of His Fate

Beginning with the confession at Cæsarea Philippi, the forecasts of Jesus' fate appear with a systematic regularity. In the first three Gospels there are three periodic prophecies of the passion.

"And he began to teach them that the Son of man must suffer many things, and be rejected by the elders, and the chief priests, and the scribes, and be killed, and after three days rise again." (Mark 8,31.)

"For he taught his disciples, and said unto them, The Son of man is delivered up into the hands of men, and they shall kill him; and when he is killed, after three days he shall rise again." (Mark 9,31.)

"Behold, we go up to Jerusalem; and the Son of man shall be delivered unto the chief priests and the scribes; and they shall condemn him to death, and shall deliver him unto the Gentiles: and they shall mock him, and shall spit upon him, and shall scourge him, and shall kill him; and after three days he shall rise again."[37]   (Mark 10,33-34.)

For the casual reader of Mark's story these three prophecies of the passion are clear enough, for he reads as Mark wrote—in the light of the events of the passion week itself. But when we seek to reset ourselves in the situation of Jesus and the disciples during the last weeks, these prophecies of the passion create all sorts of historical and psychological difficulties. They are unhistorical for the following reasons:

---

[37]Other forecasts of a similar character are found in Luke 17,25; Matt. 17,9; Mark 9,9; Matt. 17,12b; Mark 9,12; Matt. 27,63.

In the first place, all three are cold and formal and, in the light of other words and scenes, the historical student can not imagine Jesus forecasting his fate in any such indifferent fashion.

In the second place, the systematic regularity of their appearance speaks against them as actual allusions of Jesus to his approaching death. This periodic element shows clearly that they are a part of Mark's program in preparing his readers for the catastrophe that is soon to come. They are really foreign to the actual dramatic developments that bring Jesus to the cross.

In the third place, all three are made up of details from the passion story itself and are written in the light of what has already taken place. All three look back on the passion story as closed. The third prophecy in Mark is really a miniature passion narrative.

In the fourth place, in the course of the three forecasts there is no growth in the understanding of the disciples. In fact, there is an anticlimax in the state of the disciples' mind; they become increasingly dull as the prophecies progress. They understand Jesus' first forecast so well that Peter undertakes to rebuke him for the thought and to turn him from the passion path. (Mark 8,32-33.) But the disciples' reaction to the second prophecy is a surprising lack of understanding and courage,

"But they understood not the saying, and were afraid to ask him." (Mark 9,32.)

The first two prophecies fall late in Galilee, but the third comes when they are well on the way to Jerusalem. To the third, Mark reports no reaction of the disciples, but Luke adds,

"And they understood none of these things; and this saying was hid from them, and they perceived not the things that were said."   (18,34.)

The historical fact seems to be that the disciples arrived in Jerusalem unconvinced of the necessity of Jesus' death, as the three prophecies were supposed to convince them. Whatever Jesus' words to his disciples regarding his fate may have been, it is quite clear that the disciples were not prepared for the event itself, and that his death left them in a state of hopeless despondency. *They had hoped . . . but . . .* (Luke 24,21.)

In the fifth place, these prophecies do not prepare Jesus himself for his fate. After reading these three feelingless forecasts, we might expect him to go to his death unflinchingly and unfalteringly. But the severest struggle regarding his fate overtakes him on the last night of his life when the authorities are already on the way to arrest him. It is only in the very last hours that the full weight of the issue strikes him down to his knees.

In the sixth place, these three prophecies of the passion reflect nothing of the turbulent state of soul in which Jesus faced his fate. All three are devoid of those emotional elements that we find in the Gethsemane scene where the issue is unmistakable. All three are impersonal, betraying nothing of the severe struggle through which Jesus passed on the way to the cross. The tense personal elements are gone.

The three prophecies of the passion are of Christian origin and they belong to early Christian apologetics. They are one early Christian way of saying that Jesus' death did not take him by surprise, that his fate was not the result of a curious chain of circumstances, that he was not the victim of chance or accident, that he went consciously and willingly to his end. All three present the Christian view of Jesus' approach to his fate rather than the painful path which Jesus actually traversed. Their present position and arrangement in the Gospel story is the editorial work of Mark who is preparing his readers for the thing that came to the disciples with a shock and that threw Jesus himself into the throes of severest struggle down to the very last.

We do possess in the first three Gospels, I believe, the historical forecast with which Jesus referred to his approaching fate. There is only one such forecast. It comes on the way to Jerusalem. In it Jesus alludes to his fate in only the most general way, giving no details that suggest a review of the passion week, and employing a double figure—the cup and the baptism. The text of Mark reads,

"Are ye able to drink the cup that I drink? or to be baptized with the baptism that I am baptized with?" (Mark 10,38b.)[38]

That this figurative forecast is historical is clear for the following reasons:

In the first place, it comes in the form of figures, and such figurative language is characteristic of Jesus.

In the second place, on the last night of his life, in Gethsemane, Jesus makes an unmistakable allusion to his death in the figure of the cup. (Mark 14,36.)

---

[38]Matthew in his parallel passage has only the figure of the cup. (20,22b.) Luke also has but one of the two figures, that of the baptism, from another source. (12,50.)

In the third place, both figures contain a strong per-sonal element; both reflect an intense state of soul; they are not unfeeling and formal, but spontaneous outbursts of a severe inner struggle such as we find in Gethsemane where Jesus is torn by the strongest emotions. This tense emotional element is especially clear in Luke's form of this forecast,

"But I have a baptism to be baptized with; and how am I straitened till it be accomplished." (12,50.)

Jesus' Aspiration in Death

When and where and under what conditions the thought of a violent death came to Jesus we are not in a position to say. Toward the close of the Galilean days his thought seems to be developing out in a new direc-tion; a new and tragic note finds its way into his words to the twelve, and he strikes in on a new course of action— the journey to Jerusalem. The one unmistakable fore-cast of his fate comes on the way to the Holy City (Mark 10,38), and we may be sure that Jesus went up to the Passover with the thought of a fatal issue in his mind.

Mark strikes upon the natural psychological moment for the introduction of this tragic element when he has Jesus first forecast his fate as a part of his response to Simon's confession of his messiahship. Mark interprets Jesus' attitude as affirmative: He is the Messiah, but he is the suffering Messiah. This was the later Christian method of reconciling Jesus' death with his messiahship, a solution that very probably never crossed the mind of Jesus himself. There was nothing in messianic tradition to suggest to Jesus the possibility of a fatal outcome. It was only during the first and second decades after his death that the early Christians found an Old Testament basis on which to set the facts. (Isaiah 53.) But there is no indication that Jesus himself so understood Isaiah 53, or that a similar understanding was entertained by the twelve or any of Jesus' contemporaries during his lifetime.

The thought of a violent end appears more as a personal religious intuition of Jesus. How he came by it we do not know. He seems to have kept it well submerged in his own mind except when the inner pressure became too great and it forced itself to the surface as in Luke 12,50 and in Gethsemane. These spontaneous outbursts show that it was deeply personal, and Jesus seems to have made no systematic effort to prepare his disciples in the event that his intuition should materialize.

The thought of a tragic fate in the mind of Jesus was not a fixed idea; he was not determined upon his death, as Schweitzer portrays. His prayer in Gethsemane shows clearly enough that he reckoned with his fate as highly probable, yet as still tentative. Down to the last twenty-four hours he seems to consider the whole issue as not yet closed, as still open to the divine revision. He seems to leave Gethsemane in the conviction that he must die; he is clear and certain; he faces his end with a magnificent calm and courage; yet with his latest breath in Mark (15,34) we see him struggling with his God.

The problem of his fate was for Jesus far more than a question of living or dying. It was an issue that moved in the super-ranges of religious experience. Jesus' desire is neither to die nor to live. His single aspiration is to discover the divine will for himself and to mobilize the morale necessary to meet the divine demands placed upon him. The veil drops only twice, but each time we are permitted a fleeting glance into the very depths of his religious consciousness. In Mark 8,33, when Simon would turn him from the passion path, Jesus replies,

"Thou mindest not the things of God, but the things of men."

And in the Gethsemane prayer we see the utter religiousness of Jesus' feeling on this point; a single religious aspiration holds him to the very last—the discovery and performance of the divine will,

"Abba, Father, all things are possible unto thee; remove this cup from me: howbeit not what I will, but what thou wilt."   (Mark 14,36.)

In such a scene our vision is lifted to the most exalted heights of religious aspiration. We witness a state of soul that places its own fates and fortunes in the divine hand that has claimed and commissioned it to the championship of the divine cause at all costs. In Jesus' Gethsemane submission we strike upon that rare element in religious experience, an element too delicate and fine for the religious senses of a prosaic piety—the experience of God as Holy Will.[39] It appears sporadically in specially sensitive souls of whom Jesus is the rarest. When it does appear it is less for our imitation, more for our

---

[39]We strike a strain of this in the religious experience of Sadhu Sundar Singh: "If I have left India to come into Tibet on His behalf to claim souls for Him, it is not a great thing to do; but if I had not come, it would have been a dreadful thing, for this is the divine command." (Parker, *Sadhu Sundar Singh*, p. 130).

illumination, and we feel that for this moment at least we have stood directly in the presence of the Divine.

We have discussed the pressing personal problems of Jesus—cures and cause, the messianic issue and the problem of the passion path. However, these three problems may not be separated the one from the other or divorced from the total body of Jesus' religious experience. They are simply three different phases of the quest of a super-soul that was in every sense an organic unity. They were not unconnected in his experience. Two of them may have set upon him at the same time, or the solution of one may have led to the appearance of the other. Jesus' cures on his first day in public may have forced him to think of himself. (Mark 1,21-38.) He began the day in the consciousness and conviction that he was the called prophet, the commissioned preacher, of the kingdom of God. It was this consciousness and conviction that brought him to this day. But with the appearance of his extraordinary endowments and equipments his person may have become problematic for him. His cures may have thrown a new light on his person, and henceforth he may have been forced to reckon increasingly with the possibilities of his person in the divine plan and purpose.

The exact subject-matter of the divine will for himself concerning which Jesus struggled through to clearness and certainty and final triumph is nowhere explicitly given, and we are not sufficiently informed to define it in detail. There are four possibilities on the basis of the meager materials furnished us by the first three Gospels: first, that Jesus at some time or other became convinced that he was God's chosen Messiah; second, that he sooner or later became convinced that he was to be

the Messiah in that glorious future when God would
intervene and establish His kingdom; third, that Jesus
rejected the messianic idea utterly; fourth, that Jesus
toward the close of the Galilean days learned, we know
not how, that he must serve God to the very end and die
a martyr to the divine cause. We can only conjecture.
There may have been a combination of the messianic
issue with the problem of a tragic fate in Jesus' understanding of the divine will for himself. (All we know
with any measure of certainty is that Jesus sought to
learn and did perform the divine will, and as long as this
fundamental fact is clearly established in the Gospel account nothing else matters greatly, at least from the
standpoint of our own practical piety and the tasks that
such an example sets before us.)

The problems of Jesus were peculiar to his own personal experience. In the concrete, they are not problems
that confront the average run of men. Cures and cause,
the messianic issue and the facing of a tragic fate transcend the temptations that beset the ordinary type of
piety. Such issues are peculiar to the calling and commission of Jesus, but it is just in their peculiarity that they
have their special pointedness for his followers. All of
Jesus' personal problems are moral in that they involve
his character and conduct, and they are fundamentally
religious in that they involve the quest and performance
of the divine will. His personal problems move on a
high plane often demanding a choice between two *goods*,
as the choice between healing and preaching as the essence of his mission. Their exalted character seems to
carry them far above our prosaic piety that must forge
its religious life between the fires of good and evil. But
fundamentally, his personal problems are characteristic

of the genuinely religious consciousness wherever and whenever it appears—the quest and performance of the divine will. Their exalted character does not strip them of their real religiousness, and in their essential content they put Jesus for ever on the side of struggling human beings who seek to know their Maker.

It will stand for ever as the glory of the writers of the first three Gospels that they, with all of their enthusiastic and devoted faith, never rob Jesus of his deeply religious consciousness but present it, unconsciously to be sure, as the constant and unbroken continuity in all that he says and does.

CHAPTER V

Visions and Voices[1]

IN THE EXPERIENCE OF THE RELIGIOUS GENIUS

THE religion of some great men goes back to a single, outstanding experience. In the heat of one great moment, with a single blow, their hitherto indistinct and submerged desires, hopes, premonitions, personal possibilities and probabilities are welded into a solid substance of soul. They may bring with them their individual constitution, the essential elements of their training, the traditions of their past; the atmosphere of their previous life may remain with them, but the distinctive features of their personal religion are given, once for all, with this great upheaval that revolutionizes, completely changes, the whole of their life. These moments draw a sharp and distinct line that divides the old from the new, the past from the present; there is a clear consciousness of antithesis between what once was and what now is; henceforth everything dates before or after this great hour. The contribution of this striking experience is so solid and substantial that the subject feels that the whole of his life has been changed; he has become a new creature.

No student of the psychology of religious experience

---

[1]For an especially fine discussion of this problem, *see:* Wilhelm Mundle, *Die religioesen Erlebnisse: Ihr Sinn und ihre Eigenart. Ein Beitrag zur Frage nach dem Wesen der Religion.*

questions the reality of these experiences for the subject, nor does he question the contribution made by them to the life of the subject himself. The psychologist will not name these experiences as the subject does, nor will he ascribe to them the same origin. But, for both the subject and his psychologist, the change has taken place. The subject does experience a fresh and new content of religious consciousness. Certain old elements are expelled for ever, and such old elements as remain lose control of the subject's life and fall into the background. The subject feels that a whole new realm of religious values, hitherto unsuspected, is opened up to him and has become his very own. The former objects of his faith often turn into nothingness, new objects of religious reverence take their place, and, if they do not supplant the old objects entirely, they take their place beside the old as equally commanding, and usually the new predominates over the old. This one great moment results for the subject in the erection of a new set of religious standards and authorities. The subject is amazed at his former blindness, for with the new insight the old standards and authorities appear as hopelessly inadequate. The whole of his life is trained on a new objective. In brief, the character and content of this single experience becomes the center, the polar and pivotal point, about which the subject's life henceforth turns. It becomes the key to his personality, to all the principal elements in his subsequent career.

These great religious moments, in their higher forms, are usually exalted ecstatic states of consciousness in which the subject enters into a world of experience quite foreign to that of every-day life. There are visions and voices that make very clear communications to the subject. In such moments of high revelation very definite disclosures of divine origin and content are made. God is revealing His plan and purpose to the experient; it is His call to His chosen champion. These moments, for the great geniuses of religion, are more than just calls in general; in them the subject receives his commission to a very definite task; he receives the message which he, in turn, is to bring to his contemporaries. The experience ends, sooner or later, with complete clearness on the part of the subject with regard to what he is to do and to say for God. This divine call usually includes a personal response on the part of the subject; often it comes in the form of a prompt acquiescence, but in some cases the subject utters a protest based on various difficulties in the way of his acceptance and he must be persuaded or convinced. But, almost without exception, there is a response of some sort.

There is usually just one such experience in the subject's life. Sometimes it has its less pretentious forerunners, and often it is followed by others less significant. But the one great experience is usually initial and inaugural, imparting something new, original and different. It clears up any preceding premonitions of a similar character, and it is never wholly eclipsed by other great moments that may follow. Subsequent experiences of similar character usually have a more local significance. They are often numerous and come at critical junctures to determine the subject's decisions, to control his conduct in particular instances of momentary emergency. But these subsequent visitations are always subservient to the initial experience, and they usually tend to reinforce the subject's confidence in it. It continues to stand out as the one great milestone and norm by which the subject tests and measures the whole of his life. This one great experience becomes a source of almost inexhaustible personal power of which the subject was formerly incapable. The experience usually generates within the subject a set of religious convictions and certainties that never leave him. He may meet with discouragement and disappointment, he may struggle in dire distress, he may go straight through to disaster, but the confidence born in the initial vision, if he is true to the type, carries him through to religious triumph.

This initial experience is of greatest personal importance for the subject in the accomplishment of his work. It becomes a part of his message, and it reveals its importance for the subject both in the frequency and in the relish with which he recounts it. On all critical occasions he recites it with full detail, or refers to it in an unmistakable way. When he meets with question or opposition in his work, he rehearses it as the divine credential of his call and career. This great experience has left no doubt in his mind concerning the divine truth revealed. If it has convinced him once for all, why should not the recital of this great moment convince others and win them to the cause he champions, both friend and foe? Thus the confession of personal religious experience becomes, for the great geniuses, a source and means of religious conviction for others, who have not shared in such exalted moments.

IN THE RELIGIOUS EXPERIENCE OF ISRAEL'S PROPHETS

Visions and auditions, heavenly elevations of spirit and ecstatic states, are the normal experiences of the Old Testament prophets.[2] The accounts of such experiences

---

[2]For an especially fine and scientific discussion of the psychic phases of the prophetic personality, *see* Professor Gustav Hoelscher's work, *Die Profeten: Untersuchungen zur Religionsgeschichte Israels.*

are so numerous that even the casual reader of the prophetic writings can not fail to notice them. Whole sections of Amos, Ezekiel and Zechariah present the
prophetic message in long series of visions. Some of this
extensive visionary matter may be literary style, but all
of it goes to prove the prophets' familiarity with the
visionary type of experience, and the intimate detail in
these sections points quite naturally to a personal participation on the part of the prophet. But in practically
every prophetic writing we find visionary matter presented as the prophet's personal experience. It is more
prominent in some than it is in others, but in no great
prophet is the visionary and ecstatic constitution entirely
missing. Visions with a prophet like Ezekiel take on a
pathological phase; his psychic states result in a temporary physiological, partial or total, paralysis. (3,15-
16 25-26; 4,4-8.) Even in a prophet like Jeremiah,
in whom we see the first conscious effort to suppress the
ecstatic element in personal religious experience, ecstasy
is still so strong as to suggest hallucination.[3] But even
in those prophets where the ecstatic element recedes, we
usually have from them the account of the great visionary
moment of their call.

Among the prophets who recount the occasion of
their call to a career for God, that of Amos is the most
prosaic and is unusually brief as compared with some of
his great colleagues.

"I was no prophet, neither was I a prophet's son;
but I was a herdsman, and a dresser of sycamore-trees:
and Jehovah took me from following the flock, and

---

[3]Cf. Jer. 3,21; 4,13 15 18-21 23-26 31; 8,16 19-20; 10,22, etc.

Jehovah said unto me, Go prophesy unto my people
Israel." (7,14-15.)

Amos does not go into detail with regard to this great
moment in his life, but it is clear enough that he receives
a very definite call to the career of a prophet. For Amos
it was an unexpected turning-point in his life, and he em-
phasizes the fact that he is a prophet by divine call, not
a prophet by profession. It is also important to note
that he recounts the moment of his call in his conflict with
Amaziah, the priest of Bethel (7,10-13), as the credential for his commission to a prophetic career in Israel.
That this moment was the birthplace of unusual personal
power, conviction and certainty is clear in Amos' classic
word on prophetic pressure (3,8):

"The lion hath roared; who will not fear. The
Lord Jehovah hath spoken; who can but prophesy?"

The most elaborate account of a prophetic call is that
of Ezekiel (1-3), a series of visions that bring the
prophet into public equipped down to the last detail, not
only with regard to his mission and message in general,
but concerning definite and single acts which he is to
execute. This vision, or series of visions, that gave
Ezekiel his call (*Berufungsvision*) has more the form of
a personal religious confession.

In the account of his call Isaiah (6,1-13) gives full
detail concerning the vision, especially concerning his own
personal reactions. In this vision Isaiah receives his call,
a concrete commission to a definite task, the specific message he is to deliver, and a further important detail is
Isaiah's personal response to the divine call,

"Here am I; send me."

That it was a moment of inrush of great personal power
is clear in his figure of the live coal from the altar placed
on his lips.

Jeremiah recounts his call at the very beginning of his
book, and the rather general habit of the prophets in
opening their writings with the account of their call and
commission in a vision makes it clear that they present
it as their prophetic credential. Jeremiah's call takes on
the form of two visions in rapid succession which furnish
him with all that he is to do and to say; it is very definite
and concrete in its instructions. To this divine call Jeremiah at first responds with a personal protest,

"Ah, Lord Jehovah! behold, I know not how to
speak; for I am a child." (1,6.)

But this lack of self-confidence is overcome by the touch
of the divine hand, and henceforth Jeremiah is the fear-
less champion of Jehovah, a prophet of the highest order.

The call of the sixth-century Isaiah we have in Isaiah
40,6-8. It is typical and characteristic—a voice in a
vision, a call, a commission and a personal response on
the part of the prophet.

The ecstatic and visionary element belongs to the very
nerve and fiber of Israel's great eighth- and sixth-century
prophets. It was a vital and integral element in the prophetic constitution and genius. Almost without exception, the prophets of Israel had their visionary calls, clear
communications from Jehovah, disclosures of the divine
plan and purpose, inspired impartations of message, com-
missions to definite tasks for God in behalf of His people.

These moments were for the prophets unfailing springs of personal power; they resulted in an inner psychic pressure that drove them to their tasks and that carried them through, a pressure that was even painful at times, for the hand of Jehovah was heavy upon them.[4] These inaugural experiences furnished them with conviction, certainty and courage. When the day is black for the professional prophet, and the seers and diviners cover their lips, Micah speaks out of his own personal experience,

"But as for me, I am full of power by the spirit of Jehovah, of judgment, and of might, to declare unto Jacob his transgression, and to Israel his sin." (3,8.)

The ecstatic element is more or less constant in the career of the individual prophet. Various subsequent visions, often very numerous, instruct them to carry out special things, and tell them how to act, what to do and to say in particular instances. Often these subsequent visions result in an alteration either of the subject-matter or the tone, or both, of the prophet's message. Always, for the prophets, their visions and voices are a vital part of their messages, and the inaugural vision is always for them the confirmation of their credentials to the prophetic commission and career. Such experiences are the source-springs of their personal piety and religion, and almost without exception the Old Testament prophets, fortunately for us in our study of them, have the habit of self-revelation. Without hesitation, they disclose

[4]Cf. Isa. 8,11; Jer. 4,19; 6,11; 20,8-9; Ezek. 1,3; 3,14 22; 8,1; 37,1; 40,1.

their most intimate religious experiences either as **credentials or as personal religious confessions.**[5]

IN THE CHRISTIAN EXPERIENCE OF PAUL

Before turning to Jesus to determine the rôle which the visionary and ecstatic element of the prophetic genius played in his religious experience, it is necessary to sketch the psychic phases of Paul's piety. A comparative study of Paul and Jesus in this respect is too instructive to be omitted. It is instructive, not only because of the light it throws on Jesus, but also because we possess relatively extensive materials on Paul. The major part of the book of Acts is devoted to Paul's Christian career in the East, and we have a number of Paul's own letters which contain many spontaneous testimonials fresh from his own personal religious experience. Paul had the habit of self-revelation when some occasion called such forth in a natural way, or when a situation demanded a purely personal statement.

In the history of religious genius it would be difficult to find a man whose religious life centered so completely on one great moment, and in whose religious experience the visionary and ecstatic element played a more prominent rôle than in the Christian life and experience of Paul, that is, if we remain within the borders of healthy-mindedness.[6] The whole of Paul's Christianity, his entire faith in Christ, rests upon a single experience, a

---

[5]This inclination toward personal religious confession is clearest and strongest in Jeremiah; see 11,18*ff*.; 12,1*ff*.; 15,9-10; 17,12-28; 18,18*ff*.; 20,7-18.

[6]For a recent study of Paul, especially fine in its analysis and appreciation of his personal religious experience, see Wilhelm Mundle, *Das religioese Leben des Apostels Paulus.*

heavenly vision on the Damascus road before the gates of the city. (Acts 9,1-10.) The Damascus experience is the keystone of Paul's Christian life and consciousness; if we remove it, the whole structure of his faith tumbles down. It was in this high hour that the conflicting forces within his religious life, of which he was keenly conscious and which caused him deep inner distress, were forged into a single solid substance.

Certain of the pre-Damascus phases of Paul's religion remained with him: his faith in the living God of Israel, his glowing passion for religion, his intolerance for faiths at variance with his own, his reverence for his people's Scriptures, the messianic hope, and so forth. But these old elements that were retained were seen in a new light, enriched and enhanced, or they were given a new objective and endowed with a new power. In his Christian life, Paul remained a Hellenistic Jew in training, thought and temperament; but the whole of his life was thrown into a religious channel that carried him away for ever from Judaism. The Damascus experience brought a very definite break in his religious life; it drew a sharp line of division between the old and the new.

"The old things are passed away; behold, they are become new." (II Cor. 5,17b.)

"The principal orientation points of his life, his general disposition in matters of religion remained the same for Paul the Jew and for Paul the Christian. But his life acquired a new center and between the two worlds, that of the Jew and that of the Christian, there yawned a deep chasm that was fixed and unbridgeable."[7]

---

[7] Mundle, *Das religioese Leben des Apostels Paulus*, p. 60.

The contribution of this one moment of experience was so solid and substantial that Paul felt his whole life changed both in character and in content. He had become a new creature. (II Cor. 5,17a.) This one experience resulted in a new content of consciousness—in Paul's own words,

"It is no longer I that live, but Christ liveth in me." (Gal. 2,20.)

It would be difficult to imagine a more radical revolution in a healthy consciousness. Paul regarded "his call to Christ as a dissolution of his old ego which was replaced by a new ego which Paul identified with Christ Himself."[8]

For Paul the Damascus experience meant the disclosure of a whole new realm of religious values which, in turn, resulted in the depreciation of things formerly held as central. A new object of religious faith presented itself to him, as clear as it was commanding. Christ, in the faith of Paul, becomes a religious object in the full sense of the term, exalted at the right hand of God. His conversion resulted in the erection of a new set and standard of religious authorities. Faith in Christ came to supplant the law, and what Paul formerly had regarded as the crown of Israel's religious life became its curse. Paul's vision on the Damascus road gave a new objective to the whole of his life, an objective that required a complete reversal from persecutor to propagandist.

The Damascus experience was for Paul a clear communication, a concrete commission to a definite task. It

[8]Bundy, *The Psychic Health of Jesus*, p. 230.

was this clear consciousness of call and commission that gave him the courage to carry on in spite of every obstacle and hindrance. It was a perennial source of personal power, and when his gospel to the Gentiles is called in question Paul ascribes to it a divine origin,

"Neither did I receive it from man, nor was I taught it, but it *came to me* through the revelation of Jesus Christ." (Gal. 1,12.)

Thus the Damascus vision becomes the key to the whole of Paul's Christian career. It was the birthplace of his new faith, the ground of all his religious certainty and conviction. His Damascus experience became a vital part of his Christian message. He recounts it frequently both as personal religious confession and as the credential of his call and commission.[9] The opening greeting of nearly every letter of Paul contains a reference to, one often feels, an emphasis upon, his divine call.

The Damascus vision was not the only striking psychic visitation that came to Paul. Both in the Acts account and in his letters we see that he had many such experiences—dreams, trances, visions, voices, revelations and states of ecstasy. Paul himself speaks of the "exceeding greatness of the revelations" (II Cor. 12,7) that have been his. Some are of a highly ecstatic character; he is caught up into the third heaven, sees visions, hears voices, in a state of lost bodily consciousness. (II Cor. 12,2-4.) Voices break into his prayer-life. (II Cor. 12, 8-9.)

Paul seems to have been quite dependent on these sub-

[9]Cf. Acts 22,6-11; 26,12-19; I Cor. 9,1; 15,8; II Cor. 4,6; 12,1; Gal. 1,16-17; Eph. 3,3; Phil. 3,12.

sequent experiences for light and strength; he ascribes
great importance to them. He often acts according to
their indications; they determine his decisions at important junctures in his career; they control his conduct,
impart his messages and bring personal reassurance in
particular instances. He carries his message to European
soil for the first time in response to a vision. (Acts 16,
9-10.) In Corinth a vision reassures and encourages
him. (Acts 18,9-10.) In Jerusalem he falls into a
trance and is warned to flee from the city. (Acts 22,17-
21.) In the Roman quarters there, while a prisoner, a
vision forecasts his journey to Rome. (Acts 23,11.)
In the midst of the storm at sea a vision assures him of
safety for himself and all on board. (Acts 27,23-24.)
According to his own word, it was by revelation that he
went up to Jerusalem to defend his gospel. (Gal. 2,2.)
But with all their frequency and importance these subsequent visions and ecstatic states never dimmed the
original revelation on the Damascus road; rather they
reinforced it and sustained all that Paul had won from
it. In the distinctive elements of his religious experience
we may say, and without exaggeration, that Paul was the
man of a moment.

IN THE RELIGIOUS EXPERIENCE OF JESUS

Upon turning to the religious experience of Jesus for
the discovery of visionary and ecstatic elements such as
belong to the genius of the prophets and Paul, we find
that all of the first three Gospels writers ascribe such
experiences to him.[10] These visionary elements are not

---

[10]For a complete list of these materials and a discussion of the
pathological problem connected with them, *see* Bundy, *The Psychic
Health of Jesus*, pp. 206-213.

extensive and are limited to two or three principal scenes in Jesus' life.

Some of this material is so patently legendary that it may be dismissed at once without discussion. Such is the case with the vision which Luke ascribes to Jesus in the Gethsemane struggle. (22,43.) Matthew and Mark, who give much fuller detail in their accounts of the Gethsemane scene, have no such vision, and in even the best manuscripts of Luke verses 43 and 44 are missing. The appearance of the angel and the sweating of blood are later legendary additions.

A special body of visionary and ecstatic materials may be grouped together as Satan scenes—the series of three in the temptation of Matthew (4 1-11) and Luke (4,1-13), and a word of Jesus found only in Luke,

"I beheld Satan fallen as lightning from heaven." (10,18.)

The threefold temptation with its spirit that drives or leads, with the period of fasting, the appearance of angels, wild beasts (Mark) and Satan, with its fantastic shifts of scene, with its dramatic developments in dialogue, suggests at once the visionary and ecstatic type of experience. But when we consider the fact that Mark does not present these experiences in visionary form, yet has Jesus in these very dilemmas, facing these same problems, reaching identical conclusions, however, in actual historical situations in which he finds himself, then we begin to doubt the visionary nature of the threefold temptation.

Mark has historical parallels to all three temptations, but in Mark these experiences are just plain, prosaic struggles of Jesus devoid of all ecstatic and visionary elements. Further, if we leave Mark's historical parallels out of consideration and confine our attention to the three temptations as such, we find that the rational (Jesus' reflection, soundness of judgment and clearness of conception) and ethical (Jesus' choices and decisions) elements are so strong that the ecstatic element is suppressed entirely. Even Professor Holtzmann, who has sought to establish the ecstatic type of experience as an essential feature in Jesus' personality, is forced to admit that the temptation ends, not with an augmentation of the ecstatic element, as is typical of this psychology, but with its suppression,[11] and, we might add, with its elimination. At best the three temptations are visionary in form only; they are not visionary in content. We realize how widely they are separated from genuine visionary and ecstatic states when we compare them with Ezekiel's inaugural vision (1-3) or with Paul's visit to the third heaven in II Cor. 12,2-4.

In the fourth Satan passage (Luke 10,18) Jesus says to his disciples as they return from their mission, highly elated over their successes,

"I beheld Satan fallen as lightning from heaven."

Because of his use of the word "beheld," not a few students of the life of Jesus have concluded that in this brief statement he is rehearsing or referring to some personal visionary experience. But the very brevity of Jesus' statement is against a visionary or ecstatic state. The seer and ecstatic are never satisfied with such a simple

---

[11]See Professor O. Holtzmann's interesting study, *War Jesus Ekstatiker?*

sentence; they go into the most elaborate descriptive detail and build up a great scenic structure. Their interest centers even more on the form of the experience than on its content. Jesus' simple statement here gives only the bare substance of a personal religious conviction in figurative language.

For Jesus, Satan was as real as for any of his contemporaries. Satan was the source of the physical ills, the psychic afflictions and the moral evil in man's life, and Jesus often speaks of Satan as such. In the contention concerning the source of his power to cure the ailments with which Satan had afflicted men, Jesus says:

"How can Satan cast out Satan? . . . If Satan hath risen up against himself, and is divided, he can not stand, but hath an end." (Mark 3,22-30.)

When he says to one of his own trusted disciples,

"Get thee behind me, Satan" (Mark 8,33),

or,

"Simon, Simon, behold, Satan asked to have you, that he might sift you as wheat; but I made supplication for thee, that thy faith fail not" (Luke 22,31-32a),

there can be no reasonable thought that Jesus is referring to visionary or ecstatic experiences. For Jesus, Satan was the source of seductive suggestion and temptation, and in all of these Satan scenes and passages we meet the native language, the simple mother-tongue of religious experience. In the threefold temptation and in Luke 10,18 we are confronted with figures in Jesus' religious language and style rather than with psychological phases of his religious experience.

There is one incident in the life of Jesus, however, reported by all of the first three Gospel writers, which has the form of a vision of which Jesus is quite clearly presented as the subject—the vision at the Jordan (Matt. 3,13-17; Mark 1,9-11; Luke 3,21-22). That Jesus is intended as the subject of the vision, that it is his personal and private experience, is clearest in Mark's account:

"And it came to pass in those days, that Jesus came from Nazareth of Galilee, and was baptized of John in the Jordan. And straightway coming up out of the water, he saw the heavens rent asunder, and the Spirit as a dove descending upon him; and a voice came out of the heavens, Thou art my beloved Son, in thee I am well pleased."

The account is true to the visionary type of experience in its form; it is Jesus who sees the heavens open and the dove descend, and the voice is addressed directly to him in the second person.

That the Gospel writers intend this Jordan incident as important in their accounts of Jesus and as of great significance for him personally, is clear in the place in which they report it and in the understanding they have of its meaning. All three report the vision in connection with Jesus' first personal appearance in their accounts of his public life. In all three the vision is initial and inaugural, and all three regard it as a primary promoting factor that brought him out of private into public life. Their accounts of Jesus' public life begin with this vision, and its very position shows that the Gospel writers attach great importance to it, both for their stories and for Jesus personally.

Its importance is also clear in the significance which the Gospel writers attach to the incident. For Matthew and Luke, in particular, the vision contains a very clear communication; here Jesus learns that he is the Messiah. For Matthew and Luke, then, the Jordan incident is a messianic moment; it is the birth-hour and birthplace of his messianic consciousness; it is at the baptism that Jesus arrives at the messianic conviction for himself, and this new content of consciousness is imparted in a vision and a voice.

The messianic significance of the experience at the Jordan is not inherent in the account of the incident itself. That Matthew and Luke have a messianic understanding of this experience is clear in what follows immediately in both—the threefold temptation which, by its very themes, presupposes that Jesus is in full possession of the messianic consciousness, conviction and call. The great majority of the students of the life of Jesus share this understanding of Matthew and Luke.

But if we look carefully into the baptism incident itself, apart from the three temptations that follow in Matthew and Luke, we see that the incident, in and of itself, contains nothing distinctly messianic. The only messianic light that falls on the incident comes from behind, from the three tests that follow in Matthew and Luke. Further, Mark does not regard the Jordan experience as messianic. He has no series of messianic tests following at once upon the baptism; in 1,12-13 Mark gives us no hint as to the character of Jesus' temptations, only the most general sort of notice to the effect that he was tempted of Satan. The Jordan experience can not be messianic in Mark, unless we revise completely the whole of his Galilean life of Jesus, according to which, as we saw in the preceding chapter, the first definitely messianic moment comes in 8,27-30. The place which Mark gives the Jordan incident in his introduction to Jesus' public life (1,2-20) shows that he regards it as a high moment in the personal experience of Jesus himself. In Mark, as in Matthew and Luke, the Jordan vision is inaugural, and it comes to Jesus upon his first personal appearance in Mark's narrative. Mark places it at the head of the promoting factors that bring Jesus out of private into public life. In short, Mark sees in the Jordan vision Jesus' own personal call from God to a public career as the commissioned prophet of His kingdom. But in Mark the messiahship is not an evident element in Jesus' experience of call and commission, a strange sort of contrast to Matthew and Luke, who regard it as the exclusive factor in the Jordan experience.

The meaning of the Jordan incident for the Gospel writers is quite clear. For Matthew and Luke, it is messianic. But as we saw in the preceding chapter, the messianic question was not one of general calling and career for Jesus, but a purely personal problem of his own religious consciousness. For Mark, the Jordan vision is Jesus' call to the public work which he begins almost immediately, and it is this understanding of the Jordan vision that is of interest to us here in our quest of the sources of Jesus' religious convictions and certainties.

Just such a visionary experience amounting to a personal call from God as Mark here ascribes to Jesus we find in the life of practically every great founder and figure of religion. We have seen it in the prophets and in Paul, and it is equally true of other great Biblical characters. Outside of the Bible are Buddha, Mohammed, Luther, St. Teresa, George Fox and a host of others. From such great moments of revelation, involving an upheaval in the personal life, the great figures in the history of religion have received the decisive impulses and incentives that have brought them into and carried them through their life's work. And not a few modern students of the life of Jesus agree that the Jordan experience is a psychological necessity for Jesus, because the aggressiveness of his approach to his work and the intensity of his consecration to his cause must have had their source in the deepest and strongest impulses, such as are born usually in critical hours. That Jesus did feel himself called and commissioned is as clear as crystal in the Gospel picture. The aggressive and uncompromising character of his message and mission, the fact that he broke with home, family and trade, that he set his life at stake for the cause he chose and that chose him, make it clear that Jesus acted and lived under the pressure of the deepest and strongest of religious impulses. But that his call and commission came to him at the Jordan in a vision, that his experience there was the source of his deepest religious impulses and convictions, is not at all a necessary conclusion for the following reasons.

In the first place, when we come to look carefully into the content of the Jordan experience, we see that the most characteristic and essential elements of the prophetic vision of call are missing: an individual personal call, a concrete commission to a definite task, a clear communication of message and a personal response on the part of the subject. At the Jordan Jesus receives no such personal call and concrete commission to a definite task as Isaiah receives in 6,9-13; Jeremiah, in 1,4-5 7-10; and Paul, in his clear call to the Gentile mission in Acts 9,15-16 and 26,16-18. Jesus, as we see him in action, felt called and commissioned to the concrete task of preaching the kingdom of God, but in the Jordan experience there is no clear communication of message; the special work of Jesus and his call to it do not figure at all. The Jordan voice has nothing definite and specific about it. Still less is it imperative and commanding for Jesus personally, and visions of call, as we learn to know them in comparative religious psychology, regularly result for the subject in an unconditional, unescapable imperative. Further, the Jordan experience contains no personal response of Jesus to a call and commission such as Isaiah's "Here am I; send me" (6,8); as Jeremiah's personal protest in 1,6; as Paul's "Who art thou, Lord?" (Acts 9,5; 22,8; 26,15) and his "What shall I do, Lord?" (Acts 22,10). We read in the Gospels of personal responses of Jesus to the divine will for himself, the greatest of which is his Gethsemane submission, "Not what I will, but what thou wilt" (Mark 14, 36), but in the Jordan experience no such element is discoverable.

In the second place, the Jordan experience not only lacks the psychological elements that belong to the prophetic call, but it also has nothing of the personal importance for Jesus in his later self-consciousness, convictions, conduct and career that the true call of the prophet regularly has. The Jordan vision occupies no such place in the subsequent life of Jesus as does the Damascus vision in the Christian life of Paul. Jesus never refers to it as the moment when he received his call and commission. It is not revolutionary in his life; it is not a milestone in his experience before and after which all else dates; it is not the polar and pivotal point about which his whole subsequent life turns as was the Damascus experience in the life of Paul, who refers to, reminisces upon and rehearses the Damascus vision upon the slightest occasion.

Unlike Amos, Isaiah, Ezekiel and Paul, Jesus never tells when, or where, or how his call came. It is not a part of his message. In his contentions with his opponents, even in the Beelzebub conflict, where everything that he holds most sacred is called in question,[12] Jesus does not cite his call as the credentials of his commission. When, where and how Jesus received his call we do not know. It never escapes his lips in the form of a personal religious confession. It remains hidden for ever in the depths of his own consciousness. Jesus did not share the prophetic habit, the Pauline inclination toward self-revelation. The Jordan experience may have been the moment of his call to a public career, for he does not reveal the promoting factors that furnished him with the impulse to do this or that. But from the standpoint of the unimportance of the Jordan vision for Jesus personally in his later life and conduct, we might well doubt its historicity.

In the third place, Jesus is only nominally the subject of the Jordan vision. Although the voice addresses itself to him in the second person, it really utters a

[12]Cf. Matt. 12,22-37; Mark 3,19b-30; Luke 11,14-26.

declaration about him. The vision seems to be for the
benefit of others in their thought about Jesus rather
than for the benefit of Jesus himself. Even Mark finds
here a foundation for his faith about Jesus rather than
a foundation for Jesus' own personal faith. For Mark's
faith, the Jordan experience is the moment when Jesus
is selected and elected as the Son of God, which he becomes by virtue of his endowment and equipment with
the divine Spirit. The whole scene is depicted from the
point of view of its meaning for the early Christian
faith; it is not depicted from the point of view that would
show what it meant for Jesus personally. Thus the
Jordan experience, in the light of psychology, resolves
into a vision in form only; it is without content for Jesus
himself, devoid of all substance for its reported subject.

THE SOURCES OF JESUS' RELIGIOUS CERTAINTY

The author would regret it very much if he were to
leave the impression that he is determined upon the elimination of all visionary and ecstatic matter from the religious experience of Jesus. In fact, the author would be
glad to recognize such elements. But, on the basis of
scientific psychology, these materials are not forthcoming.
The visionary materials in the Gospels confine themselves
at most to sporadic details and language, or to visionary
forms without visionary substance for Jesus the subject.
As Professor W. M. Horton writes, "For the scientific
psychologist, the life of Jesus is a singularly unattractive
subject; the data are totally inadequate."[13] In the psychic
phases of his piety Jesus is not a fruitful subject for the
student of the psychology of religion.

---

[13]*The Journal of Philosophy*, XXI, 19, p. 528.

The Gospel records of Jesus are not rich source-books
for the study of religious experience of an unusual type
such as we find in the New Testament materials dealing
with Paul and from Paul's own hand, such as the confessions of Augustine, or the autobiography of St.
Teresa. In Jesus' experience we discover no complicated
psychotechnique such as is typical of the visionary and
the ecstatic. In his religious language there is nothing
of the elaborate architechtonic symbolism, nothing of
the fantastic figures and gaudy allegories that come from
Ezekiel's visionary world.   There is no notice of Jesus'
entrance into or emergence from a state of vision or
ecstasy.[14]   In his religious experience we find no partial
or complete alterations of the conscious state such as
is common in the experience of the Old Testament
prophets, Paul and many other religious geniuses.[15] There
are no visions that endanger the integrity of relations to
the actual world, that often result in the falsification of
either the objective or the subjective consciousness. To
the psychology of the ecstatic type of piety, from the
scientific point of view, Jesus has nothing to contribute.

I am not able to discover in the religious experience of
Jesus the prominent visionary element that some of the
liberal German theologians find. In the religious experience of Paul we do find an important visionary and
ecstatic element, but in the case of Jesus visions of a real

[14]Cf. Ezek. 1,3; 3,22; 8,1; 33,22; 37,1; 40,1; Isa. 8,11.

[15]For a fine example of the ecstatic and visionary element in a pro-
foundly religious personality, *see* the now rather extensive literature on
SADHU SUNDAR SINGH, who, in the author's opinion, is one of the two
greatest of our contemporary Christians. The two best accounts are:
The Message of Sadhu Sundar Singh, by Professor B. F. Streeter, and
Sadhu Sundar Singh: Ein Apostel des Ostens und Westens, by Pro-
fessor Friedrich Heiler; now in English, abridged translation by Olive
Wyon, *The Gospel of Sadhu Sundar Singh*.

religious content fall completely into the background as stimulating and supporting factors in the content of his consciousness and in the control of his conduct. In fact, I am not able to convince myself that Jesus was subject to visionary visitations of any kind, for the reason that they do not play the prominent part in his religious experience that they regularly play, according to psychological observation, in the life of the religious subject who speaks and acts according to their dictation and direction. I am not able to determine upon a single conviction or choice of Jesus that was the result of an ecstatic or visionary state, as any student of Paul can do in numerous cases. When visions and ecstatic experiences enrich the content of the religious consciousness, or when they control the conduct of the religious subject, then we may speak of them as playing a prominent rôle in the religious life and experience of the individual and as essential elements in both. In the religious life and experience of Jesus I am unable to find such.

It is only as we seek to determine the contribution of visions and ecstatic states to the religious life of Jesus that we realize fully how unimportant this type of experience was for him, if he *ever* shared in it. As we have already pointed out, Jesus appears before us only as a mature man of full and finished faith. What transpired in his personal experience prior to his coming to John at the Jordan, we have no way of finding out. Jesus' inner life is of a single solid substance, but there is no reason for supposing that this was welded in the heat of a great moment or series of moments. In his known life there is no special moment when an entirely new content captures and controls his consciousness. There is no vision in which a new realm of religious values, hitherto unknown, dawns upon him, henceforth to become the burning center of his life. There is no change in Jesus' objects of worship, no shift in the seat and sources of religious authority, such as we see in Paul's religious life. We witness no radical transformations in his religious attitudes, no reversals in his scale of religious values.

Jesus' distinctive religious consciousness does not seem to have had its origin in visions and voices. It was not supported, reinforced or bolstered up by them. Jesus may have had his visions and special inner experiences, but they never have a regulative or reassuring influence in either his character or his conduct. He never shows himself dependent upon them at important junctures in his public career. He never refers to his call as coming, to his message as imparted, at some special time or place, in some striking psychic manner. His utterances never betray a visionary origin; Luke 10,18 is the only possibility.

Jesus' consciousness of call, his conviction concerning his commission, rested upon something far deeper and more fundamental than the work of a single special moment, or series of ecstatic states. All the way through the Gospel account we see that, for Jesus, the psychological weight was on his choice of God and His cause rather than on God's choice and call of himself. Jesus often expresses his consciousness of call and his conviction of divine commission. But these expressions come in the form of single crisp sentences, the thought and point of view of which pushes his own person into the background, submerged by the cause which he champions.

"Let us go into the next towns, that I may preach there also; for to this end came I forth." (Mark 1,38.)

"I came not to call the righteous, but sinners."
(Mark 2,17b.)

Even in a word like Luke 12,49,

"I came to cast fire upon the earth,"

Jesus is thinking of the firebrand, not of the one who hurls it.[16] Such simple statements are wholly foreign to the visionary temperament, yet in the experience of Jesus they are clear crystallizations of a great body of personal religious conviction and certainty.

Of the nature and number of his outstanding religious experiences we learn practically nothing from Jesus himself. The inclination and habit of self-revelation, so characteristic of the great geniuses of religion, Jesus did not share. At least he does not practise it, and in this respect he stands virtually unique in the history of religious genius. The journals, diaries, autobiographies, confessions and personal correspondence of the great religious geniuses contain almost innumerable rehearsals of visionary moments when God was, to use their own language, specially clear, near and dear to them. But Jesus seems to have possessed the very opposite inclination, and no one knows this better than the serious student who has sought to gain an adequate conception of what and how he thought of himself.

If Jesus did experience special moments, visions and voices, they are shrouded in darkness because he left them there, and none but he could have dispelled this darkness. This he did not choose to do. Even when it

---

[16]For similar statements of Jesus, *see* Matt. 5,17; 10,34-36; Luke 12,51-53; Matt. 20,28; Mark 10,45; Luke 19,10.

comes to those intimately personal phases of his piety that are not visionary in form or substance, he seldom reveals them. We know well enough that there were moments in Jesus' religious experience when his emotions were lifted, his convictions deepened, when his devotion was intensified. The very character of certain of his words shows that they were uttered at high moments of feeling and faith. But Jesus does not connect them with visions and ecstatic states. He tells us nothing of their origin. In these intimate matters there stands the reticence of Jesus, and we can not break it down, even if we would. The same sensitive reserve that marked others of Jesus' religious attitudes extended over the field of special types of religious experience—if he *ever* had such.

We are now in a position to draw our conclusions on one of the principal elements that went into the production of a religious personality like Jesus, his personal heritage from the prophets.[17] We may say that Jesus was a genuine prophetic personality, the heir of the highest and best in the religious genius of his people. He is the prince of all the prophets, the culmination and perfection of this strange and sensitive strain of religious genius.

In only one major respect is Jesus untrue to the general character of the prophetic type of religious genius—in the psychic phases, visions and ecstasy. In his religious experience we see a practical, if not a complete elimination of the ecstatic element in prophecy. But even here Jesus is not without a great predecessor among the prophets. As early a prophet as Jeremiah is skeptical regarding

[17]*See* the author's companion study, *The Religion of Jesus*, pp. 31-38.

visions and the religious certainty and conviction they
may impart. For some of his visions at least, he awaits
the confirmation of fact. (32,6-15.)[18] In Jeremiah's
religious experience we see that rational reflection begins
to invade and inhibit ecstasy. The prophetic consciousness of call and commission begins to prevail over momentary emotional uplifts and depressions. The relationship between God and His prophet becomes more
constant.

This is exactly what we see in the case of Jesus. There
is no reason to suppose that this suppression of the visionary and ecstatic element was conscious and deliberate
on his part. We are not even sure that there was an
ecstatic and visionary strain in his personality. In Jesus
we see no consciousness of conflict between ethics and
ecstasy such as we find in the religious experience of Paul.
(I Cor. 14,18-19.)   The absence of the visionary type
of experience in Jesus' religious life appears more natural.
The whole temper of his personality seems opposed to
such. He seems to have been too practical and realistic
a nature to furnish a fertile soil for the appearance of
such psychic phenomena.

This conclusion has its direct bearing on the sources
of Jesus' personal piety. We may say that Jesus does not
seem to have found the visionary type of experience a
source of spiritual stimulus and personal power, as did
Paul with his visions, dreams, trances, revelations and
states of ecstasy. The personal piety of Jesus seems
to have taken on the form of a deep experience of religion rather than of striking religious experiences which,
for most religious geniuses, constitute breaks that sep-

---

[18]Cf. Hoelscher, *Die Profeten*, p. 294.

arate the new from the old, pivots about which the whole of the religious life turns, milestones that mark long strides in personal progress toward God.

Jesus had his sources of spiritual stimulus, his sources of personal power that supported and sustained him, that reinforced his convictions, that controlled his conduct and that directed his decisions at important junctures in his life. These were not located in visions and voices, but in prayer and communion with God. In his religious experience, in its sources and psychic phases, Jesus did not feel himself separated from the average run of men as did the old prophets and seers, the later Jewish and Christian apocalyptists. In the psychic phases of his piety Jesus belongs to that group of plodding, yet patient souls who struggle long and hard in quest of the divine will, and who, once they are clear regarding this will for themselves, find themselves at the beginning of that painful path of obedience, which they traverse only by renewed effort and severe struggle.

CHAPTER VI

More about the Praying of Jesus

THE INDIVIDUAL RETREATS[1]

It is indeed surprising that Luke preserves so many notices of retreat for prayer and precisely at those critical junctures when personal pressure was heaviest upon the soul of Jesus. Some of these notices are perhaps editorial, settings supplied independently by Luke's own hand. (9,18 28-29; 11,1.) But this literary possibility does not in the least prejudice the reliability of the tradition to the effect that Jesus in hours of stress and strain, when confronted with specially pressing problems, sought out solitude and seclusion, there to be alone with his God, to seek His will and to strive to perform it. If we may be sure of anything in the Gospels, we may be sure that prayer was a religious resort and recourse of Jesus. If Luke does supply some of the situations, it is only further evidence of the fact that he was deeply impressed by what had come down to him as the distinctly devotional life of Jesus. Further, in Luke these notices appear at those psychological moments when we would naturally expect them to appear.

At the Baptism

The *first* notice of Jesus' praying is found in Luke's

---

[1]For a list and brief discussion of Jesus' retreats for prayer, *see* the author's companion study, *The Religion of Jesus*, pp. 189-195.

298

account of the baptism. Matthew (3,13-17) and Mark (1,9-11) have no notice of the prayer in connection with this incident. Luke's text reads:

> "Now it came to pass, when all the people were baptized, that, Jesus also having been baptized, and praying, the heaven was opened, and the Holy Spirit descended in bodily form, as a dove, upon him, and a voice came out of heaven, Thou art my beloved Son; in thee I am well pleased." (3,21-22.)

Luke's notice of prayer here is only natural. Jesus is taking a religious step, undergoing a religious rite which meant infinitely more to him than the Gospel writers cause to appear. Just all that was in the mind of Jesus on this occasion we are not able to say; just all that John's baptism meant for him we do not know. But it is certainly a religious act on the part of Jesus which he performs in all spiritual sincerity, and any one who has any insight at all into his religious life can not imagine him in any other attitude at the Jordan than that of prayer. Luke does not report Jesus' prayer on this occasion, and we are no wiser than Luke.[2]

Apart from Simon's House

The *second* notice of Jesus' praying is found only in Mark. (1,35-38.) Matthew nowhere reports this retreat, and Luke, to our surprise, reports this retreat from Simon's house but gives no notice of prayer. (4, 42-43.) Mark's text reads:

---

[2]The retreat to the wilderness which follows at once upon the baptism was probably a period of intensive prayer, although none of the Gospel writers gives a notice to this effect.

"And in the morning, a great while before day, he rose up and went out, and departed into a desert place, and there prayed. And Simon and they that were with him followed after him; and they found him, and say unto him, All are seeking thee. And he saith unto them, Let us go elsewhere into the next towns that I may preach there also; for to this end came I forth."

With the exception of the Gethsemane struggle, this is the most detailed and intelligible of all the retreats reported. It comes at the close of Jesus' first day in public, and we have an unusually full account of the events and experiences that led up to it. (Mark 1,21-34.) His first day has been a day of cures, resulting in a tremendous popularity which is disappointing to him personally. His ability to cure strikes him with surprise, and this, with his popularity, throws his mind into a state of serious solicitude concerning the essence of his mission—cause or cures. From Mark's account we might think that this personal problem pressed upon Jesus' mind throughout the night, for "in the morning, a great while before day," he retreats from Simon's house to a desert place, there to pray. Jesus' prayer on this occasion is not preserved to us, but the result of the retreat is quite clear. When Simon and his companions find him, he is already clear and certain as to the course he will pursue: He will go to the next towns and preach rather than return to Capernaum and cure. This retreat for prayer results for Jesus in clearness and certainty concerning his mission: His great task is to preach the kingdom of God. This retreat is one of the most dramatic situations in the whole of the life of Jesus known to us, and the drama reaches back to the very soul of Jesus himself.

After the Cleansing of the Leper

The *third* retreat for prayer is reported by Luke only and is connected with the cleansing of the leper. (5,12-14.) Matthew (8,1-4) and Mark (1,40-45) have no retreat for prayer in connection with this cure. Mark has Jesus retreat to "desert places," but has no notice of prayer. Luke's text reads,

> "But he withdrew himself in the deserts, and prayed." (5,16.)

Luke supplies no special reason for this retreat unless it is the thronging of the multitudes. (5,15.) Luke 5,16 may be only the delayed notice which Mark reported earlier. (1,35-38.)

Before Choosing the Twelve

The *fourth* retreat for prayer is also peculiar to Luke and falls on the night preceding the choice of the twelve. Matthew neglects the choice of the twelve as a definite act of Jesus and reports only the catalogue of their names in connection with their mission. (10,1-4.) Mark reports the choice of the twelve, but gives no notice of prayer in connection with this choice. (3,13-19a.) Luke's text reads:

> "And it came to pass in these days, that he went out into the mountain to pray; and he continued all

night in prayer to God. And when it was day, he called his disciples; and he chose from them twelve." (6,12-13a.)

In Luke, then, the choice of the twelve appears as a distinctly religious act of Jesus, and from Luke we should suppose that not only the act of choosing twelve permanent companions but the selection of the personnel of the group was the result of a night of prayer. The choice of the twelve was a very important decision of Jesus, and we can not imagine his failing to seek the divine guidance.

After Feeding the Five Thousand

The *fifth* retreat for prayer is passed over by Luke. It is Matthew's only Galilean retreat (14,23) and the second of Mark, whose text reads:

"And straightway he constrained his disciples to enter into the boat, and to go before *him* unto the other side to Bethsaida, while he himself sendeth the multitude away. And after he had taken leave of them, he departed into the mountain to pray." (Mark 6, 45-46.)

Matthew and Mark supply no special motive for this retreat. It follows at once upon the feeding of the five thousand and provides the setting necessary for the walking on the water—Jesus alone on the land and the disciples together in a boat contending with a heavy sea.

At Cæsarea Philippi

The *sixth* retreat is peculiar to Luke and is reported in connection with Peter's confession at Cæsarea Philippi. Matthew (16,13-20) and Mark (8,27-30) have no notice of prayer on this occasion. The text of Luke reads,

> "And it came to pass, as he was praying apart, the disciples were with him: and he asked them, saying . . . " (9,18a.)

This is the high point in the Galilean life of Jesus, and Luke reports this notice of prayer at a good psychological moment, although he gives no specific motive for this particular retreat.

At the Transfiguration

The *seventh* retreat for prayer is also peculiar to Luke, in connection with the transfiguration. Matthew (17,1-8) and Mark (9,2-8) have no notice of prayer in their accounts of the incident. The text of Luke reads:

> "And it came to pass about eight days after these sayings, that he took with him Peter and John and James, and went up into the mountain to pray. And as he was praying, the fashion of his countenance was altered, and his raiment *became* white *and* dazzling." (9,28-29.)

This is another of the high moments in the experience

of the disciples, and a notice of Jesus in prayer increases the effect; at least, this appears as the point of view of Luke. Any one who surveys the stress that must have been on the soul of Jesus during the last of the Galilean days, when the thought of his fate seems to have struck him, would be surprised to find no retreats for prayer. In this notice of prayer and in the preceding, Luke's insight into the religious life of Jesus is accurate and true to fact.

At the Giving of the Lord's Prayer

The *eighth* retreat for prayer is also peculiar to Luke. It is a part of his long and eventful journey to Jerusalem. (9,51-19,28.) Luke's text reads,

> "And it came to pass, as he was praying in a certain place, that when he had ceased, one of his disciples said unto him, Lord, teach us to pray, even as John also taught his disciples." (11,1.)

This notice is probably editorial, a fitting setting in which Jesus gives the *Lord's Prayer* to the disciples. (11,2-4.) Nevertheless, Luke in this appropriate setting shows his skill as an editor as well as his genius for sensing one of the great secrets of power in Jesus' exclusively religious personality. However, it may be historical. It does have about it a native naturalness—Jesus' own praying suggests to the disciples the request for a prayer for themselves. The allusion to the practise of prayer by John and his disciples certainly conveys reliable historical information. (Luke 5,33.)

In Gethsemane

The *ninth* is the most familiar of all of Jesus' retreats for prayer, the Gethsemane retreat, reported in detail by all of the first three Gospel writers.[3] It is the pressure of impending events that brings Jesus to his knees on this occasion. The hour has come; he must face his tragic fate. In Gethsemane Jesus is seeking final assurance concerning the divine will and a moral mobilization of personal powers to meet the most terrible issue of his life. The text of Mark reads in part:

"And they come unto a place which was named Gethsemane: and he saith unto his disciples, Sit ye here, while I pray. And he taketh with him Peter and James and John, and began to be greatly amazed, and sore troubled. And he saith unto them, My soul is exceeding sorrowful even unto death: abide ye here, and watch. And he went forward a little, and fell on the ground and prayed that, if it were possible, the hour might pass away from him." (Mark 14,32-35.)

This is the only retreat of the nine in which Jesus' prayer is reported. (Mark 14,36.) Matthew and Mark have Jesus retreat from the three disciples three different times, and each time engage in prayer; Luke, however, has only one retreat for prayer in Gethsemane and that directly from the twelve. The results of this retreat are clear enough: Jesus is certain that he must die, and he faces his fate with a courage that is born of a deep religious conviction won on his knees.

[3]Matt. 26,36-44; Mark 14,32-42; Luke 22,40-46.

THE PERSONAL PRAYERS OF JESUS[4]

In the personal prayers of Jesus we come upon some of the most genuine words of his that have been preserved to us. These tense, terse utterances did not lend themselves so readily to the Christianization process as did his general religious message. Further, some of them are so firmly imbedded in certain concrete situations that they could not be easily extracted. To be sure, we do not possess every prayer of Jesus, nor every word just as he prayed it. Matthew's form of the *Lord's Prayer,* so easily repeated, in all probability owes its present smoothness to frequent use in the early Christian circles from which it came. Jesus' prayer of praise, as we shall see, has acquired a later Christian supplement. But judged in the light of all that we know of him, the seven personal prayers of Jesus that have survived bear the distinctive stamp of his thought and style, and in their essential substance they appear as wholly true expressions of his own religious feeling and faith.

The reported prayers of Jesus are his very own, yet one is at once impressed with their genuine Jewishness. Two of the seven are extracts from the prayer-literature of his people. Judged in the light of the sources, objects and issues of the religious experience from which they come, there is nothing in them to sever the organic bond that holds them firmly to that great and living body of Israel's religious faith. Further, the genuine Jewishness of Jesus' personal prayers would only increase our confidence in their essential reliability.

---

[4]For a list and brief discussion of Jesus' prayers, *see* the author's companion study, *The Religion of Jesus,* pp. 195-209.

The Lord's Prayer

The *Lord's Prayer* is one of those settingless words of Jesus that has come down to us with no definite indication as to when, where or why Jesus spoke it. Matthew reports it in his Sermon on the Mount in connection with a general discussion of prayer. (6,5-8.) But it is quite inconceivable that Jesus should have uttered this most intimate of all his words upon the very first occasion of his appearance in public as Matthew represents. (5-7.) It certainly belongs to the later life of Jesus. The very character and content of the prayer demand an intimate and trusted audience which Jesus did not have at the time of the delivery of the Sermon on the Mount, when as yet, in Matthew, he has about him only four recently called fishermen. According to Luke, Jesus is on his way to Jerusalem when he gives his disciples this famous prayer (11,2-4) in response to their request,

"Lord, teach us to pray, even as John also taught his disciples." (11,1.)

Whether Luke gives the historical occasion for the *Lord's Prayer* we shall never be able to say. As we noted in the preceding section, Luke's occasion may be editorial, but it possesses a naturalness that is a tribute to Luke's editorial skill and psychological insight. We may be certain that the *Lord's Prayer* is a genuine word of Jesus, but of the occasion out of which it arose, when and where it was spoken, we are not certain.

The *Lord's Prayer* is reported only by Matthew and Luke. It is very surprising that such a significant word escaped Mark. But even this gem from the religious experience of Jesus has not come down to us in its purity. Matthew and Luke report it in two quite different forms. Matthew's form includes seven petitions,[5] that of Luke only five. Scholars generally at present, in contrast with the older consensus of opinion, regard Luke's form as the more original. Matthew's form, so familiar to us, has about it a literary smoothness, an almost liturgical character due probably to frequent repetition. Luke's form is more abrupt and broken, and has the marks that suggest the impromptu and extemporaneous speech of Jesus.

Matthew 6,9-13	Luke 11,2-4
Our Father who art in heaven.	Father,
Hallowed be thy name.	Hallowed be thy name.
Thy kingdom come.	Thy kingdom come.
Thy will be done,	
as in heaven, so on earth.	
Give us this day our daily	Give us day by day our daily
bread.	bread.
And forgive us our debts,	And forgive us our sins;
as we also have forgiven	for we ourselves also forgive
our debtors.	every one that is indebted to us.
And bring us not into temptation,	And bring us not into temptation.
but deliver us from the evil *one*.[6]	

---

[5]The Jewishness of the *Lord's Prayer* in Matthew has been pointed out by Rabbi Gottlieb Klein, of Stockholm. He writes: "According to Matthew, the *Lord's Prayer* consists of seven petitions; according to Jewish precept, a prayer should have just seven. Further, the proper prayer should be made up of three parts. It should begin with a hymn praising God, *Schebach*. Thereupon the personal portion of the prayer should follow, the *Tefilla*, and the prayer should close with a doxology, *Hodaja*. The *Lord's Prayer* follows this order and arrangement. Finally, a prayer, even that of the individual, should be in the plural. Such is the case in the *Lord's Prayer*." (*Ist Jesus eine historische Persoenlichkeit?* p. 35.)

[6]Some manuscripts of Matthew conclude the *Lord's Prayer* with the familiar doxology. The majority however omit this, and textual criticism has come to reject it as a later liturgical addition. Historical research, however, could state with confidence that the Jewish prayers of the period often closed with a doxology (*Hodaja*). The student of

In our discussion at this point we are interested in the *Lord's Prayer* only as it relates itself to Jesus' prayer-experience as a whole. Orthodox theology in the past has cut off this prayer from the experience of Jesus, claiming that it is not a prayer that Jesus could or would pray for himself and that it fits only the situation of the disciples for whose benefit alone he gave it. This objection is based solely on the petition for forgiveness of sins which orthodox theology feels would compromise its doctrine of the sinlessness of Jesus.

He who raises theoretical objections to the propriety of Jesus praying entirely as he prays in the *Lord's Prayer,* who sees in it only a prayer for his followers and not for himself, has his eyes blinded for ever by a theoretical theology that hides from him the very soul of Jesus' personal piety—in fact, he has lost the real Jesus of history who feared, loved and prayed to God. There can be no real religious objection to Jesus having prayed the *Lord's Prayer* as his own. The only possible objection is purely theoretical, based upon a theoretical sinlessness of Jesus rather than an actual sinlessness of religious accomplishment, which no historical student denies. It is universally true of the religious consciousness that the subject with the clearest conscience is the first to pray for forgiveness. His very humanity, his native sense of distance between himself as man and his Maker, excludes the possibility of the omission of such a petition. The deeply religious consciousness that remains healthy

---

the psychology of religion could add that there is nothing in the expression—*For thine is the kingdom, and the power, and the glory. Amen*—to take it from the lips of Jesus. Judged in the light of the religious objects addressed and the religious attitudes expressed, this doxology fits into the personal piety of Jesus as organically as any other part of the prayer.

may not entertain the thought of its own sinlessness without thereby compromising its purity of heart.

The *Lord's Prayer* differs from the other prayers of Jesus in that it is consciously didactic; it is given for instruction and contains a reflective element. However, it still remains a devotional, a prayed prayer of Jesus, and it sprang from the very depths of his religious experience. It is the richest single word of his that has come down to us. No other one passage gives us so much of Jesus himself. Into no other utterance did Jesus pour more of his own life, thought, feeling and faith. It contains the supreme religious values which he himself sought, and as such it is the direct issue of his own prayer-experience. It is an invaluable testimony of what Jesus himself sought in prayer. In it Jesus gives us his best, and it stands as the richest and ripest fruit of his own prayer-life. Rabbi Gottlieb Klein writes: "It is the most personal reminiscence from Jesus that we possess. All the hopes and desires of his God-filled heart are here concentrated in a single utterance."[7]

Jesus' Prayer of Praise

Jesus' second prayer is a prayer of praise and thanksgiving. It is distinctly personal and devotional. Just when and where Jesus uttered this prayer is also uncertain. Matthew (11,25-26) reports it in a more or less meaningless connection where there are no immediate antecedents that would lead up to such an enthusiastic outburst. He introduces it in a matter-of-fact way, "And at that season Jesus answered and said." Luke, however, seems to sense the exalted state of soul out of which it

---

[7]*Ist Jesus eine historische Persoenlichkeit?* p. 34.

sprang and to feel the sweep and swing of emotion that
carries it along. (10,21.) He introduces it with the
more noteworthy notice, "In that same hour he rejoiced in the Holy Spirit, and said." However, Luke
supplies a general setting out of which the prayer came.
It follows at once upon the mission of the seventy and
their return (10,1-20), and Luke seems to intend to
say that the enthusiastic report of the returning disciples
occasioned this prayer of praise. But there are technical
literary difficulties in the way here, and the historical
student finds in this prayer another of the many genuine,
but settingless words of Jesus. However, the strong
emotional element with which the prayer is charged
shows that it comes from some high moment in the religious experience of Jesus, even though we are not in
a position to locate and identify it. The text of Matthew
and Luke reads verbatim,

"I thank thee, O Father, Lord of heaven and earth,
that thou didst hide these things from the wise and
understanding, and didst reveal them unto babes: yea,
Father; for so it was well-pleasing in thy sight."

The following passage in both Matthew (11,27) and
Luke (10,22) is commonly regarded as the organic
continuation of this prayer. The text of Matthew reads,

"All things have been delivered unto me of my
Father: and no one knoweth the Son, save the Father;
neither doth any know the Father, save the Son, and
he to whomsoever the Son willeth to reveal *him*."

There is an intended literary continuity that brings these

two passages together. Otherwise, however, they constitute in no sense an actual unity of utterance from a
living personality. The first passage is in the first person of direct address, the true form for purely personal
prayer, but the second passage drifts off into the third
person of impersonal discourse and thus gradually de-
parts from the intimate intercourse which personal
prayer demands. In the first passage Jesus is a true
religious subject pouring out a prayer of praise to the
Father, but in the second passage he becomes a religious
object who is discoursed about. The first passage is a
terse utterance, tense with deep and strong emotion,
but from the second passage the flood of feeling is gone
and we have only an abstract Christological statement
that betrays nothing of the warmth which we sense at
once in the first. The first passage is a true prayer in
form, thought and feeling; the second, however, is of
Christian origin, a deposit of early Christian conviction
and thought. The first passage is a personal religious
confession from Jesus' own experience; the second is a
confession of early Christian feeling and faith concerning the relation of the Son to the Father and of the
Father to the Son.

Professor Deissmann speaks of this prayer as Jesus'
"most compact confession of his experience of God."[8] It
is a spontaneous outburst of Jesus' religious feeling, expressing his exalted faith in the Father. Here we meet
the naked substance of his confidence and trust in God, a
praising of His will and way.

When we survey the nature of Jesus' experience in
public, we may say that this prayer of praise and thanksgiving springs perhaps from the joy of conquered dis-

----

[8]*Evangelium und Urchristentum*, p. 103.

appointment, conquered because such was the will and way of the Father. Jesus' disappointment would come from the facts of his general experience in public; his joy would come from his faith that had surmounted all fact. At any rate, the prayer seems to express a conviction born of sudden insight, and it is to be appreciated as such rather than analyzed. Of this prayer Johannes Weiss wrote: "Before us we have a hymn of exalted inspiration that owes its existence to an hour of deepest spiritual seizure and that must be measured with other standards than are applied to the more didactic words of Jesus: It must be sensed and shared."[9]

Jesus' Prayer for Simon

The third prayer of Jesus we have only in substance. It is found in Luke alone (22,31-32) in the form of a word addressed to Simon when Jesus is at the table with the twelve. Luke's text reads,

> "Simon, Simon, behold, Satan asked to have you, that he might sift you as wheat; but I made supplication for thee, that thy faith fail not."

When and where Jesus prayed for Simon we do not know, but the character of his allusion as well as historical probability would put it in only the most immediate past, perhaps on that very night, even at the table. There is not much that we can say about this prayer, but we know Simon, and it helps us to a fuller knowledge of Jesus. This brief word throws a whole flood of light on the intimate bond that drew and held Jesus to his chosen

---

[9]*Die Schriften des Neuen Testaments*, I, p. 309.

companions. His attachment to them is most deep and devoted; their personal fates and fortunes become themes of his petitions to God; he knows their weaknesses and prays for the firmness of their faith in time of test and trial.

ꜜ *Jesus' Prayer of Submission*

The fourth prayer of Jesus is the famous Gethsemane prayer. It is the first of the only two prayers reported by Mark, and the only prayer reported by all of the first three Gospel writers. According to Matthew and Mark, Jesus prays this prayer three times; in Luke, however, only once.[10] The occasion of this prayer is perfectly clear. Jesus here is struggling with the immediate prospect of his fate to which he refers as a cup, and he has hardly finished praying before the authorities are upon him and place him under arrest. In this prayer Jesus petitions that the cup may pass from him, but above this petition he prays for the divine will for himself even to the drinking of the cup. The text of this prayer varies slightly in the first three Gospels, but not enough to affect either its thought or its point. The text of Mark reads:

"Abba, Father, all things are possible unto thee; remove this cup from me: howbeit not what I will, but what thou wilt."

No prayer of Jesus reaches deeper or reveals more clearly the very soul of his personal piety. In it there is no doctrine, no dogma, no theology, no soteriology. To seek to fit such a prayer into a system or scheme of salvation is to tear out its heart. It must be approached from

---

[10]Cf. Matt. 26,39 42 44; Mark 14,36 39 41; Luke 22,42.

the standpoint of the psychology of a living personality, the very core of whose being was exclusively religious. In this prayer there is no fanaticism seeking a tragic fate; there is also no fatalism that goes to its end in a feeling-less fashion. Jesus' Gethsemane prayer is the sponta-neous outburst of a torn human heart that can reconcile itself to its fate only because such appears as the divine will. This conviction becomes a religious certainty which issues in an heroic submission. Jesus' submission in Geth-semane is his supreme religious act and, we might add, the most exalted altitude ever attained by a human re-ligious subject. Professor Heiler speaks of this prayer of Jesus as "the highest and purest prayer in the history of religion,"[11] "the sublime summit in the history of prayer."[12] Of it Professor Hoeffding wrote: It is "the most profound religious word that was ever uttered."[13]

5 Jesus' Prayer of Forgiveness

The fifth prayer of Jesus is peculiar to Luke also. (23, 34.) It reads,

"Father, forgive them; for they know not what they do."

Textual criticism has had many a skirmish over this word of Jesus because it is not found in some of the best manuscripts of the third Gospel. But textual criticism has its very serious limitations when it comes to deter-mining the genuineness of Biblical passages. There is

---

[11]*Das Gebet*, p. 93.
[12]*Ibid.*, p. 239.
[13]Quoted by Heiler, *Ibid.*, p. 239.

nothing in the form or thought of this word that would take it from Jesus. It is as true as steel to the best of his spirit and is in every sense a true prayer of petition. At a very early date this prayer was fixed upon the mind of the early Christian community as one of his dying words. In one of the most primitive pieces of tradition in the book of Acts Stephen is pictured as dying in imitation of his Lord with His prayer on his lips,

"Lord, lay not this sin to their charge."   (7,60.)

Forgiveness is the very heart of Jesus' teaching on human relationships; he presents it as indispensable to men who must live together and die at the hands of one another. His words on love and forgiveness to enemies are the product of such prayer as appears here. That Luke is here modeling Jesus' conduct on the cross to correspond to certain of his teachings is a most puerile type of criticism. It is in this word on the cross that the purity and power of Jesus' prayer-experience have their issue in a corresponding purity and power of character and conduct. In such a prayer we meet the absolute climax of ethical conception: a content of character, a code and control of conduct, that enable a man to die at the hands of his enemies and yet forgive them fully in the presence of God with his latest breath.

Jesus' Prayer of Protest

The sixth prayer of Jesus is found only in Matthew and Mark, and is verbatim from Psalms 22,1. This prayer and the following are involuntary invasions from the prayer-life and literature of Jesus' people. It is not a conscious citation; Jesus does not reflect and select, but into this ancient cry he pours the whole of his distress. On the cross Psalms 22,1 becomes his very own. Mark's text (15,34) reads,

"My God, my God, why hast thou forsaken me?"

This prayer is a cry to God *de profundis*. In direst distress, in the midst of terrible tension of soul, in the throes of physical agony, Jesus prays. It is not a cry of despair and defeat. It is a prayer of protest. In Jesus we do not see an utterly dumb devotion, but a reverent reaction to the requirements of the divine will. In this prayer we meet a "self-assertion with a consciousness of complete dependence."[14] The horrors of the hour do not rob Jesus of his faith in God. He does not desert God, but asks why God has deserted him. His own personal faith is firm to the last, and this cry on the cross springs from a tremendous strength of soul. Behind such a protest there lies the solid substance of a soul that knows the sustaining power of prayer. "If religious faith were dependent upon experience, the many unanswered prayers would have led along ago to the end of all religious life. . . . The strongly religious personality will find in unanswered prayer, in experiences that call the certainty of his faith in question, only an augmented impulse to hold all the more firmly to the reality of the Eternal."[15]

Through such a cry as comes from the cross faith doubles its power, and such a prayer restores calm and composure. This cry stands as the final affirmation of

---

[14]Hocking, *The Meaning of God in Human Experience*, p. 438.
[15]Mundle, *Die religioesen Erlebnisse*, pp. 48, 49.

Jesus' faith in God. "Exactly this last cry is a final confession of Jesus to the omnipotent will of God."[16] "It is indeed wonderful how he, in the throes of suffering, feeling that he is deserted of the Divine, at the very last takes his flight to none other than the heart of his God."[17] In Mark Jesus dies as he has lived, in the throes of struggle with his God. There is no force that can tear him from his faith, from his quest of the Divine. He refuses the numbing drink (Mark 15,23), preferring to fight the last great fight of his faith in clear consciousness, in full possession of all his faculties. In such an hour, with such a prayer on his lips, Jesus simply staggers us with the virtue and volume of his faith in God.

Jesus' Prayer of Commitment

The seventh and last prayer of Jesus is found only in Luke. In Matthew (27,50) and Mark (15,37) we have only an inarticulate cry. The text of Mark reads,

> "And Jesus uttered a loud voice, and gave up the ghost."

But in Luke (23,46) this last cry becomes articulate and expresses itself, with the exception of the first word, in the language of Psalms 31,5a. Luke's text reads,

> "Father, into thy hands I commend my spirit."

In Luke Jesus dies as he has lived, dispensing forgiveness to his enemies, promising Paradise to a fellow-victim,

---

[16]Wernle, *Jesus*, p. 55.
[17]*Ibid.*, p. 63.

and at the last calmly committing himself to the One whom he has always trusted. The contrast between the pictures of the dying Jesus in Mark and Luke we pointed out before.[18] Both are probably true to historical fact. Mark's cry of distress had its origin in a firm faith that pours forth its need to God in its darkest hour. The release of soul in such a cry restores a calm and a composure that allow it to withdraw from the scene of history, committing itself with confidence to the Father-God of its faith.[19]

---

[18]*See* the author's companion study, *The Religion of Jesus*, p. 25*f.*

[19]"Vor dem ganz unbegriffenen offenbar-unoffenbaren Geheimnis kniet man, gestillter Seele, sein Wie erfuehlend, und darin sein Recht." Otto, *Das Heilige*, p. 101.

BIBLIOGRAPHY

BIBLIOGRAPHY

BOUSSET, W. *Jesus* (3te Auflage, Tuebingen: Mohr, 1907).

Das Wesen der Religion (4te Auflage, Tuebingen: Mohr, 1920).

BULTMANN, R. *Jesus* (Berlin: Deutsche Bibliothek, 1927).

Die Geschichte der synoptischen Tradition (Goettingen: Vandenhoeck & Ruprecht, 1921).

Die Erforschung der synoptischen Evangelien (Goettingen: Vandenhoeck & Ruprecht, 1925).

"The New Approach to the Synoptic Problem," *Journal of Religion* (Chicago: University of Chicago Press), VI, July, 1926.

BUNDY, W. E. *The Religion of Jesus* (Indianapolis: Bobbs-Merrill, 1928).

The Psychic Health of Jesus (New York: Macmillan, 1922).

"The Meaning of Jesus' Baptism," *Journal of Religion* (Chicago: University of Chicago Press), VII, January, 1927.

CASE, S. J. *Jesus: A New Biography* (Chicago: University of Chicago Press, 1927).

"The Alleged Messianic Consciousness of Jesus," *Journal of Biblical Literature*, XLVI (1927).

COE, G. A. *The Psychology of Religion* (Chicago: University of Chicago Press, 1921).

DEISSMANN, A. *Evangelium und Urchristentum* (Muenchen: Lehmann, 1905).

"Der Beter Jesus," *Christliche Welt* (XIII, 1899, cols. 701*ff.*).

DUPONT, G. *Le Fils de l'Homme* (Paris: Fischbacher, 1924).

GUNKEL, H. *Die Propheten* (Goettingen: Vandenhoeck & Ruprecht, 1917).

HEILER, F. *Das Gebet. Eine religionsgeschichtliche und religionspsychologische Untersuchung* (4te Auflage, Muenchen: Reinhardt, 1923).

Der Katholizismus. Seine Idee und seine Erscheinung (Muenchen: Reinhardt, 1923).

Sadhu Sundar Singh. Ein Apostel des Ostens und Westens (2te Auflage, Basel: Reinhardt, 1924); abridged English translation by Olive Wyon, *The Gospel of Sadhu Sundar Singh* (New York: Oxford University Press, 1927).

HOCKING, W. E. *The Meaning of God in Human Experience* (New Haven: Yale University Press, 1912).

HOELSCHER, G. *Die Profeten. Untersuchungen zur Religionsgeschichte Israels.* (Leipzig: Hinrichs, 1914).

HOLTZMANN, O. *War Jesus Ekstatiker?* (Leipzig: Mohr, 1903).

KLEIN, G. *Ist Jesus eine historische Persoenlichkeit?* (Tuebingen: Mohr, 1910).

LEIPOLDT, J. *Vom Jesusbilde der Gegenwart* (Leipzig: Doerffling & Franke, 1913).

LIETZMANN, H. *Der Menschensohn* (Leipzig: Mohr, 1896).

LOISY, A. *The Gospel and the Church* (New York: Scribners, 1912), translation from the French by Christopher Home.

My Duel with the Vatican (New York: Dutton, 1924), translation from the French by R. W. Boynton.

LOOFS, F. *Wer War Jesus Christus?* (Halle a. d. S.: Niemeyer, 1916), being the German revision of *What is the Truth about Jesus Christ?* (New York: Scribners, 1913).

MUNDLE, W. *Das religioese Leben des Apostels Paulus* (Leipzig: Hinrichs, 1923).

Die religioesen Erlebnisse. Ihr Sinn und ihre Eigenart (Leipzig: Hinrichs, 1921).

"Der Christus des Glaubens und der historische Jesus," *Zeitschrift fuer Theologie und Kirche*, Hefte 3 und 4. (Neue Folge, 1921.)

OTTO, R. *Das Heilige. Ueber das Irrationale in der Idee des Goettlichen und sein Verhaeltnis zum Rationalen* (9te Auflage, Breslau: Trewendt & Granier, 1922). English translation by John W. Harvey, *The Idea of the Holy. An Inquiry into the Non-rational Factor in the Idea of the Divine* (3d impression, London: Oxford University Press, 1925).

PARKER, Mrs. A. *Sadhu Sundar Singh* (4th edition, New York: Revell, 1923).

PFANNMUELLER, G. *Jesus im Urteile der Jahrhunderte* (Leipzig u. Berlin: Teubner, 1908).

SCHWEITZER, A. *Die Geschichte der Leben-Jesu-Forschung* (2te Auflage, Tuebingen: Mohr, 1913). English translation of the first edition, *Von Reimarus zu Wrede* (1906), by W. Montgomery, *The Quest of the Historical Jesus* (2d edition, London: A. & C. Black, 1911).

Das Messianitaets- und Leidensgeheimnis (Tuebin-

gen: Mohr, 1901); English translation by Walter
Lowrie, *The Mystery of the Kingdom of God*
(Dodd, Mead & Co., 1914).

Die Geschichte der Paulinischen Forschung (Tue-
bingen: Mohr, 1911); English translation by
W. Montgomery, *Paul and His Interpreters*
(London: A. & C. Black, 1912).

Die psychiatrische Beurteilung Jesu (Tuebingen:
Mohr, 1913).

The Decay and Restoration of Civilization (London: A. & C. Black, 1923).

Civilization and Ethics (London: A. & C. Black
1923).

*On the Edge of the Primeval Forest. Experiences
and Observations of a Doctor in Equatorial
Africa* (London: A. & C. Black, 1922).

Aus meiner Kindheit und Jugend (Bern: Haupt,
1924).

Mitteilungen aus Lambarene (3 Hefte, Bern:
Haupt, 1928).

STRAUSS, D. F. *Das Leben Jesu kritisch bearbeitet* (2te
Auflage, Tuebingen: Osiander, 1837).

STREETER, B. H. *The Message of Sadhu Sundar Singh*
(New York: Macmillan, 1922).

WEINEL, H. *Biblische Theologie des Neuen Testaments*
(3te Auflage, Tuebingen: Mohr, 1921).

Jesus im 19. Jahrhundert (3te Neubearbeitung,
Tuebingen: Mohr, 1914).

WEISS, J. *Die Schriften des Neuen Testaments* (3te
Auflage, Goettingen: Vandenhoeck & Ruprecht,
1917), Band I, *Die drei aelteren Evangelien.*

WELLHAUSEN, J. *Einleitung in die drei ersten Evangelien* (2te Ausgabe, Berlin: Reimer, 1911).

Das Evangelium Mathaei (2te Ausgabe, Berlin:
Reimer, 1914).

Das Evangelium Marci (2te Ausgabe, Berlin: Reimer, 1909).

Das Evangelium Lucae (Berlin: Reimer, 1904).

Das Evangelium Johannis (Berlin: Reimer, 1908).

WERNLE, P. *Jesus* (Tuebingen: Mohr, 1916).

WINDISCH, H. *Johannes und die Synoptiker. Wollte der vierte Evangelist die drei aelteren Evangelien ergaenzen oder ersetzen?* (Leipzig: Hinrichs, 1926).

WREDE, W. *Das Messiasgeheimnis in den Evangelien* (Goettingen: Vandenhoeck & Ruprecht, 1901).

INDEX OF SUBJECTS

INDEX OF SUBJECTS

Abraham 25, 44

Acts
   See Index of Scripture Passages
"Alleged Messianic Consciousness
   of Jesus, The" 218

Amos 188, 272, 289
   See Index of Scripture Passages

Apostles' Creed 9

Asia Minor 114

Aus meiner Kindheit und Jugend
   77, 161

Beelzebub 289

Bethlehem 87, 196

*Biblische Theologie des Neuen
   Testaments* 144

Boston University Bulletin 190

Bousset, W.
   Das Wesen der Religion 3
   Jesus 90, 137, 145, 249

Brightman, E. S.
   Boston University Bulletin 190

Buddha 287

Bultmann, R.
   *Die Erforschung der synop-
      tischen Evangelien* 102
   *Die Geschichte der synoptischen
      Tradition* 102, 218
   Jesus 102, 137, 218
   "The New Approach to the
      Synoptic Problem" 101, 218

Bundy, W. E.
   "The Meaning of Jesus' Bap-
      tism" 138
   The Psychic Health of Jesus
      181, 197, 255, 280
   The Religion of Jesus ix, 10, 43,
      185, 200, 238, 295, 298, 306

Cæsarea Philippi 215, 216, 221,
   230, 237, 240, 243, 244

Cana 50

Capernaum 50, 82, 143, 205, 207,
   209, 211, 229, 300

Case, S. J.
   Jesus: A New Biography 130,
      137, 218
   "The Alleged Messianic Con-
      sciousness of Jesus" 218

Catholic Church 10

Christianity
   and Easter experiences 98*f.*
   and Fourth Gospel 60-61
      See Fourth Gospel
   and Jesus
      and passion path 260-261, 262
   Christianization of
      See Jesus, Christianization
         of
   fear of studying 11
   gap between 7*ff.*, 106, 126
   loyalty to 12
   religious approach of 2, 135
   return of 63
   and messianic issue 213*ff.*, 226
   and modern mind 19
   and Orient 8
   and Paul 1
   and John 1
      See Fourth Gospel
   and Synoptics 65-66
   conservatism of 106
   Jewish religious experience in
      107-108
   need of to-day 18
   pessimism in 164*f.*
   piety of 112

Christology 28, 35

Church
   and learning 2
   and study of Jesus 3
   as prophet 2
   ministry of 4-5
   See Christianity

Civilization and Ethics 191
Coe, G. A.
  The Psychology of Religion 153
Colossians
  See Index of Scripture Passages
I Corinthians
  See Index of Scripture Passages
II Corinthians
  See Index of Scripture Passages
Cornelius 215

Damascus 32
Daniel
  See Index of Scripture Passages
Das Evangelium Johannis 102
Das Evangelium Lucae 102
Das Evangelium Marci 102
Das Evangelium Mathaei 102
Das Gebet 73, 315
Das Heilige 319
Das Messianitaets- und Leidens-geheimnis 76, 214
Das Messiasgeheimnis in den Evangelien 101, 214, 215, 225
Das religioese Leben des Apostels Paulus 276, 277
Das Wesen der Religion 31
Deissmann, A.
  "Der Beter Jesus" 137
  Evangelium und Urchristentum 36, 122, 312
"Der Beter Jesus" 137
"Der Christus des Glaubens und der historische Jesus" 101
Der Katholizismus 190
Der Menschensohn 248
Die Erforschung der synoptischen Evangelien 102, 218
Die Geschichte der synoptischen Tradition 102
Die Profeten 271, 296
Die Propheten 73
Die psychiatrische Beurteilung Jesu 76
Die religioesen Erlebnisse 268, 317
Die Schriften des Neuen Testaments 247, 313

Dupont, G.
  Le Fils de l'Homme 248

Easter experiences 98, 215
Einleitung in die drei ersten Evangelien 101, 218
Elijah 36, 108, 221
Ephesians
  See Index of Scripture Passages
Eschatology 76, 178*ff.*
Evangelium und Urchristentum 36, 122, 312
Evolution
  and human progress 183*f.*
  contribution to religion 183
Ezekiel 272, 273, 291
  See Index of Scripture Passages

Faith
  and fact 180
  and life-of-Jesus research 127-128
  in Christianization of Jesus 97
  in church 3
  in Easter experiences 98
  of Jesus
    See Jesus, faith of
Fiction
  in Baptist's birth 109
  in life-of-Jesus research 84-91
  in Narratives of the Nativity 87*ff.*
Fourth Gospel
  as Christian confession 61
  commands of Jesus in 59
  cures in 50, 53
  disparity with Synoptics
    chronological 41-42
    historical 41-42
    psychological 42
  early Christian attitude toward 40
  fate of Jesus in 54-56
  Gethsemane in 52
  human features of 48-49
  Jesus as religious object 43, 60
  God and his kingdom in 45-48
  lacks personal problems 53

Fourth Gospel—*Cont.*
limitations of power in 50
messianic issue in 54, 234
metaphysical knowledge in 46
omniscience in 49
parables in 42
popularity of 106
religious experience in 44-45,
48, 56-58
sinlessness in 51
Strauss' alternative 62
temptation in 52
wonder-works in 53
words of Jesus in 42
See Index of Scripture Passages
Fox, George 5, 287

Galatians 23
See Index of Scripture Passages
Galilee 32, 93, 114, 213, 259
Geschichte der Leben-Jesu-Forschung 68
Geschichte der Paulinischen Forschung 76
Gethsemane 38-39, 52, 57, 58, 82,
116, 201, 260, 261, 263, 281, 305,
314
God
and evolution 183*ff.*
and visions and voices 270
as Father 45, 148, 162, 189
in Christian faith 104
in faith of Jesus 10, 42, 104*f.*,
177, 184
See Jesus, attitudes of
in life of Israel 175-176
in religious experience of Jesus
136
in social teachings of Jesus 176*ff.*
Golden Rule 10, 172, 192
Gospel and the Church, The 131
Gospels, Synoptic 3, 4, 12, 15, 20,
34, 39, 64, 67, 68, 69, 71, 72,
79, 81, 84, 92*ff.*, 100*ff.*, 144, 153.
Christianity's religious experience in 109*ff.*

Gospels—*Cont.*
contrast with Fourth Gospel 41-
62
fact in 122*ff.*
faith in 92-121
fiction in 84-91
See Life-of-Jesus research
Jesus' religious experience in
109*ff.*
Jewish type of religious experience in 107-109, 110
Greece 32, 93
Gunkel, H.
Die Propheten 73

Hebrews
and humanity of Jesus 38
contrast with James 38
theology of 37
See Index of Scripture Passages
Heiler, F.
Das Gebet 73, 315
Der Katholizismus 190
Sadhu Sundar Singh 212, 291
Herod 196
Hitzig 42
Hocking, W. E.
*The Meaning of God in Human
Experience* 149, 317
Hoeffding 315
Hoelscher, G. 271
Die Profeten 271, 296
Holtzmann, O.
War Jesus Ekstatiker? 282
Horton, W. M.
The Journal of Philosophy 290
Hosea
See Index of Scripture Passages
Huggard, W. A., ix

Isaiah 273, 288, 289
See Index of Scripture Passages
Israel 104, 108, 109, 158, 159, 170,
175-176
Ist Jesus eine historische Persoenlichkeit? 308, 310

Jairus 85

James 232

James, Epistle of
    analysis of 36
    contrast with Hebrews 38
    Jewishness of 35
    kinship with Jesus 37
    religious point of view 35-37
    See Index of Scripture Passages

Jeremiah 221, 259, 260, 261, 272, 274, 288, 295-296
    See Index of Scripture Passages

Jerusalem 56, 108, 116, 212, 222, 232, 233, 280

Jesus
    and creed 9-10
        See Apostles' Creed
    and Easter experiences of disciples 98f.
    and Fourth Gospel
        See Fourth Gospel
    and historical student 202-203
    and layman 16
    and messianic issue
        and cures 237, 241f.
        and passion path 262
        and religious consciousness 249ff.
        and temptation 235f.
        and triumphal entry 222-223
        at Jordan 235f., 285ff.
        background of 213f., 215ff.
        confession of Peter 230-231, 242ff.
        confessions of demoniacs 240f., 323-333
        controversy over 214
        eschatology of 218f.
        in conception of disciples 228ff.
        in Fourth Gospel
            See Fourth Gospel
        in New Testament 62-63
        in public mind 219ff.
        linguistic approach to 248-250
        materials of 219

Jesus—Cont.
    and messianic issue—Cont.
        messianic consciousness of 54, 116f.
        request of James and John 231ff.
        solution of 255-256
        and modern mind 19, 139ff., 150ff., 178-179
    and New Testament
        Hebrews 37-39
        James 35
        John
            See Fourth Gospel
        Synoptics
            See Gospels, Synoptic
    and paradox 189
    and passion path
        and Christianity 260-261
        aspiration in 263f.
        forecasts of 257-258, 261
        historical 261f.
        unhistorical 258-260
        thought of 263
    and the Passover 116
    and Paul
        comparison of religious experience 29
        See Paul
    and religion of the group 149ff.
    and Satan 282ff.
    and theology 126, 132
    and visions and voices
        at Jordan 285ff.
        attitude of Jesus toward 288
        importance of 287-288
        in Gethsemane 281
        lack of 290ff.
        material of 280-281
        Satan passages
            at threefold temptation 281, 284
            "I beheld" 282
        unimportance of 292ff.
    and wealth 188
        See Jesus, social teachings of

Jesus—*Cont.*
application of tests to 11-12
approach to
  historical 129-131, 135
  human 131
  literary 129
  psychological 131-132
  religious 132-138
as Christ of faith 92-121, 136
as High Priest 37
aspiration of 85
as prophet 158*ff.*, 295-296
as religious genius 141-143,
  144*ff.*, 294
as religious object
as religious subject 30, 43, 125,
  136-138
  See Jesus, Christianization of
as Risen Lord 104
  See Jesus, Christianization of
attitude of family toward 143-
144
attitudes of
  toward God 136, 104*f.*
    See Fourth Gospel
  toward Jordan experience
    288*ff.*
  toward Kingdom of God 119,
    148
  toward life 168, 190
  toward mankind 168, 171*ff.*
  toward present 181*f.*
  toward world 166*ff.*
baptism of
  and messianic issue 235, 236,
    285*ff.*
  Christianization of 114*ff.*
  in Fourth Gospel 56
  prayer at 298-299
Beelzebub conflict 289
call of 286*ff.*, 293
characterization of 132
Christianization of
  and Kingdom of God 120
  and Son of man 121
  as Christ of faith 136

Jesus—*Cont.*
  Christianization of—*Cont.*
    as Risen Lord 104
    in background 115-116
    in early Christian faith 104*f.*,
      114
    in Gospels 95*ff.*
      See Fourth Gospel
    in major phases 116
    in religious outlook 109*ff.*
    neglect of actual situations
      112*ff.*
    personal religious experience
      of 117*ff.*
    religious message 117*ff.*
  cleansing of temple 56
  commands of 10, 59
  cures of 50, 53
    and personal popularity 208-209
    and science 202-203
    attitude toward 208
    demoniacs 224*ff.*
    frequency of 212
    importance of 210
    instances of 205, 211, 212
    method of 203
      See Jesus, personal problems of
  death of 260
    See Jesus, and passion path
  demands of 17, 127, 139
    and modern mind 139*ff.*
    autobiographical nature of 141
    interpretation of 147
    loyalty to God in 141*ff.*
    selectivity of 146
    social implications of 186
      See Jesus, social teachings of
  emotions of 95-96
  eschatology of 178*ff.*
    ethical element in 180-181
    evangelical element in 184
    in messianic issue 218
  estimate of self 254*f.*
  faith of 105
    confidence of 184

Jesus—*Cont.*
  faith of—*Cont.*
    defies fact 180
    form of 178-179
    in mankind 170
  fanaticism of 147
  fate of 116
    See Jesus, personal problems
      of
  first day in public 204*ff.*
  gives Peter surname 49
  Golden Rule 172
  happiness of 144
  healing ministry of
    See Jesus, cures of
  humanity of 48-49
  in Gethsemane 38-39, 52-53, 82,
    116, 172, 201, 260, 261, 263,
    281, 305
  in New Testament
    Acts 33-35
    object of faith 20
    Paul's letters
      See Paul, letters of
    Peter 33
  interpretation of
    See Jesus, social teachings of
  Jewishness of 108
  journey to Jerusalem 116
  literature about 136
    See Bibliography
  message of
    Christianization of 117
  mission of 207
  Narratives of the Nativity
    See Narratives of the Nativity
  of fiction 84-91
  of history 122*ff.*
  on cross 82
    See Jesus, prayers of
  parables of 169, 188
  personal problems of 53, 128
    cause 212-213
    characteristics of 266
    cures 202-212
    fate 54, 257-264

Jesus—*Cont.*
  personal problems—*Cont.*
    meagerness of material on 198-
      199
    messianic issue 233-256
    nature of 200
    personal popularity 208-209
    religiousness of 251*ff.*
    temptation 200*f.*
    time of meeting 201*f.*
  philosophy of 201
  piety of 43, 108, 135, 149-150,
    163, 198
    Jewishness of 31
  prayer-experience of 56-58
  prayers of 201
    as source of strength 297*ff.*
    for Simon 313
    Lord's Prayer 307
    of commitment 318-319
    of forgiveness 315-316
    of praise 310-313
    of protest 316-318
    of submission 314-315
  public career of 116
  religiousness of
    comparison with early Christi-
      anity 104
    in estimate of world 166*ff.*
    in reply to sons of Zebedee
      253
    in temptation 253
    neglect by world 21
    on last night 254
    problems of
      See Jesus, personal problems
        of
    sources for 64
  religious reference of
    and quest and performance of
      divine will 186*f.*
    for history 175*f.*
    for humankind 168-173*ff.*
    for world 165-168, 173*ff.*
  retreats for prayer
    after cleansing leper 301

Jesus—*Cont.*
retreats for prayer—*Cont.*
after feeding five thousand 58, 302
apart from Simon's house 299-301
at baptism 298-299
at Cæsarea Philippi 303
at giving of *Lord's Prayer* 304
at transfiguration 303
before choosing the twelve 301-302
in Gethsemane 57-58, 263, 264, 305
self-consciousness of religiousness of 251*ff.*
self-revelation 294
sense of limitations in 50
Sermon on Mount 105, 213, 217
sinlessness of 39, 51
social teachings of
and uniform wage 156
and militarism 156
and religious obligation in civil life 156
as anti-social 160*f.*
disappointments in 156-157
doctrine of poverty 155
doctrine of wealth 154-155
lack of definiteness 192*ff.*
lift burden of existence 167
Lord's Prayer 162
meagerness of 157*ff.*
on divorce 157
relation of church and state 155
religious reference 163*ff.*
See Jesus, religious reference of
selectivity of 187
sources for 79, 81, 122
teleology of 180
temptation 38, 52, 235, 236*ff.*
religiousness of 252*f.*
See Jesus, personal problems of

Jesus—*Cont.*
triumphal entry of 222-223
See Life-of-Jesus research
Jesus (Bultmann) 90, 102, 145, 218, 249
Jesus (Wernle) 73-74, 75, 131, 137, 150, 317
Jesus: A New Biography 130, 137, 218
Jesus im 19. Jahrhundert 68
Jesus im Urteile der Jahrhunderte 68
Job 36
Johannes und die Synoptiker 41
John (Gospel) 1, 8, 18, 92
See Fourth Gospel
See also Index of Scripture Passages
John (son of Zebedee) 232
John the Baptist 221
and the messianic issue 54
baptizes Jesus 56, 114-115
birth of 108
fiction in 109
instructions of 157
practise of prayer 304
religious reference of 188
Jonah 177
Jordan 114, 116, 248, 284
Joseph (father of Jesus) 87
Journal of Philosophy, The 290
Judaism 179, 277
Judas 49, 55
Judea 196

Kingdom of God 10, 11, 30, 88
and birth of John the Baptist 108
and poverty 155
and wealth 154-155
as social experience 177-178
in faith of Paul 105
in Fourth Gospel 45-48
Jesus' relationship to
as quest and performance of divine will 184*f.*

Kingdom of God—*Cont.*
  Jesus' relationship to—*Cont.*
    consecration to 141*ff.*, 148, 163
    eschatology of 178*ff.*
    faith in 105, 119
    meaning of 43, 177
I Kings
  See Index of Scripture Passage
Klein, G.
  Ist Jesus eine historische Per-soenlichkeit? 308, 310

Lazarus 48, 50, 53, 58
Le Fils de l'Homme 248
Leipoldt, J.
  Vom Jesusbilde der Gegenwart 68
Lietzmann, H.
  Der Menschensohn 248
Life of Jesus 67, 74
Life-of-Jesus research
  and Gospels
    fact in 122-138
    faith in 92-121
    fiction in 84-91
  and prejudice 71*ff.*
  and psychology of religion 133*f.*
  and theology 126*f.*
  approach of
    historical 129-131, 135
    human 131
    literary 129
    psychological 131-132
    religious 132-138
  method of 68-70
  problems of 128
  representatives of 101*ff.*
  requirements of 79, 127
  results of 72-79, 81, 126*f.*
  skepticism in 101*ff.*
Loisy, A.
  My Duel with the Vatican 73
  The Gospel and the Church 131
Loofs, F.
  Wer War Jesus Christus? 68

Lord's Prayer 10, 162, 304, 306, 307
  Jewishness of 308
  meaning of 309
  objections of theology to 309
  See Jesus, prayers of
Luke
  See Gospels, Synoptic
  See also Index of Scripture Passages
Luther, Martin 5, 17, 35, 287

Mark
  See Gospels, Synoptic
  See also Index of Scripture Passages
Martha 54
Mary (mother of Jesus) 87
Matthew
  See Gospels, Synoptic
  See also Index of Scripture Passages
Meaning of God in Human Experience, The 149, 317
"Meaning of Jesus' Baptism, The" 138
Melchizedek 37
Message of Sadhu Sundar Singh, The 208, 291
Messianic issue
  See Jesus, and the messianic issue
Micah 275
  See Index of Scripture Passages
Miletus 35
Misereres 170
Modern mind
  and evolution 183-184
  and social teachings of Jesus
  See Jesus, social teaching of
Mohammed 287
Mosaic law 34
Mundle, W.
  Das religioese Leben des Apostels Paulus 276, 277

Mundle, W.—*Cont.*
"Der Christus des Glaubens und der historische Jesus" 101
Die religioesen Erlebnisse 268, 317
My Duel with the Vatican 73
Mysticism of St. Paul 76

Narratives of the Nativity 87*ff.*
as folk-lore 89-90
fruit of Christian piety 89
religious substance of 90-91
Nathaniel 49
Nazareth 32, 87
"New Approach to the Synoptic Problem, The" 101, 218
New Testament 2, 4, 5, 8, 12, 14, 16, 17, 20-21, 35, 36, 37, 39, 44, 67, 68, 71, 76, 77, 80, 91, 92, 126, 135, 164-165, 170, 190, 218, 219, 220
See Gospels, Synoptic
See also Jesus, and the New Testament
See also Fourth Gospel
See also Index of Scripture Passages

Old Testament 67, 68, 262
See Index of Scripture Passages
On the Edge of the Primeval Forest 77, 78
Orient
and Christianity 8
Otto, R.
Das Heilige 319

Palestine 180
Papias 63
Parables 88
Parker, Mrs. A.
Sadhu Sundar Singh 145, 208, 264
Passover 56, 116, 262
Paul 8, 92, 97, 98, 108, 110
and Christianity 1, 31
and cross 24

Paul—*Cont.*
and Lord's Supper 23
and Luther 17
and obedience 25
and temptation 24-25
and visions and voices
comparison with Jesus 291*f.*
Damascus experience 276*ff.*
importance of 279
results of 278
other experiences 279-280, 287, 288, 289
source of strength 296
at Miletus 35
attitude toward Jesus
acquired on Damascus road 28
identification of Lord with God 28-29
neglect of historical Jesus 21*ff.*
conception of world 164-165
emphasis on future 26-27
faith of 25, 29-31, 104-105
letters of 39, 134
piety of 24, 29, 31
prayer-life of 25
religious experience of 215
comparison with Jesus 29*ff.*
old elements in 277
sources of 291
studied by ministry 5
use of words of Jesus 23
Pentecost 215
Peter (Apostle) 54, 85, 146, 206, 207, 300
and the Christ of faith 33
confession of 216, 230*f.*, 262
and messianic issue 215, 242*ff.*
influence on Mark 63
Jesus' prayer for 313
surname given 49
II Peter
See Index of Scripture Passages

Pfannmueller, G.
 *Jesus im Urteile der Jahrhun-
  derte* 68
Pharisees 147
Philippians
 See Index of Scripture Passages
Philosophy of Civilization 76
Psalms
 See Index of Scripture Passages
Psychic Health of Jesus, The 181,
 182, 197, 255, 280
Psychology of Religion, The 153
Prayer
 of Jesus
  See Jesus, prayers of
 of Solomon 176

Quest of the Historical Jesus, The
 68, 72, 74
Religion of Jesus, The ix, 10, 43,
 44, 45, 46, 47, 48, 49, 51, 56,
 57, 59, 185, 200, 238, 295, 298,
 306
Renan 213
Romans
 See Index of Scripture Passages
Rome 280

Sadhu Sundar Singh (Heiler) 212,
 291
Sadhu Sundar Singh (Parker)
 145, 208, 264
St. Augustine 5, 134, 291
St. Teresa 134, 287, 291
Satan
 in religious experience of Jesus
  283
Schweitzer, A. 75-79, 161, 217, 218,
 219, 227, 248
 Aus meiner Kindheit und Jugend
  77, 161
 Civilization and Ethics 76, 78, 191
 *Das Messianitaets- und Leidens-
  geheimnis* 76, 214, 225
 *The Decay and Restoration of
  Civilization* 76

Schweitzer, A.—*Cont.*
 *Die psychiatrische Beurteilung
  Jesu* 76
 *Geschichte der Leben-Jesu-For-
  schung* 68
 *Geschichte der Paulinischen
  Forschung* 76
 Mysticism of St. Paul 76
 *On the Edge of the Primeval
  Forest* 77, 78
 *The Quest of the Historical
  Jesus* 68, 72, 74
Second Isaiah 176, 181
Sermon on the Mount 10, 36, 172,
 213, 217
Simon
 See Peter
Skepticism
 in life-of-Jesus research 101*f.*
Singh, S. 145, 208, 291
Solomon 176, 177
Soteriology 32, 314
Stephen 34, 316
Strauss, D. F. 62, 79
 Life of Jesus 67-68, 74
Streeter, B. H.
 *The Message of Sadhu Sundar
  Singh* 208, 291
Syria 114

Temple
 cleansing of 56
Tertullian 190
Theology 2*ff.*, 126*ff.*
I Thessalonians
 See Index of Scripture Passages
II Thessalonians
 See Index of Scripture Passages

Visions and Voices
 in experience of Jesus
  See Jesus, and visions and
   voices
 in experience of Paul
  See Paul, and visions and
   voices

Visions and Voices—*Cont.*
  in experience of prophets 271-276
  in experience of religious genius 270-271
Vom Jesusbilde der Gegenwart 68
Votaw, C. W. ix

War Jesus Ekstatiker? 282
Weinel, H.
  Biblische Theologie des Neuen Testaments 78
  Jesus im 19. Jahrhundert 68
Weiss, J.
  Die Schriften des Neuen Testaments 247, 313
Wellhausen, J.
  Das Evangelium Johannis 102
  Das Evangelium Lucae 102

Wellhausen, J.—*Cont.*
  Das Evangelium Marci 102
  Das Evangelium Mathaei 102
  Einleitung in die drei ersten Evangelien 101, 218
Wernle, P. 75
  Jesus 73-74, 75, 131, 137, 150, 317
Wer War Jesus Christus? 68
Wesley 5
Windisch, H.
  Johannes und die Synoptiker 41
Wrede, W. 216, 218, 219, 227, 231, 247, 248
  Das Messiasgeheimnis in den Evangelien 101, 214, 215, 225

Zechariah 272

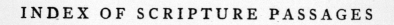

INDEX OF SCRIPTURE PASSAGES

INDEX OF SCRIPTURE PASSAGES

OLD TESTAMENT

I Kings	Page	Jeremiah	Page
3, 7-9	176	11, 18*ff.*	276n
Psalms		12, 1*ff.*	276n
14	170	15, 9-10	276n
22, 1	316	17, 12-28	276n
31, 5	318	18, 18*ff.*	276n
58	170	20, 7-18	276n
82	170	8-9	275n
Isaiah		32, 6-15	296
6, 1-13	273	**Ezekiel**	
8	288	1-3	273, 282
9-13	288	1, 3	275n, 291n
8, 11	275n, 291n	3, 14	275n
40-66	176	15-16	272
40, 6-8	274	22	275n, 291n
53	262f.	25-26	272
Jeremiah		4, 4-8	272
1, 4-5	288	8, 1	275n, 291n
6	274, 288	33, 22	291n
7-10	288	37, 1	275n, 291n
3, 21	272n	40, 1	275n, 291n
4, 13	272n	**Daniel**	
15	272n	7, 14	178
18-21	272n	**Hosea**	
19	275n	4, 9	5
23-26	272n	**Amos**	
31	272n	3, 8	273
6, 11	275n	7, 10-13	273
8, 16	272n	14-15	272f.
19-20	272n	**Micah**	
10, 22	272n	3, 8	275

NEW TESTAMENT

Matthew	Page	Matthew	Page
1-2	87	4, 1-11	200, 235, 255n, 281
3, 13-17	235, 284, 299	3-4	204, 211
14-15	114f., 235n	4	211

Matthew	Page
4, 18-22	299
23-25	203
5-7	307
5, 3-12	172
11	113
17	294n
32	22n, 157n
48	173, 192
6, 3	148
5-8	307
9-13	307f.
10	185
22	143
24	22n
25-34	147
34	201
7, 1-2	22n
8	71
8, 1-4	301
9, 14-15	257n
9, 35-11, 1	113
10, 1-4	301
10	22n
17-18	113
23	110, 179, 232
32-33	120f.
34-36	294n
34	156
37-38	120
39	118n
11, 2-19	246n
23-24	209f.
25-26	310ff.
27	111, 311f.
28-30	111f.
12, 6	177
11	172
22-37	289n
27	242
35	169f.
41-42	177
13, 33	22n
44	169
14, 1-2	221n
23	302
33	246n
16, 13-14	221n
13-20	230n, 235, 303
17-19	243

Matthew	Page
16, 25	118n
17, 1-8	303
9	258n
12	258n
18, 20	110
19, 9	22n, 157n
11-12	146
29	119n
20, 1-16	156
20-21	232n
22	261n
28	294n
21, 1-9	222n
10-11	223
14	212
21-22	22n
23, 8	78
37-39	108n
24, 14	110
26, 36-44	305n
39	314n
42	314n
44	314n
59-66	235, 244n
27, 50	318
51-53	86
63	258n

Mark	Page
1, 1	64f.
2-8	65
2-20	286
9-11	65, 114, 236, 284, 299
12-13	65, 200, 236, 238, 286
14-15	65
15	117f., 232
16-20	65, 115, 229
21-28	205, 224, 227
21-34	204f., 300
21-38	65, 82, 201, 205, 265
23-24	224n, 240n
24	224
25	224n, 240n
29-31	205
32-34	205
34	224n, 240n
35-38	205, 207, 211f., 238n, 239, 299f., 301
38	206, 241, 293

Mark   **Page**

1, 40-45 ....211, 301
   40-45 ....211, 301
   43-44 ....241n
2, 17 294
   18-20 257
3, 11 ....224n, 240n
   11-12 224
   12 ....224n, 240n
   13-19a 301
   16 49
   19b-21 143
   19b-30 ....289n
   22-30 283
   30-35 143
   35 144
5, 6-7 ....224n, 240n
   8 ....224n, 240n
   43 ....241n
6, 8-9 114
   14-15 221
   45-46 302
7, 1-23 166
   3-4 166
   10-13 148
   15 166
   15-23 ....22n
   32-37 203
   36 ....241n
8, 11-12 ....238n
   22-26 203
   26 ....241n
   27 ....242n
   27-28 221
   27-30 ...216, 230, 237, 240,
        242 255n, 256, 286, 303
   29 ....242n
   30 ....243n
   31 258
   32-33 ....238n, 259
   33 ....263f., 283
   35 118
   36 146
   38 ....121n
9, 1 ....110, 179, 232
   2-8 303
   2-10 ....243n
   9 ....258n
   12 ....258n

Mark   **Page**

9, 31 258
   32 259
   41 190
   43-47 ....140, 143
10, 11-12 ....22n, 157n
   18 50
   23 154
   25 154
   29-30 ....118f.
   33-34 258
   35-40 232
   38 ....232, 261f.
   40 253
   45 ....294n
   46-52 212
11, 1-10 ....222n
12, 17 ....22n, 155
   37 16
   38-40 159
13, 3-37 110
14, 10-11 ....255n
   32-35 305
   32-42 ....82, 305n
   34 199
   36 ...261, 264, 288, 305, 314n
   39 ....314n
   41 ....314n
   55-64 ....244n, 255n
   61 244
   62 ....179, 245, 247, 254
15, 23 318
   33-37 82
   34 ....263, 316f.
   37 318

Luke

1, 5-25 108
1, 5-2, 52 87
   17 109
   57-80 108
2, 13-14 ....86f.
3, 10-14 157
   21-22 ....235, 284, 299
4, 1-13 ...200, 235, 255n, 281
   3-4 ....204, 211
   5-6 165
   31-43 229
   42-43 ....206, 299

Luke — Page

5, 1-11 229
12-14 301
15 301
16 301
33 304
33-35 .... 257n
6, 12-13 .... 301f.
20 155
24 154
29-36 .... 22n
7, 18-35 .... 246n
9, 7-8 .... 221n
18 .... 298, 303
18-19 .... 221n
18-21 .... 230n, 235
21 .... 243n
24 .... 118n
26 .... 121n
28-29 .... 298, 303f.
9, 51-19, 28 304
57-62 .... 139f., 143
58 144
62 .... 22n, 120
10, 1-20 311
7 .... 22n
18 .... 281f., 284, 293
21 .... 310ff.
22 .... 311f.
11, 1 .... 298, 304, 307
2-4 .... 304, 307ff.
11 172
14-26 .... 289n
12, 8-9 121
13-14 156
16-20 188
39-40 .... 22n
49 294
49-50 199
50 .... 232n, 261n, 262f.
51-53 .... 294n
14, 26 145
26-27 120
27 181
16, 1-7 169
13 145
18 .... 22n, 157n
17, 25 .... 258n
33 .... 118, 189
18, 1-5 169

Luke — Page

18, 13 171
28 146
29-30 .... 18, 146f.
34 259
19, 10 .... 294n
29-38 .... 222n
41-44 .... 108n
21, 20-22 .... 108n
24 .... 108n
22, 15 116
18 179
31-32 .... 283, 313
33-34 171
40-46 .... 305n
42 .... 314n
43-44 281
51 212
66-71 .... 235, 244n
23, 27-31 .... 108n
34 .... 34n, 315f.
46 .... 34n, 318f.
24, 21 .... 233, 260

John

1, 29-34 56
35-51 .... 229n
41 .... 54, 229n
42 49
43 59
45 54
47-48 49
49 54
3, 3 47
5 47
14-15 .... 59n
36 .... 59n
4, 6-7 48
18 49
24 44
26 54
29 49
34 51
46-53 50
5, 5 50
30 .... 50, 52
6, 11 .... 58n
16-21 50
29 .... 59n
35 .... 59n

John

	Page
6, 38	44n, 52
40	50, 59n
62	44n
64	50
70-71	50
7, 16	46
33	44n
7, 53-8, 11	42n
8, 14	44n
23	44n
24	59n
26	46n
28	46n
29	52n
38	46n
46	51
58	44
9, 1	50
37	54
10, 17-18	55
18	46n
30	45
36	54
11, 4	53
11-14	50
25-26	59n
27	54
35	48
41-42	58
12, 26	59
27	52, 55
27-28	57f.
30	57
41	44n
45	45
49	46
13, 3	44n
34	59
35	60
14, 1	59n
6	59n
13-14	57
24	46n
28	45
31	52n
15, 10	52n
14-17	56

John

	Page
15, 15	46n
16, 27	59
28	44n
17, 1-26	58
3	59
5	44n
24	44n
18, 11	52, 55, 58

Acts

	Page
2, 22	33
22-24	215
24	33
6, 14	34
7, 2-53	34
51-53	34
59	34
60	34, 316
9, 1-10	277
5	288
15-16	288
10, 38	33
38-42	216
40-41	33
16, 9-10	280
18, 9-10	280
20, 35	35
22, 6-11	279n
8	288
10	288
17-21	280
23, 11	280
26, 12-19	279n
15	288
16-18	288
27, 23-24	280

Romans

	Page
1, 17	17
2, 1	22n
4, 3	25
9	25
7, 14-25	170
8, 15	25
22	164
12, 14	22n
17	22n
20	22n
13, 7	22n
14, 10	22n

Romans   Page
14, 13 .... 22n
14 .... 22n
20 .... 22n
15, 3 25

I Corinthians
1, 18 24
4, 12 .... 22n
16 .... 24n
5, 6-8 .... 22n
6, 7 .... 22n
7, 10 22
25 23
9, 1 .... 279n
14 22
10, 13 25
21 .... 22n
11, 1 24
23-25 23
13 105
2 .... 22n
14, 18-19 296
15, 8 .... 279n

II Corinthians
4, 6 .... 279n
5, 16 27
17 .... 277f.
21 26
8, 9 26
12, 1 .... 279n
2-4 279
7 279
8-9 279

Galatians
1, 4 164
12 279
16-17 .... 239, 279n
2, 2 280
20 .... 24, 278
4, 6 25
5, 9 .... 22n
21 .... 22n

Ephesians
2, 12 170
3, 3 .... 279n

Philippians
2, 5-8 26
8 25
3, 12 .... 279n
13 .... 22n

Philippians   Page
3, 17 .... 24n
4, 9 .... 24n

Colossians
3, 11 30

I Thessalonians
1, 6 .... 24n
4, 13-18 27
15-18 .... 63, 104
5, 2 .... 22n
4 .... 22n
15 .... 22n

II Thessalonians
1, 5 .... 22n
3, 9 .... 24n

Hebrews
2, 18 38
3, 2 38
4, 15-16 38
5, 7-8 .... 38f.
9 39
7, 26-27 39
10, 7 38

James
1, 1 35
2-18 36
6 .... 37n
9-11 .... 37n
13-15 .... 37n
22-25 .... 37n
2, 2-3 .... 37n
8 .... 37n
10-11 .... 37n
13 .... 37n
15-16 .... 37n
3, 1 .... 37n
10-12 .... 37n
4, 2-3 .... 37n
11-12 .... 37n
15 .... 37n
17 .... 37n
5, 1-5 .... 37n
7-9 35
10-11 36
12 .... 37n
14-15 .... 37n
17-18 36
20 .... 37n

I Peter
2, 21-24 40